EUROPEAN POLITICS II

The Dynamics of Change

EUROPEAN POLITICS II

The Dynamics of Change

A Comparative Government Biennial

Edited by
WILLIAM G. ANDREWS

Contributions by

ROY C. MACRIDIS, *Brandeis University*
ROBERT T. HOLT, *University of Minnesota*
JOHN E. TURNER, *University of Minnesota*
WILLIAM G. ANDREWS, *State University College, Brockport*
GEORGE K. ROMOSER, *University of New Hampshire*
JOHN A. ARMSTRONG, *University of Wisconsin*

VAN NOSTRAND REINHOLD COMPANY

NEW YORK   CINCINNATI
TORONTO   LONDON   MELBOURNE

Van Nostrand Reinhold Company Regional Offices:
Cincinnati, New York, Chicago, Millbrae, Dallas

Van Nostrand Reinhold Company Foreign Offices:
London, Toronto, Melbourne

Published by Van Nostrand Reinhold Company
450 West 33rd Street, New York, N. Y. 10001

Published simultaneously in Canada by
D. Van Nostrand Company (Canada), Ltd.

1 3 5 7 9 11 13 15 16 14 12 10 8 6 4 2

Preface

THIS VOLUME OF *European Politics,* LIKE ITS PREDECESSOR, IS DESIGNED primarily to supplement textbook readings in college comparative government courses that include the political systems of Europe. The authors were asked to treat in depth one or two major political or constitutional developments that had occurred since *European Politics I* went to press. They were asked to write at a level somewhat above that of most textbooks but less difficult than most articles in scholarly journals. The purpose of the book is to offer students material that (1) goes well beyond the textbooks in giving them a depth of knowledge on selected narrow but important aspects of contemporary political life, (2) supplies them with detailed information on recent developments in the countries they are studying, and (3) requires them to deal with and acquire a feel for political science writing pitched a bit above the level of most textbook writing.

Professor Roy C. Macridis of Brandeis University, in the introductory essay, discusses in broad, comparative terms certain trends he discerns in the contemporary development of European political attitudes and institutions. He tests the argument that ideology is declining, using evidence from both democratic and Communist systems. Also, he discusses changes in the roles of institutions, especially executives vs. legislatures, parties, bureaucracies, and elections. He gives special attention to the concept of "plebiscitary democracy" and "new corporatism." Throughout, he stresses the parallelism with which most European countries, both totalitarian and democratic, meet and solve their problems.

In the first of the four studies that focus on single countries, Professors Robert T. Holt and John E. Turner of the University of Minnesota examine the fundamental political problems that have confronted Prime Minister Harold Wilson and the British Labour government, especially since the March 1966 elections. In particular, the authors are concerned with problems of change and rigidity in the composition and structure of the Parliamentary Labour Party and consequent effects on the general operation of the British system.

The editor treats the impact of the 1965 presidential elections on

French politics. He argues that those elections catalyzed and accelerated trends toward consolidation and simplification in party politics, especially on the Left and among the political elite. He gives special attention to patterns of candidacies and voting in elections, to the behavior of the deputies in parliament, to the formation of the Federation of the Democratic and Socialist Left, and to its alliance with the French Communist Party.

Professor George K. Romoser of the University of New Hampshire studies the decline and fall of the Erhard government and the formation and operation of the Grand Coalition that took its place. He is especially attentive to the lessons that may be drawn from the paradoxical experiment of lodging in the same government both the major parties in what operates essentially as a two-party system and the implications this has for democratic government.

Professor John A. Armstrong of the University of Wisconsin describes the political and governmental situation as the post-Khrushchev period in the Soviet Union emerged from the first shock of the fall of the old dictator. He analyzes the retreat from Khrushchev's ideological apocalypticism, and from many of his policies and practices in dealing with religion, minority nationalities, intellectuals, social nonconformism, economic and social differentiation, Libermanism, and even general economic and political structures. He emphasizes the extent to which the policies of Khrushchev's successors still represent greater continuity than change and the importance of the Party and State bureaucracy in producing the shifts that have occurred.

Throughout these essays, the authors have been especially concerned with describing and explaining the dynamics of the changes occurring in contemporary European politics; with relating short-term developments to long-term trends; with fitting the fleeting and perishable into the permanent, continuous, and durable; with discovering which events are mutations and which reflect underlying reality. If their efforts succeed in making European politics more real, more interesting, and more understandable to comparative government students, the mission of this book will have been accomplished.

WILLIAM G. ANDREWS

Brockport, New York

Contents

Contributors

WILLIAM G. ANDREWS, Professor and Chairman, Department of Political Science, State University College at Brockport (N.Y.), edited *European Political Institutions* and *The Politics of International Crises* (in press).

JOHN A. ARMSTRONG, Professor, University of Wisconsin, wrote *Ideology, Politics, and Government in the Soviet Union* and *The Soviet Bureaucratic Elite*.

ROBERT T. HOLT and JOHN E. TURNER, Professors, University of Minnesota, wrote *The Political Basis of Economic Development* and *Political Parties in Action*.

ROY C. MACRIDIS, Meyer and Walter Jaffe Professor of Politics and Chairman, Department of Politics, Brandeis University, is co-author of *France, Germany, and the Western Alliance* and *The de Gaulle Republic*.

GEORGE K. ROMOSER, Associate Professor and Chairman, Department of Political Science, University of New Hampshire, is the author of *The Politics of Resistance in Nazi Germany* (in preparation).

European Politics II

Change in Attitudes
and Institutions

by Roy C. Macridis

THE POLITICAL SYSTEMS OF THE MODERN INDUSTRIALIZED
countries of Europe are developing in a manner that indicates,
by and large, parallel institutional trends to cope with common
problems. The hard lines we drew between totalitarian and democratic systems some ten years ago, on the assumption that totalitarianism and democracy obeyed laws that were "inherent" to
each of them, has given place to a more relaxed and discriminat-
ing approach. The reason for this is primarily the recent body of
theory and research on political development, that subsumes, at
least in part, both democratic and non-democratic systems. When
all the relevant quantitative data is collected and tabulated, the
Soviet Union and many of its eastern satellites appear to be as
"developed" and "modern" as many of the countries of western
Europe, especially when contrasted with the hard realities of under-
development that plagues most of the world. They fit Lipset's
"profile" of modernity.[1]

Many western democracies have crossed, apparently irre-
versibly, the line that distinguishes private from public property.
They have set up large administrative entities to perform important
economic activities for the public—in transportation, energy, production of goods, the provision and administration of services. As
a result, the problems of organization, consultation of interests
involved, responsibility and control of decision-makers and efficiency do not differ significantly between democratic and non-
democratic systems. Similarly, the prevalent theme of Marxist and
left-wing analysis of democratic politics—class struggle—seems

1

to be abandoned progressively. Affluence and the development of genuine mass consumption economies seem to have mitigated, from an objective standpoint, class conflict, and to have attenuated class-consciousness considerably. This is the case, also, in the Soviet society and some of her eastern neighbors.

Modern systems—democratic or not—appear to be following similar trends. Conflict gives place to competition, ideology to pragmatic considerations (but we shall have to qualify this), the bureaucracy has grown in numbers and scope, decision-making is concentrated increasingly in the hands of the executive with a corresponding diminution of the powers and prerogatives of representative assemblies; correspondingly, interest groups have shifted their attention to the executive and the bureaucracy, while political parties become more inclusive and pragmatic. Also, a common and pervasive theme in democratic and non-democratic systems alike is concern with individual rights and liberties and the right to dissent.[2]

It would be impossible to cover all these developments in this introductory essay. In the first part we shall discuss the evolving pattern of political attitudes—the political culture—and the changing ideological climate. In the second part we shall deal more specifically with institutional changes.

I. IDEOLOGY AND POLITICAL CULTURE

According to many, one of the most prevalent phenomena in the development of European politics is the "decline of ideology." The argument is too familiar to require discussion. It can be summed up as follows: Post-World War II economic growth has created a state of affluence in most western European systems and perhaps the Soviet Union and some of the eastern satellites, too. Also, a number of divisive issues, especially those pertaining to the running of the economy, have been resolved in favor of nationalization and bureaucratic control. The old issue of free enterprise vs. socialism does not agitate and divide any more. The result has been the lowering of political conflict, the decline of ideological confrontations between classes or groups, and the development of a political climate which resembles the market—subject to bargaining and compromise in an effort to provide for allocation of benefits and resources. In essence, the argument stipulates the end of revolutionary politics because of the success of the economy, thanks in part to its own resiliency, but also because reforms in the directional planning and nationalization have been realized.[3]

This thesis depends primarily on the definition given to ideology. It can be defined solely in terms of its integrative function, i.e., a set of beliefs, ideas, and norms that are shared widely by all, thus keeping the society together; or as a highly divisive force, i.e., a set of beliefs and ideas shared by some for the purpose of changing the society radically and often forcibly. In this narrow sense, ideology has utopian and revolutionary traits. Professor LaPalombara, who agrees more with the argument that ideology has declined, defines ideology as "a philosophy of history, a view of man's present place in it, some estimate of probable lines of future development, and a set of prescriptions regarding how to hasten, retard and/or modify that developmental direction. . . . Ideology . . . tends to specify a set of values that are more or less coherent and that it seeks to link given patterns of action to the achievement or maintenance of a future, or existing, state of affairs." [4] In that sense, he argues rightly that ideology is far from dead and illustrates this by indicating its persistence and strength in the Italian political system, especially the Italian Left.

In our discussion, we use a narrow definition, according to which ideology is a set of ideals that have, as Manheim put it, a distinct utopian character calling for direct action to change the existing environment in favor of the utopian goals. It purports to change society drastically rather than play an integrative role through a set of collective values and ideas that hold a society together. In this sense "ideology" may be on the decline.

In all the modern societies, the evolving political culture begins to show striking similarities. Status and traditional politics have given place to egalitarian values. Differentiation in the norms and values of different groups gives place to a growing homogeneity. The new industrial order emphasizes mass performance, mass satisfaction of wants, social discipline, and equality. The expansive education, growing urbanization, reality of social mobility and relative bridging of the sharp differences in opportunities and consumption that characterized the past create a similarly-minded body politic. The political awareness and participation that result, however, lower the emotional involvement and commitments in politics. As Otto Kirchheimer put it, the individual becomes "privatized" increasingly, i.e., within a given context whose existence is not threatened he can pursue his own individual interests.[5]

Increasingly, decisions are made through collective bargaining and give-and-take among the spokesmen of large groups—trade unions, business, farmers, the bureaucracy, and many others. Group politics guarantee to the individual the defense of his own interests without calling for individual action. As we shall see, a new form of corporation is in the making. In the collectivist era, as Professor Beer called modern politics in Great Britain,[6] the decisions are made through confrontation and bargaining among large collectivities within the system. The individual who wishes to step from his private world into political action usually finds it very difficult to affect seriously the highly structured group relations through which decisions are made.

Thus, the political culture of modern industrialized society allows for political participation, but makes it less effective. It provides what may be called a broad common denominator of attitudes and expectations from which decisions normally are expected to flow. It introduces a process of bargaining among groups in order to reach political decisions, and hence removes the individual increasingly from the participation that is open to him. This is not to say that what the French call *les grandes options* have disappeared. Still, we have not resolved matters of war and peace, nationalism and internationalism, the control of the physical environment that is required for the expanded population to survive; the fate of the underdeveloped world; the conquest of space through collective effort; and harnessing new energy resources for purposes other than war. They are likely to become the basic political issues in the near future and to inject an element of passion and commitment that is so lacking today. But perhaps these are problems of the 21st century.

1. The French Case

Both the themes of ideological controversy and the intensity with which ideologies were held by various groups and classes almost certainly have weakened in France over the last three or four decades. A recent book entitled *Les Familles Politiques*[7] *en*

France, discusses four basic ideological themes which divided the French political society before the Third Republic. In terms of awareness, intensity of feelings, and saliency, all these themes appear to play a far less important role today than in the past. The authors identify the following issues: the clerical issue; the

ATTITUDE WITH REGARD TO AUTHORITY OF STATE

	Extreme Left 100%	Moderate Left 100%	Moderate Right 100%	Extreme Right 100%
Authority of state should be maintained	19	30	54	62
Lessen power	73	58	30	26
No opinion	8	12	16	12

AID TO PAROCHIAL SCHOOLS SHOULD BE SUPPRESSED

	Extreme Left 100%	Moderate Left 100%	Moderate Right 100%	Extreme Right 100%
Agree	63	31	8	12
Disagree	33	54	82	82
No opinion	4	15	10	6

LARGE PRIVATE ENTERPRISES SHOULD BE NATIONALIZED

	Extreme Left 100%	Moderate Left 100%	Moderate Right 100%	Extreme Right 100%
Agree	58	34	25	29
Disagree	22	42	50	47
No opinion	20	24	25	24

CONSTRUCTION OF SOCIALISM IS NECESSARY

	Extreme Left 100%	Moderate Left 100%	Moderate Right 100%	Extreme Right 100%
Agree	84	69	38	32
Disagree	6	11	21	31
No opinion	10	20	41	37

manner in which the authority of the state is viewed by the individual; nationalization of the large private enterprises; and the "construction of Socialism." They conclude, as the tables above indicate, that none of these issues divide the French sharply. Only residual attitudes remain, which continue to be reflected in the identification of the individuals with the Left, Center and Right spectrum and the corresponding political parties.

A survey undertaken by the author, particularly among elites, also illustrates a relative—but only relative—decline of ideological themes in the narrow sense of the term.[8] The distinction between Left and Right continues to be significant, but the intensity of feeling and identification with either camp has declined. The pervasive ideological conflicts of Church vs. State, the individual vs. the state, and capitalism vs. socialism have been attenuated significantly. However, as Professor LaPalombara has argued with regard to Italy, broader ideological themes have reappeared. But, in contrast to the past, they are not utopian nor are they clearly associated with a single group, class, or party. Such themes as "Europe," greater group participation in decisions ("democratic participation"), and the desire to develop consultative channels between the bureaucracy and the interests are reformist rather than utopian or revolutionary, and are shared by parties of the Left, Center, and Right and by respondents who identify themselves with Left, Center, and Right. Thus, when asked what they thought were the most important cleavages and conflicts in French politics of today, eight per cent of those interviewed said class, 24 per cent said ideological, 27 per cent said domestic political issues, six per cent said current issues, and five per cent nationalism vs. supranationalism. Asked if conflict between Left and Right was "important" today, 48 per cent said yes, 46 per cent said no, one per cent did not know, and another five per cent was not ascertained. As for the "old parties," 24 per cent replied that they were dead, 70 per cent replied that they were not, two per cent did not know, and the remaining four per cent were not ascertained. Only two per cent of the elite respondents enthusiastically favored a revival of a Popular Front, with another 15 per cent in favor (three per cent moderately so, and 12 per cent in favor but with reservations), while 57 per cent were against it—28 per cent of them "vehemently," 22 per cent not vehemently, and seven per cent disfavored it in general, but would favor it under certain conditions. A significant percentage—27 per cent—saw only superficial differences among the parties, 35 per cent detected important differences on domestic policy issues, but only 12 per cent noted ideological differences, ten per cent mentioned foreign policy issues, and a mere five per cent regarded class differences as constituting areas of vital disagreement among the parties. The majority of the respondents believed that the parties would play an equal or greater role after De Gaulle, eight per cent saying that they would dominate the political scene, 41 per cent that they would be much more important than at present but not as important as under the Fourth Republic, and 24 per cent that they would play about as important a role as in the Fifth Republic. De Gaulle's death appeared to be the most serious single internal problem for 33 per cent of the respondents (29 per cent inferred the death of a national leader while the other four per cent said a domestic political crisis), and 43 per cent envisaged no specific type of upheaval in their society or even denied the possibility of one. Only about ten per cent evoked the possibility of a depression, and only one per cent mentioned possible world war.

2. *The German Case*

As with France, any firm conclusion about West Germany should await the end of the provisional situation the country is in now. Only when the matter of unification is settled, one way or another, shall we be able to tell whether certain trends have crystallized. But present developments cannot be ignored. Pragmatic politics seem to have replaced conflict. The amputation of the Prussian territories, the degradation of the Junkers who had provided the heart of the officer corps, the unprecedented prosperity that followed the chaos of defeat, the ascendancy of the industrial and bourgeois order, appear to have changed the climate of politics radically and to have transformed the political culture.

Nothing illustrates this better than the internal development of the political parties and the change in their goals. Both major parties attempt to attract as many votes as possible and, in so doing, shy away from ideologies. The SPD has become a cautious reformist party, thus completing its transition from the years before the turn of the century, and, like the British Labour Party, has decided to abandon a commitment to socialism. The CDU, on the other hand, has become progressively inclusives and national, and has shown a rather unanticipated ability to provide for limited reforms in domestic politics. Extremist parties have shown, until recently, great weakness. Even if the Communist Party had not been outlawed, it is doubtful that under the present circumstances it would recuperate even one-hundredth of its pre-Nazi strength. Characteristically, the present situation in Germany is referred to as "consensus" politics[9]—broad agreement about ends and minor disagreements on policy issues which are, however, susceptible to compromise and negotiation. The coalition government formed by the SPD and the CDU has put the official stamp on consensus politics. As with France, the old quarrels about capitalism vs. socialism, about authoritarianism vs. democracy, the Army vs. the State, the industrial power vs. the middle classes and the working class seem to have been seriously attenuated. Barring unforeseen developments—and the problem of reunification may prove to be crucial—the German political culture seems to display a degree of consensus that no political scientist would have ventured to predict a few years ago.

Yet, while the French appear to be seeking a new synthesis to transcend the present Gaullist arrangements, German politics are based exclusively upon an attachment to the status quo—the system has worked and probably will be accepted as long as it works. Any serious failure, however, may bring forth developments to shatter the present consensus. Old and new ideologies— but mostly old—may yet reappear, armed with the same vision and dedication that characterized the German past.

3. The Soviet Case

The evolution of the Soviet political culture, at least with respect to ideology as defined in narrow terms, is equally striking. In fact, the evolution of the system is the story of a utopian and revolutionary ideology being nationalized and legitimized to become an integrative political force; adjusting to many of the historical, cultural, and social realities of the past; and adapting itself to new problems and socio-economic developments. The transition from revolutionary Marxism to "socialism in one country"; from rigid egalitarianism to the acceptance and legitimation of inequalities; the access to decision-making and elite status of new groups; particularly the managers, bureaucrats and officers; the subtle replacement of the term class by stratum; the rationalization of the need of a growing state apparatus—all these changes indicate how revolutionary ideology can become a unifying and integrative force.[10]

The Soviet system is the victim and the beneficiary of one of its most cherished goals—mobilization of the individual. A series of links in the chain of Soviet history relate to it. Mobilization requires that the citizen be inculcated with incentives and interest. Ideological motivation, essential at the start, cannot sustain this over a long period of time. Positive response by the government to those who are asked to participate becomes essential. In the last analysis, this response can take only one form—government performance to meet popular demands. For the government to associate the vast majority of the citizens with its goals, two things are needed—communication between governors and governed and a minimum of response by the people to the signals that come from the government. Such response cannot be assured unless the people attain a sufficient level of awareness of the government, develop some affective ties to it, and are assured of some benefits. This, again, means that the government must, through performance, satisfy the demands of many. Thus the coercive elements that stemmed from an imposition of values and prescriptions during the first stages in the Soviet history give place to incentives and force is transformed into a complex set of rules and symbols that politicize the citizen and secure his allegiance. At this stage—through which the Soviet system is going now—ideology sheds its utopian and messianic character to become an integrative force and to provide the solidarity of the system. But the more integrative it becomes the more it loses its "ideological" component in the narrow sense of the term. What, then, are its new traits and how does it relate to the political culture?

Clearly, "socialism," in the sense of the ownership by the State of the major means of production is generally and overwhelmingly accepted today, with some serious qualifications about agricultural production and the manner in which farmers can be given additional incentives for their work. Hence, the manner in which the economy will be run is no longer an ideological issue. Rather, it has become a policy issue viewed in terms of efficiency: the reassessment of the manager's role, the development of new methods to provide for "profit" and allow for competition within a given parameter, and the growing consideration of consumer choices. Secondly, bureaucratic imposition has given place, again within limits, to a consultative process in which the major interests, including the consumer, are consulted before policies are elaborated. Thirdly, within both the Party and the society at large, the allocation of different incomes and rewards to different occupations and roles is accepted widely and expected—in fact, is desired. Fourthly, social mobility on the basis of achievement has become a generalized value and any interference with it, by political or bureaucratic fiat, is bound to cause serious and adverse reactions. Finally, in an industrialized society, two other things are beginning to be valued increasingly: the inviolability of social and economic roles (managerial, professional, educational, scientific, research, etc.) and a growing desire for abundance and well-being. Both create attitudes that lead to a limitation of the role of the State in certain domains, i.e., a demand for increased freedoms, and to what we might call the "demystification" of the government and the Party. From a bearer of ideology and the purveyor of coercion and control, the Party is viewed increasingly as an instrument to satisfy the quest for abundance and well-being. Autonomy of roles, i.e., freedom, is being sought increasingly. Despite a number of backslides, the direction is clear for the scientist, the artist, the musician, the university student, the manager. I say the "direction," because the very agitation about these freedoms and the claims of autonomy is more revealing than the fact that they are not met fully or are at times rejected by the Party and the State apparatus. Further, the instruments of coercion appear to have been weakened considerably while the legitimation of the political and socio-economic roles develops. The weakening of the Soviet Empire carries the same logic for the authoritarian institutions at home and the "autonomy" claimed by the satellites is reflected in similar claims by many groups that perform specific roles and functions within the Soviet society.

Such claims not only are heard by the Communist Party, but often find reconciliation and compromise within the Party. As with democratic parties, interests and groups vie for influence by attempting to gain as many governmental favors and rewards as possible through the party. As with democratic parties, the Communist Party has to accommodate as many as possible rather than allow itself to be bent to the will of one or to the combination of the will of the most powerful ones. This changes totally the attitudes of the leaders at the various layers of the Party pyramid— the ideologue gives place to the politician, the commissar to the manipulator, the hero to the ward healer. This does not imply that the Party did not have many politicians, manipulators or ward healers in the early years, but rather stresses that the shift in ideology tends to legitimize *them* rather than the hero, the ideologue, and the commissar! Thus, the Soviet citizen develops a market mentality and attitude toward the Party. He is satisfied with compromises and incremental benefits that represent a common denominator of many conflicting group expectations. These preoccupations affect the top echelons of the party leaders also and the meetings of the Politburo resemble meetings of company directors—assessing demands, satisfying interests, and providing policies with an eye to efficiency and performance. If this is the case, the Soviet system may well be at the threshold of significant political changes in the direction of a more pluralistic, pragmatic, and open polity.

II. THE POLITICAL INSTITUTIONS

The changing ideological context of contemporary politics may well account for a parallel trend in the evolution of political institutions. At least four major institutional trends can be identified: (a) the increasing dominance of the executive and the relative weakening of representative assemblies; (b) the changing role of the bureaucracy as new functions have been added to it; (c) the trend away from representative to what we might call, for lack of a better term, "plebiscitary" democracy; and (d) the reduction in number of the political parties—notably in Germany and France. Naturally, most of these trends are identified readily with Western democracies, but also they take into account the institutional changes in the people's democracies of Eastern Europe and in the Soviet Union. Finally, the concentration of decision-making in the hands of the executive and its political powers stemming from the plebiscitary character of election of the top political executive, has given rise to a new concern with individual liberties and renewed efforts to safeguard them.

Executive Dominance

Irrespective of crisis situations, concentration of decision-making in the hands of a very small group of men headed by a Prime Minister, a Chancellor, or a President has become the rule increasingly. Political power that derives ultimately from popular support has also become increasingly personalized and concentrated in the hands of one man.

The reasons stem either from the simplification of the party system or the direct election of the top executive leader, as is the case with France today. In all systems, the parties nominate and limit to a few candidates the choice available to the people in electing the "government." Once such a choice is made in periodic elections, decision-making is in the hands of one man and his immediate advisers. Though collegiality continues to play an important role in some smaller democracies and, to some extent, in the Cabinet systems of Western democratic systems, the trend has been toward one-man political leadership and control. Momentous decisions have been made by a single man—or a very small number of the Cabinet members. Decisions to produce nuclear weapons, to mount military expeditions, to install ballistic missiles, or to wage war by virtue of ambiguous legislative authorization have been made by one or a handful of men.

The corresponding diminution of the legislative powers of control and policy-making stem fundamentally from the same reasons that account for the ascendancy of the executive. The majority party is the legislature. But also, the business of government has become extremely complex and has assumed regulatory economic tasks that call for a high level of expertise. Gone are the days when the problems facing the government were only political questions and matters of foreign policy. Expert knowledge and direction within the framework of general policy directives often is the essence of government and of performance. Legislation has become, in effect, the task of the executive and of the various ministerial or interministerial committees. Almost everywhere, the legislature's function is to say "yes." Given the party discipline, the "yes" is said with a monotony reminiscent of the acquiescence by the Supreme Soviet and its equivalents in the satellites to legislation proposed by the party leaders in charge of the executive branch.

Where party support cannot be counted on—either because the parties are not disciplined enough or because the executive derives his powers from other sources, which is at least in part the case for France—other devices to limit the legislature are introduced: its legislative functions are limitatively defined; its ability to censure the government is circumscribed carefully; its power to debate issues that lead to a vote are curtailed; the requisite majority to overthrow the Cabinet is defined constitutionally to make it difficult for the opposition to overthrow the Prime Minister; its powers to amend government bills is qualified and the scrutinizing and deliberative functions of the legislative committees are limited. All these provisions are in the Constitution of the Fifth Republic where the legislature operates under the shadow of a Presidency with powers that even the American President may envy: to dissolve and call for an election at any time; to declare an emergency and rule by executive ordinances; and to call for referenda on virtually any question of policy which, if approved, can set aside legislation or even constitutional provisions.[11]

In West Germany, the so-called "constructive vote" or a motion of confidence makes it impossible for the legislature to overthrow a Chancellor unless those who vote against the incumbent agree on his successor. This has never occurred yet and changes of Chancellor—from Adenauer to Erhard to Kiesinger—have taken place by prior party agreement and consultation rather than and through parliamentary designation and deliberation.

But the supremacy of the executive power is also grounded on what may be called purely managerial considerations—the running of the economy in the Soviet Union and the satellites, the regulation, control, and planning of a great array of economic activities in the western democracies, including the nationalized industries and many services. The legislature cannot scrutinize these activities that are delegated generously to the executive and to independent regulatory or administrative bodies. In England, but also in France, the economic plan or the operations of the nationalized industries come up for debate only once a year—

usually on the Estimates or the Annual Reports of the boards of nationalized industries—and scrutiny of anything, other than the broadest policy directives issued by the Cabinet or the Prime Minister to such units, is impossible. Sub-delegation by the executive is the rule and control is mostly hierarchical, i.e., can be exerted only by the political executive which is responsible theoretically to the representative assembly. The task of providing controls for the managerial state is as difficult in democracies as in totalitarian states. Consultation with the interests affected is a safety device to obtain support before a decision is made, rather than to institute control of the decision-makers.

The Simplification of the Party System[12]

In two countries, France and West Germany, the number of parties has declined or they have consolidated into larger groupings. In both countries, electoral devices have played some role and the constitutional reform of 1962 in France, limiting the number of candidates for the popularly-elected Presidency of the Republic to only two on the second ballot, is important.

The simplification of the party system stems fundamentally from a combination of the changes in the electoral methods and in the growing erosion of ideological and party differences. Where the proportional representation system remains, as in the Scandinavian countries, Holland, and Belgium, to safeguard ethnic and religious minorities or powerful groups that identify themselves with a party, simplification of the parties has not occurred and inter-party agreements have been responsible for the formation and stability of the Cabinet. On the other hand, where the ideological differences have been attenuated and the electoral system provides for a straight or a qualified single-member majority system the trend has been toward simplification.

Fewer in numbers and well-organized, the parties have taken over some of the functions of the legislature. They nominate the leader who, if he receives majority support, becomes the head of the political executive; they deliberate on policy and suggest reforms on the program to be followed after the elections and, thanks to their discipline, they sustain the Cabinet in office. If we were to ignore the lack of an opposition in the Soviet Union and the satellites, the single parties there perform fundamentally the same functions. Dissensions within them will spell the collapse of the political executive in the same way that dissensions within a majority party will spell the end of the political executive in democracies—without necessarily giving way to the opposition party.

Plebiscitary Democracy

The growth of national and better-disciplined parties, the trend toward two-party systems, and the strengthening of the leadership and decision-making functions of executives have been in great part responsible for the development of plebiscitary democracy. Its main trait is that all intermediary representative bodies are by-passed or diminished in power in favor of personalized leadership that stems from direct popular support provided in periodic elections. In France under the Gaullist constitution, the President, as the political leader and head of the governmental machinery, derives his powers from direct elections; the same is true of the American Presidency and of the British Cabinet under the leadership of the Prime Minister, i.e., the leader of the majority party. The political parties select and nominate political leaders who can appeal to the public directly. They set broad policy guidelines. But the personal appeal of the leader and his ability to attract widespread support may be, in the last analysis, the decisive factor for victory or defeat at the polls and for continuation in office.

While, as with France, plebiscitary government has an old and venerable lineage in the Bonapartist tradition, also it reflects profound social changes that have created increasingly a homogeneous body politic to which the parties could no longer sell their differentiated ideological or policy programs. Large national formations vie for support on the basis of what increasingly are becoming broadly similar appeals. As a result, identification with the party becomes weaker and weaker or, to put this in a different way, the personality of a leader or the incumbent may become the crucial variable. Correspondingly, the ratio of party members to voters, for the whole community and for each party, declines while the number of independents or "floaters" grows. The personality of the candidates often decides the issue—as the victories of Eisenhower, De Gaulle (both non-party men), and, on three occasions, Adenauer clearly showed.

The basic difference here between western democracies and totalitarian systems is primarily that the latter exclude any competition and use the election as a well-controlled plebiscitary instrument while the democracies give the citizens choices that are becoming, however, limited more and more. All other things being equal, the leader in the people's democracy and in the Soviet Union is more likely to emerge after he has proven his credentials within the party, which remains a powerful screening and recruitment agency. In western democracies, excepting England, nonparty men may, without prior screening or testing, avail themselves of the plebiscitary character of the election.

The logic of plebiscitary democracy applies to both western democracies and totalitarian systems. The intermediary organs— even the parties—are weakened, the representative assemblies diminished, and political power is concentrated overwhelmingly in the hands of the political leaders.

No institutions to countenance the tremendous concentration of political and decision-making powers in the hands of a plebiscitary leader have developed yet. The traditional 19th century safeguards—legislative assemblies, committees, responsibility of the executive to the legislature, judicial review, recall and referendums on policy questions, federalism and local government—either are dead or are going through a careful period of reconsideration.

The Changing Nature of the Bureaucracy[13]

The most significant change, reflecting profound modifications in the political culture of contemporary modern societies, is in the bureaucracy. We are referring not only to its sheer growth or to the multiplication of its functions, but particularly to profound internal changes of values and perceptions. Traditionally "bureaucracy" has been viewed only as an instrument to enforce and execute the law. Impartial and neutral—at least in theory— it was also remote, incarnating the authority and majesty of the State. Structured internally on the basis of superior-inferior relations with clear-cut functional division of labor, it remained the most solid bastion of the statist tradition in all European countries including Russia. It emphasized legality rather than equity, rule application rather than innovation, continuity rather than change. The civil servants remained aloof from everyday affairs, saw more files than citizens, and made quasi-judicial decisions. The "mandarin," as the French called the civil servant, lived and flourished in the interconnected bureaus and pigeon-holes of the Weberian model of a legal-rational organization.

This model no longer applies. The increase in numbers and the expansion of functions provided a serious quantitative change. The civil servant became ubiquitous, and as a result, the aloofness and remoteness that characterized his occupation and status were qualified. The performance of new functions brought far-reaching qualitative changes. The bureaucrat was transformed from the guardian of the law to a quasi-legislator; his quasi-judicial functions were slowly transformed into decisions that had immediate consequences in the lives of large groups and affected the social environment directly; his world became enlarged and broadened and he began to view his constituency, not as a host of individual plaintiffs who sought redress in accordance with the law, but as groups and interests that pressed for decisions affecting the very fabric of social relations. The passive administrator assumed an active posture and the neutral and impartial observer found himself confronted with conflicts and interests that called for discretion and choice among alternatives. While still clinging to the tradition of statism and neutrality, the bureaucracy became permeated with pressures and forces that called for positive action and discretion. Also, the instruments available to the bureaucracy have changed. The bureaucracy makes almost nine-tenths of the rules and regulations that the State machinery spawns every year in any developed industrialized society.

The civil servant's mentality and role became transformed inevitably when he entered the realm of direct action in the world of economy, labor, commerce, banking, and production. The skills required to regulate, let us say, credit are vastly different from those needed to decide on the applicability of a law to individual cases. The man responsible for using atomic energy to produce electricity, constructing new cities, producing cars, settling labor disputes that involve large groups and interests, producing coal, maintaining full employment is vastly different from his 19th century counterpart. Knowledge, expertise, originality, and inventiveness, but also ability to gain cooperation and support from the interests involved became crucial. The civil servant who is responsible for economic planning must not only know his job, but must be in touch with the interests affected by planning.

Consultation and mutual interpenetration of interests and civil servants, has become the rule. The old bureaucracy based upon "imperative coordination" has become transformed into a "consultative" bureaucracy that acts over vast domains of social life and is permeated thoroughly by the interests it serves and by the need to serve the citizen-customer. The more it does so, the more open and responsive it becomes and the more blurred become the lines that separated it from the community. The reader may well argue that this is not necessarily new, that interests always controlled and even colonized important sectors of the bureaucracy. This argument misses the point. I am pointing to something entirely different—an open consultative process between civil servants and interests for the purpose of reaching a decision through a process of deliberation and often confrontation, an open dialogue that changes the attitudes of both parties. The colonization by powerful interest groups of the bureaucracy or some of its bureaus or departments was nothing but an effort to use its authority and alleged impartiality for their own ends or to neutralize it. Interests pursued their purpose behind the cloak of bureaucratic anonymity. Now the dialogue is open, the anonymity is lacking, the possibility for all interests to be heard is much greater. The civil servants who make decisions engage their responsibility—not legal or hierarchical but down-right political responsibility. The very orientation of the civil servant toward the customer-citizen carries implications of change that also worked for the political parties. The civil servant will want to hear as many customers as possible before he decides what product to make, what service to perform, and what decision to make.

The "New Corporatism"

The new relations between interest groups and the bureaucracy also account for a radical transformation in the mentality, attitudes, and manner of action of the interests. A new relationship has evolved and is in the process of being institutionalized, calling for an open and continuing dialogue—a "New Corporatism."

"Corporatism," repugnant so long to liberal political thought and castigated by the Marxists, was, at heart, a doctrine giving the State authority and control over powerful interests—notably labor—that were threatening the status groups in the 19th century. It stipulated that interests, defined by the State arbitrarily in terms of certain economic activities—industry, agriculture, transportation, etc., would be elevated to the status of "corporations" with quasi-public functions. Such bodies would be widely representative of the individuals that performed any type of work that fell within the economic activity as defined by the State and would, always under the authority of the State and the bureaucracy, perform certain stated functions: consultation, regulation, and deliberation with other similarly organized interests. The overriding trait of the corporatist thinking was the dominance of the State. "Guild socialism," in contrast, was aimed at emancipating all associations and economic interests from the control of the state. It was an explicit attack against sovereignty and authority in the name of pluralism. While the proponents of corporatism aimed to dominate the interests and harness them to the purpose of the State, guild socialism was dedicated to liberating the interests and the occupational groups so that they might pursue their respective goals through an ill-defined system of consultations and deliberations.

"New corporatism" is a cross between the two and refers to the institutional changes that are unfolding before us, rather than being a well-developed body of theory as were corporatism and guild socialism. It can be understood best simply by pointing out that both corporatists and guild socialists proved to be right in part: the State, through the executive and the bureaucracy, has become stronger, as the corporatists wanted, but the interests have become more independent, autonomous, and strong as the guild socialists desired. In fact, both the interests and the State are stronger and better organized than ever before. What is more, probably they have drawn strength from each other and their development has been parallel, despite periods of conflict.

Generally, interests are attracted to the centers of power and decision-making. The growth of the executive branch, the concentration of rule-making powers in the bureaucracy, the direct or indirect control by the State over the economy, and, last but not least, the benefits that the state can dispense or withhold, in the form of subsidies, tax rebates, tariffs, purchases, etc., have attracted inevitably the attentions of the interest groups. In the past—at least in most of the continental democracies of Western Europe and to a large extent in England—their efforts were directed toward the legislature where the decisions were made, while they shied away from the often intractable or impotent bureaucracy. The focus of attention has changed as the locus of power changed. We can trace the shifting attitude of the interest groups and study their relationships with the executive and the bureaucracy in terms of the following stages: mutual aversion and hostility, pressure group tactics, the beginning of a dialogue, and finally the development of permanent and organic relations that amount to both the politicization of the bureaucracy and to the full domestication of the interest groups. The last stage corresponds to what we have called the "new corporatism."

The change occurred when the bureaucracy and the executive branch assumed policy-making functions and took control of many economic activities. The interests found themselves in a position where executive spending and control became the very essence of their own welfare. Gradually, and sometimes rapidly, they abandoned the legislative chambers and committees in favor of the previously awesome chambers of the bureaucracy. The dialogue had begun but in a manner that was most propitious to both sides. While the interests depended upon the manner in which the bureaucrat dispensed his largess, the latter was extremely sensitive to the support he would receive from them in the performance of his new technical functions. Also, he depended, to a great degree, upon advice and cooperation—as demonstrated clearly by the early New Deal years and by economic planning in France and England since World War II. But the civil servant also was concerned with satisfying as many demands as possible and with eliciting as much support as he could in making decisions that affected large aggregates of the population.

At this point, we enter the present stage. Interests and bureaucracy locked in a permanent dialogue not only bridge the distance that separated them, but become so deeply interconnected and intermingled as to lose, properly speaking, their respective identities. The bureaucracy becomes open to the interests, but at a price; and the interests welcome the new instrumentality that sustains them, but at a sacrifice. Bureaucracy extracts the price of openness in the dialogue and the requirement that all interests be heard before a decision is made; the interests sacrifice by accepting compromise and the realization that a common denominator is better than insistence upon exclusiveness. The new corporatism erases the sharp lines between the State and economic interests, and creates a climate that institutionalizes dialogue, compromise, and give-and-take between the two for the pursuit of goals and objectives that concern both. The "mandarin" becomes the "manager." The executives of private corporations and the spokesmen of interest groups find themselves much more in tune with the new officialdom in status, background, education—if not always income—to make the dialogue both easy and productive. Not really until the end of the forties did the congruence of the objectives of the State and the interest groups become apparent and the overt or latent hostility between the two give place to cooperation. Friction may be generated by the varying policy goals and objectives, but the realization that cooperation is necessary to achieve them, whatever they may be— economic planning, urban redevelopment, health measures, medical insurance, full employment, relocation of marginal enterprises, etc.—no longer escapes anybody.

NOTES

1. S. M. Lipset: *Political Man* (1960). For a sharp differentiation between totalitarian and democratic forms, see C. J. Friedrich and Z. Brzezinski: *Totalitarianism* (1955).

2. M. Massenet: "L'Avenir de la liberté politique," in *Bulletin SEDEIS,* December 1962, Paris.

3. K. Manheim: *Ideology and Utopia* (1936); Daniel Bell: *The End of Ideology* (1960); S. M. Lipset: *Political Man* (1960); Georges Vedel (ed.): *La Dépolitisation—Mythe ou réalité* (Paris: 1962); Léo Hamon: *Les Nouveaux Comportments de la Classe Ouvrière* (Paris: 1962); R. Aron: "Société industrielle, ideologies, philosophie," *Preuves,* Jan., Feb., and March 1965; H. Steck: "The re-emergence of ideological politics in Great Britain: The campaign for Nuclear Disarmament," *Western Political Quarterly,* 18 (1), March 1965: 87–103; R. E. Lane: "The decline of politics and ideology in a knowledgeable society," *American Sociological Review,* 31 (5), October 1966: 649– 662. For a discussion and a dissenting view, Joseph LaPalombara: "Decline of Ideology: A Dissent and an Interpretation," *American Political Science Review,* March 1966, pp. 5–16.

4. LaPalombara, *op. cit.*

5. Otto Kircheimer: "The Waning of Opposition," *Social Research,* Vol. 24, No. 2 (1957).

6. Samuel H. Beer: *British Politics in the Collectivist Age* (1965).

7. E. Deutsch, D. Linden, P. Weill: *Les Familles Politiques Aujourd'hui en France* (Paris: 1966).

8. K. Deutsch, L. Edinger, R. Macridis, and R. Merritt: *France, Germany and the Western Alliance* (1967), particularly pp. 25–117.

9. K. D. Bracher: "Problems of Parliamentary Democracy" and A. Grosser: "The Evolution of European parliaments," in *Daedalus: The New Europe,* Winter 1966, pp. 179–198 and 153–178 respectively. Also Bracher: "Germany's Second Democracy—Structure and Problems," in Henry W. Erhmann (ed.): *Democracy in a Changing Society* (1964), and G. Sartori: "L'avenir des parlements," *Bulletin SEDEIS Futuribles,* 20 February 1964, No. 74.

10. Isaac Deutscher: *Russia What Next* (1953); Barrington Moore, Jr.: *Terror and Progress—USSR.* Also Gordon Skilling: *The Government of Communist East Europe* (1966).

11. R. Macridis and B. Brown: *The DeGaulle Republic: Quest for Unity* (1960), and Stanley Hoffmann *et al.: In Search of France* (1964).

12. See the excellent article of Otto Kircheimer, "The Transformation of Western European Party Systems," in J. LaPalombara and M. Weiner (eds.): *Political Parties and Political Development* (Princeton: 1966), and G. Sartori, "European Political Parties—The Case of Polarized Pluralism," *ibid.,* pp. 137–176. Also R. Macridis (ed.): *Political Parties* (1967); Barnes, Grace, Pollock and Sperlich, "The German Party System and the 1961 Federal Election," *American Political Science Review,* 56 (4), December 1962, pp. 899–914; P. Pulzer, "Western Germany and the Three-Party System," *Political Quarterly,* 33 (4), October–December 1962, pp. 414–426; C. E. Frey, "Parties and Pressure Groups in Weimer and Bonn," *World Politics,* 17 (4), July 1965, pp. 635–655.

13. Many of my remarks on the role of interests and the changing nature of bureaucracy are based on the recent French experience. See particularly P. Lamerle: *La Planification en France,* and P. Viot: *L'-Aménagement du territoire en France* (Paris: Institut d'Études Politiques de l'Universite de Paris, 1964–65). Also in *Bureaucracy and Political Development,* edited by Joseph LaPalombara (1963), Fritz M. Marx, "The Higher Civil Service as an Action Group on Western Political Development," pp. 62–95; Merle Fainsod, "Bureaucracy and Modernization: The Russian and Soviet Case," pp. 200–232; and Carl Beck, "Bureaucracy and Political Development in Eastern Europe," pp. 268–300; and Brzezinski, "Cincinnatus and the apparatchik," in *World Politics,* 16 (1), October 1963, pp. 52–78; and B. Gournay, "Un groupe dirigeant de la société française—les grands fonctionnaires," *Revue Française de Science Politique,* 14 (2), April 1964, pp. 215–242.

Change in British Politics:
Labour in Parliament and Government*

by Robert T. Holt and John E. Turner

IN THE EARLY MORNING HOURS OF APRIL 1, 1966, LONDON newspapers carried banner headlines announcing that the Labour Party had won a smashing victory by piling up a majority of about 100 seats. Prime Minister Harold Wilson knew the result before he retired early that April morning. Now he could rest easily with the knowledge that the nightmare of having to govern with a slender margin was over at last.

After Labour's narrow victory in October 1964, the Government had a hairline majority ranging from five to three. Yet it managed not only to survive, but also to enact the bulk of its legislative program. The task of keeping the Labour banner at full mast in the division lobbies, however, had not been easy. For some crucial votes, ailing Labour members were brought to the precincts of the Palace at Westminster by ambulance in order to preserve the Government's majority. The Liberals, to be sure, often voted with Labour, but a governing ministry

* This study was carried out under the auspices of the Center for Comparative Political Analysis, Department of Political Science, University of Minnesota. The authors have benefitted from conversations with Professor L. J. Sharpe, Nuffield College, Oxford, and from help given by Professors Roger W. Benjamin, William H. Flanigan, David E. RePass, and John E. Schwarz, of the University of Minnesota. Mr. Richard Leonard secured some information for us on one of the Early Day Motions. Dr. Henry Durant, Director of the Gallup Poll, has kindly given us permission to cite some of the Poll findings. Special commendation is due to Mrs. Patricia Hayman-Chaffey and Mrs. Diana Rigelman, who assisted with the research.

cannot afford to rely upon the moods of another party, especially when that party dislikes some of its program—such as steel nationalization and the Land Commission. Hence, from October 1964 until February 1966 the Government had to operate under the realization that its dependable majority might be wiped out by the "Grim Reaper" or possibly even by a handful of ideological dissidents within its ranks whose strong beliefs on a given issue might prompt them to stay out of the Government's division lobby.

But even though death gradually reduced his overall majority— leading one Labour M.P. to remark that the Deity must have "Conservation leanings"—the Prime Minister skillfully held his parliamentary forces together and was able to call a new election at a time of his choosing. His sensitive political antennae enabled him to gauge the timing properly. Even before all the returns were in, he knew that his Party had a commanding lead. Exhausted from a grueling campaign, Wilson could now relax a bit; he no longer had to worry about his Government falling by accident, or as a result of persistent onslaughts from the opposition, or the rebellion of a few Labour dissidents. Barring the most exceptional circumstances, Britain would have five years of Labour government.

The textbook description of the operation of the House of Commons would justify whatever confidence Wilson gained from the electoral returns. According to typical analyses, the role of the majority party is to support the government and the job of the opposition to criticize. The problem of keeping the backbenchers in line is often treated simply as a problem of getting a three-line whip into the hands of each supporter several days before a crucial division. Apparently, unified, disciplined parties in a parliamentary system require nothing more.

Comparison with the American Congress tends to support this view. In the twentieth century, no government with a majority in the British House of Commons has fallen as a result of having been defeated in a division. Votes against the government by members of the majority party are rare; even unauthorized abstentions do not occur with great frequency.

Voting in the House of Commons, however, cannot be compared in any simple-minded fashion with voting in Congress. An American President can be defeated time after time in his efforts to push his program through Congress and still remain President of the United States. But a single defeat on a major issue will topple a Prime Minister and his government. Indeed, on some occasions, even significant dissent within his own party has led to the resignation of a Prime Minister. Witness, for example, the collapse in 1940 of the Chamberlain Government which was still able to carry the day in the division lobbies, but with a greatly diminished majority. The consequences that may follow from M.P.s voting against their leaders when their own party is in power are so great that the infrequency of such rebellions should come as no surprise; it is more surprising that they happen at all. The fact that they do occur from time to time suggests that a party is not as cohesive and unified as one might surmise from a superficial examination of the division lists on a sample of votes. Moreover, if the party embraces dissident factions, something more than a three-line whip is needed to keep the members marching into the appropriate lobby.

In this chapter we shall try to identify this "something more" and to indicate how the Labour Government in the 1966 parliament has tried to rally the support of its backbenchers behind the policies of the Cabinet. We cannot, however, launch a frontal attack upon this problem. Before we can adequately explain the approach which Mr. Wilson and his colleagues have taken to the problem of maintaining cohesion within the Parliamentary Labour Party (PLP), we must lay a rather wide foundation so that the various components of the problem will be visible clearly.

In erecting this foundation, we must first point out the difficult economic, social, defense, and international problems which have confronted Britain since the second war, and we must note the issues of public policy to which they have given rise. Without these stubborn and deeply-rooted problems, which require an assessment of priorities as well as legislative action, the task of maintaining the unified support of Labour backbenchers would be much easier for the Party leaders. Second, we must examine the major policies pursued by the Wilson Government when it held a razor-thin majority from October 1964 until March 1966. Third, we shall glance at the 1966 election campaign, noting the salience of some of these issues, as well as the sweep of the Labour Party to a larger majority.

With this segment of the foundation constructed, we shall review the actions of the Labour Government as it operated with a large majority after April 1966. We shall call attention to issues that generated dissension on the backbenches, prompting significant numbers of Labour members to register their objections in public by abstaining on crucial votes and, in one instance, by actually voting against their Government. For the student who has been led to believe that the maintenance of discipline within the Parliamentary Labour Party is an automatic process overseen as a matter of course by the whips, the actual voting records may produce some surprises. But the student may now ask some interesting questions. Why do "floor rebellions" develop? Who fosters and supports them? How do the Party leaders attempt to cope with them?

Additional background information is required to answer these questions. We need to explore the pluralistic nature of the Parliamentary Labour Party, identifying the major socio-economic groupings and the subcultures of attitudes which tend to crystallize. In order to get a better view of these, we must establish a base-point. This will be done by glancing briefly at the composition of the PLP from 1945 to 1950, examining the patterns of support for and dissidence against the Government in two major floor rebellions. With this earlier period as a benchmark, we shall have a better vantage point from which to observe the changes that have taken place in the makeup of the backbench group in recent years, as well as the changing patterns of support for Government policies.

The concluding sections of this chapter deal specifically with the problem of maintaining discipline among the rank-and-file Labour M.P.s. Here we shall observe that the old-style methods of discipline may no longer be appropriate for many new backbenchers. Apparently, the Wilson Government has recognized this problem and is trying to cope with it in markedly new ways. These new techniques of generating consensus, however, may have implications for the operation of the House of Commons that extend beyond the initial problem of preserving the unity of the PLP. But, this is too far ahead of our story. We return to the starting point of our outline, the difficult problems that Britain has faced since World War II.

BRITAIN'S POSTWAR PROBLEMS

World War II was in many respects a watershed in British history. Looking backward from 1939 toward the nineteenth century, one sees a great world power relatively secure in its insular position, with its navy still controlling the "narrow seas"— the channel, the continental outlets into the North Sea, Gibraltar, Suez, Aden, and the Straits of Sumatra. Secure in empire, strong in military power, and skillful in diplomatic dealings, Britain was always a power to be reckoned with in international affairs. At home, her industrial plant was one of the most formidable in the world and the social and political relationships which had been pragmatically worked out through the decades were widely accepted.

Late in the nineteenth century, however, indications of dramatic changes appeared. The growing strength of Germany, Japan, and the United States posed a challenge to Britain's control of the seaways, and foreign merchants provided vigorous competition in world markets. While countries with enormous industrial potential were beginning to exert more influence in world affairs (in the 1920s the USSR could be placed in this category), the British industrial plant and resource base entered a phase of relative decline. At the same time, rumblings of social discontent could be heard within the country, as new political movements— especially the Labour Party—began to attract a larger mass following. On the eve of World War II, however, the Conservatives were still the dominant party; the Empire—modified by the development of Commonwealth status—remained intact; and Britain's industrial base was powerful enough that the nation could stand virtually alone against the Nazi enemy in the opening stage of the conflict.

The forces of change were greatly accelerated by the war and just five years after the Battle of Britain the picture was entirely different. The United States and the Soviet Union were now the superpowers and were making decisions that once had been made in London, Paris, and Berlin. The fires of nationalism were smoldering in sections of the Empire. India, the crown jewel, was soon to be granted independence—a first step in the dissolution of the Empire. With the Labour Party in full control of parliament for the first time, its leaders were to introduce a set of reforms designed to change the social face of Britain drastically. The economy, badly disrupted by the war, was to reveal the fundamental weaknesses that had been concealed from most people for so many years.

Looking forward from the watershed of World War II, one sees a nation trying to carve out a new international role appropriate for a state with second-class military potential and struggling to work out a realistic timetable for granting independence to its colonies. At the same time, the economy had to be rebuilt, revitalized, and modernized, and the growing demand for a larger measure of social and economic equality had to be met without undermining standards that had been a hallmark of British society. We need to examine several of these interrelated problems in more detail in order to gain some appreciation of the difficulties that would face any political party called upon to take over the governing of Britain in the 1950s and 1960s.

Problems in the Economy and the Crisis of Sterling

International bankers, when considering support for the pound sterling, sometimes speak of the "English sickness." The symptoms of the disease are easily detectable—lagging growth rates, inflationary pressures, chronic balance of payments difficulties. From 1950 until 1962, average growth of per capita gross national product (GNP) in constant prices was only 2.1 per cent annually.[1] These rates of growth were below comparable figures for the United States, West Germany, France, and Japan. While the economy was growing slowly, the price index was rising rapidly. Taking the 1960 price index as 100, by 1965 it had risen to 118.[2] From 1960 to 1965, major balance of payments crises developed in 1960, 1964 and 1965.

The price index has increased so much faster than the growth rates because average annual income has risen much faster than productivity. From 1955 to 1965, average income for wage and salary earners increased by about 75 per cent.[3] With income rising more rapidly than production, there were bound to be inflationary pressures and increased demand for imports of consumer goods, which helped to throw the international accounts out of balance. However, if we proceed a step farther and ask why the economy has not grown more rapidly, especially during a period of full employment, the problem becomes more complicated.

Part of the answer lies in the economic costs of the war. Billions of dollars of capital assets were destroyed by the war. Billions more were lost through "disinvestment"—under the pressures of war, the people were unable to maintain capital equipment in non-essential industries, particularly those specializing in the export of consumer items. Even more important, Britain was forced to sell many of her overseas investments to help pay for the war effort. Other investments were lost in countries that were overrun by the enemy. While Britain in 1939 had been a creditor nation, using income from her overseas investments to help finance imports, Britain in 1949 was a debtor nation and had to use income from her exports to pay the interest and principal on her overseas debts. But this is not the complete picture. After all, countries like France and Germany, which also suffered heavily during the war, were able by the early 1950s to develop vigorous economies with healthy growth rates. Thus, although it must be conceded that the war contributed significantly to Britain's problems, other factors are obviously operating.

One of the most important factors is the decline in Britain's natural resource base. English iron and coal mines have been worked longer and more intensively than any others in the world and, by the middle of the twentieth century, they were rapidly becoming exhausted. Since the coal mines were deep and the seams narrow and steeply sloping, extraction costs ran far above those in the United States and in many parts of Western Europe. Moreover, iron ore had to be imported. And while the resource base that had been the foundation of the economy during the iron and steam age was being depleted, a new industrial technology based upon non-ferrous metals and petroleum was emerging. Britain did not have the raw materials for this type of technology, and was forced to import them in huge quantities—an additional debit on the international ledger.

In diagnosing Britain's economic ailments, experts call attention to other factors, the impact of which is more difficult to discern. Some analysts point an accusing finger at organized labor, criticizing the trade unions for their restrictive practices ("featherbedding," in American parlance), their lack of discipline which results in disruptive "wildcat" strikes over minor issues, and their power during full employment which sometimes enables them to extract exorbitant concessions from management. Equally frequent are the indictments of management. The British entrepreneur is occasionally portrayed as rich and lazy, more interested in price-fixing agreements than in vigorous competition, and generally prone to cautious investment policies which are not conducive to dynamic growth.

These criticisms contain grains of truth, but the fault rests not so much in personality characteristics as in certain structural features of the British economy. The rational manager in a fully-employed economy tends to "hoard" labor, and hence is relatively unconcerned about restrictive practices. Rising consumer demands usually enable him to sell all that he can produce even if the prices rise steadily. Why should he seek new, risky export markets when he can sell all of his product at home? Why should he borrow money to launch new schemes with the bank rate at six or seven per cent? The attitudes of organized labor are equally easy to understand. The memory of unemployment in the interwar years still haunts some of the trade-union branches, especially their older members. The men on the shop floor have made enormous gains since the war and they guard them jealously. The fear of technological unemployment is real and widespread. Until the workers have some guarantee of income through such devices as redundancy payments, they will defend the restrictive practices of their unions. Their concern, too, about the "capricious decisions" of management continues to incite some workers to wildcat strikes.

The remedy for these problems requires changes in the entire industrial complex, but significant change is not easy to introduce. Change is difficult because so many factors must be manipulated simultaneously. It might seem simple to lower the bank rate, making money cheaper and thereby stimulating new and productive investment. But a bank rate reduction would cause foreign holders of sterling to convert to a different currency and thus help to create another balance of payments crisis. Adequate redundancy payments, if financed by the private sector, will drive up the costs of production in the short run and thus drain needed capital away from investment. If the payments are taken over by the govern-

ment, they will either contribute to inflation (if financed by bor-
rowing) or reduce funds available for investment (if financed
by increased taxes). Obviously, if single solutions are likely to
fail, a simultaneous attack on several interrelated problems involves serious political and administrative difficulties.

While all postwar governments have tried to cope with these
problems, they have all taken actions which, however well they
may be justified on certain grounds, have tended to exacerbate
rather than to rectify the fundamental weaknesses in the economy.
On humanitarian grounds, it is easy to justify the national health
scheme, periodic increases in pensions, and the steeply progressive
pattern of taxation. But, as the income of the worker rises in an
increasingly consumer-oriented economy and when he has little
financial worry about major sickness and retirement, his propensity
to save tends to decline even as his income goes up. This helps
to dry up some of the sources for capital investment which are
necessary if the economy is to grow and provide the resources
for the humanitarian programs of the welfare state. Yet few leaders
in either major political party would advocate a reduction in welfare benefits or the social services for the purpose of strengthening
the economy. Such a policy would, in effect, place the burden of
economic expansion upon those least able to pay.

Even this brief survey of Britain's economic problems helps explain why they have commanded so much attention from every
government in the 1950s and 1960s and why they have not
yielded to quick and easy solutions. The full magnitude of the
difficulty, however, cannot be visualized unless we see how it is
interlaced with the international problems which have confronted
the British people.

Crises in Defense, Foreign, and Colonial Policy

The postwar international environment was far different from
what it had been in the first four decades of the twentieth century. It was an age of super-powers and of a bi-polar international
system. Not only had Britain's economic potential for conducting
an independent foreign and defense policy diminished in comparison with the United States and the Soviet Union, but the
technology of nuclear weapons rendered the small and densely
populated islands intolerably vulnerable in a nuclear conflagra-

tion. The channel was not what it had been in either 1860 or 1940.

Despite Britain's decline in relative power and her crushing economic burdens, the Labour Government in 1945 pursued a defense and foreign policy appropriate for a nation of the first rank. Its leaders decided to develop nuclear weapons—first atomic, and then hydrogen bombs—and to equip the defense forces with this capability. When it became apparent that the USSR posed a threat to Western Europe, Britain helped found NATO and later placed four combat divisions on the Rhine. (At the peak of its commitment the United States had slightly more than five divisions in Germany.) Even after India and Pakistan had been granted independence, Britain maintained the capability to operate East of Aden.

The development of a military establishment on the same technological level as that of the United States and the USSR soon became impossible. The Conservative Government decided to produce a missile system—the Blue Streak—to carry British nuclear weapons, but it became apparent before very long that the costs of developing what would be an obsolete system were too great and the plan was scrapped. As a substitute, the Government decided to purchase the Skybolt system from the United States, and to meld it with the "V-bombers." The United States, however, abandoned the Skybolt as too complicated and expensive, leaving Britain in the missile era with little more than a fleet of aging bombers. Hurried negotiations between Prime Minister Macmillan and President Kennedy led to an agreement that the United States would sell Polaris missiles for use in British-made submarines. Shortly after the Wilson Government came to power in 1964, it made a comparable decision to halt the development of a new multi-purpose fighter plane—the TSR-2—and to purchase the controversial TFX from the United States.

These transactions enabled Britain to maintain a formidable, technically-advanced defense force at a lower cost than if she had developed the systems on her own. But the purchases from America required hard currency expenditures, thereby contributing to the balance of payments problem.

Thus, Britain was confronted by sticky alternatives. Either she could remain a nuclear power or she could pursue a defense strategy along the lines of the Swiss or Swedish model. The former alternative required that Britain decide whether to develop and produce advanced defense systems herself at enormous cost (and perhaps, in the long run, at technologically inferior levels), or to purchase the costly equipment from the United States with hard-earned foreign currency. Each of these three possibilities had support in the Labour Party.

In the postwar period, the British have also been engaged in the disestablishment of their Empire. After granting independence to India and Pakistan, they set up a time schedule, in agreement with the colonies concerned, for orderly transfer of authority to the new countries. Although at times the transition was far from smooth, it had largely been completed by the mid-1960s—with one major exception, which posed a serious problem for Wilson's Government.

The exception was Rhodesia. Unlike many other parts of Britain's colonial empire, Rhodesia has a significant population of land-owning white people who are committed to permanent residence. Opinion in Britain favored a constitution for Rhodesia that would enable the African majority to dominate the government of the country after independence. Fearful of such an arrangement, the white minority unilaterally declared independence and established a government that would insure white supremacy. The newly independent nations in Africa—especially the new members of the Commonwealth—pressed Britain strongly to suppress the "rebels" by armed force. Although the Wilson Government was unwilling to resort to such drastic action, it did ask for economic sanctions supported by the United Nations and attempted to negotiate a compromise settlement with the Rhodesian leaders.

While colonial disengagement helped alleviate a few of Britain's problems, some of these emerging nations soon began contributing to a festering problem within Britain. The members of the Commonwealth, though independent states in every respect, have special relationships with the United Kingdom. One right they enjoyed was that their citizens could reside in Britain after passing a simple medical examination. This created no problem so far as the older Commonwealth members (like Canada, Australia, and New Zealand) were concerned. Their citizens were culturally linked with the British, and, in any event, the general movement of population was toward them and away from Britain. But special problems arose when former colonies in Africa, Asia, and the West Indies became members of the Commonwealth. Thousands of their people viewed Britain as a promised land where jobs, housing, and a better way of life were available, and a wave of immigrants drifted into London and other industrial centers. Many of the new immigrants differed from the native residents, not only in color, but also in educational attainment, cultural values, and style of living. With the influx of immigrants into crowded cities which already faced a severe housing shortage, racial tensions began to develop, culminating in minor street disturbances in some areas. In 1961–1962, the Macmillan Government sought to relieve the pressure by introducing a set of immigration controls.

Housing

While economic difficulties and problems of defense and foreign policy consumed much of the time of government leaders in the 1960s, most British citizens were more concerned about an issue closer to home (literally speaking). Housing has been scarce in the industrial cities since the war. The shortage is particularly acute in London and other parts of Southeast England, where there have been heavy movements of population. Like the other problems we have examined, the housing shortage originated in the depression years, when residential construction almost stopped, and the war, when home building was neglected and many thousands of residential units were destroyed. The housing programs of both the Labour and Conservative governments would have alleviated the shortage considerably by the 1960s if the British people had not become so mobile. The enormous population shifts to London and adjacent districts, combined with the influx of Commonwealth immigrants, prolonged the shortage and, in some places, made it worse. The Milner Holland Committee, which studied the problem in London, reported in 1964 that 1,500 families (7,000 people) were without homes and were forced to rely upon hostels and reception centers provided by the local authorities on an emergency basis.[4]

THE FIRST WILSON GOVERNMENT

The economy, defense and foreign policy, immigration, and housing became the crucial issues in Britain during the 1960s. Three of these problems—the economy, defense, and foreign policy—commanded the attention of the Wilson Government after it received a new mandate from the voters in March 1966. In order to understand the specific political problems encountered by Wilson during his second tour of office, however, it will be instructive to survey the policies of the Labour Government when it was forced to operate with a slim majority.

Although many experts questioned whether the Party, with a majority of five, could govern effectively against determined opposition efforts, the new Prime Minister proceeded as though his majority were five times as big. A coalition with the Liberals was not considered seriously. No immediate thought was given to a cutback of the more controversial parts of the Party's program. Harold Wilson was the first Labour Prime Minister in Britain since 1951 and he was determined to act like a Prime Minister.

During its first months in office, the Labour Government could devote little attention to the long-range reforms which had been stressed in the Party's campaign rhetoric. The immediate crises were too pressing. The balance of payments question was the most threatening. Wilson was not fully aware of the magnitude of the difficulty until shortly after he had taken office, when detailed reports revealed that the pound was in serious trouble and that something had to be done with dispatch. The new Prime Minister and his senior colleagues ruled out devaluation—a policy they were forced to adopt later, in the autumn of 1967—and imposed a temporary surcharge on imports, particularly manufactured and semi-manufactured items. On November 11, 1964, the Chancellor, Mr. Callaghan, introduced a supplementary budget which increased certain duties and tax assessments. A few days later, the bank rate was raised to 7 per cent. While these measures were being implemented, the danger signals on the currency reserves continued to flash. To tide Britain over the sterling crisis, the Government negotiated loans of more than $1 billion with central banks in Europe and North America. In late November, additional credit facilities of $3 billion were arranged with foreign central banks and the Bank for International Settlements. Subsequent assistance from the International Monetary Fund enabled the Government to repay the short-term credits as they fell due. These financial transactions relieved the pressure on the pound for the time being, but so far little had been done to remedy the long-run problem.

The remedy, of course, was clear enough: prices needed to be stabilized and the income from exports would have to rise much faster than expenditures for imports, foreign travel, and overseas defense. But how to achieve these results in a way that would be both economically effective and politically feasible was far from clear. After the initial sterling crisis, the first cautious step toward a solution was taken in the first real Labour budget in April 1965. Some excise taxes were increased and new taxes were levied on capital gains and corporate profits.

The budgetary intent was clearly deflationary, but the members of the Government realized that these measures were not sufficient to check the pressures of inflation. A "prices and incomes policy" was needed to link wage increases to growth in productivity and to keep prices stable so that the wage increments would retain their real value. The basic consensus for such a policy was hammered out in December 1964 when representatives from the Government, the Trades Union Congress, and several employers associations signed a declaration of intent with respect to productivity, prices, and incomes. It was later agreed that the National Economic Development Council would keep under review the general trends in prices and incomes, and a National Board for Prices and Incomes was created to consider whether particular requests for wage and price increases were in the national interest. Unions and management were to notify the Board voluntarily of proposed dividend distributions, price rises, and wage claims, and to take the Board's recommendations into account. In April 1965, it was announced that the norm for wage increments would be in the range of 3 to 3½ per cent each year, with provision for numerous exceptions.

In 1965, the Government's program was having an impact, but earnings and prices were still rising faster than productivity. If this trend continued, it would lead either to worsened economic conditions or to devaluation. But with such a slender majority, it was difficult for the Government to resort to compulsory controls. During the "July crisis" in 1965, when the pound was threatened again, it cut back or delayed non-essential public projects, placed some private construction projects under licensing controls, restricted installment buying, tightened exchange control regulations, and provided better credit facilities for exporters.

The continuing crisis in sterling, the political gloom that descended on the Party after Patrick Gordon Walker was defeated in the Labour stronghold at Leyton in the January by-election, and the strenuous effort required to work with a tiny majority all contributed to the reluctance of the Government to push through a few of its more controversial legislative proposals. On the renationalization of the steel industry, for example, the Government faced adamant opposition from two Labour members. Their recalcitrance was threatening because the Liberals opposed nationalization. Although in May 1965 the Government won House approval for a White Paper proposing to nationalize steel, it chose not to push the issue any further then. Of course, the Government with its small majority could have taken its chances and attempted to place this controversial measure on the statute books; then, if it lost in the division lobbies, it could have resigned and taken the issue to the country in a new election. This would have been poor strategy for Labour, however, as steel renationalization was not popular among the voters and was not an attractive issue on which to fight an election. Had the Government followed this course of action, it might have been issuing an open invitation to the voters to return the Conservatives to office. Naturally, some left-wing Labour M.P.s were displeased by the Government's failure to discipline its majority and to restore the steel industry to public ownership.

The left-wing Labour members were not only unhappy about the delay in nationalizing steel, but they were joined by colleagues from other sections of the Party in criticizing their leaders for supporting American policy in Vietnam. Just six months after the 1964 election, 49 Labour M.P.s tabled a motion requesting the Government to withdraw its support.[5] Some Labour members were especially incensed by the bombing of North Vietnam. In February 1966, when the United States resumed its air campaign in the North, nearly 100 Labour people sent a protest wire to Senator Fulbright.[6] About the same number, representing various shadings of socialist belief, tabled a motion to condemn the American action.[7]

The 1964–1965 parliamentary session was very demanding for all the Labour members, but the restless members of the left who had pinned their ideological hopes on a Labour government must have suffered especially long periods of frustration. The Ministry persisted, not only in supporting the action in Vietnam, but also in expending precious resources to keep British troops on the Rhine and to maintain an influence East of Suez. Moreover, it arranged to purchase expensive, multi-purpose aircraft elsewhere after cancelling contracts for British-made models. The Government, to be sure, had re-examined and trimmed some expenditures in the defense field. But, in the eyes of those members who view defense commitments as competing with the social services, the Government had not gone far enough. In contrast, however, it had not hesitated to introduce a domestic program of austerity restricting wage increments, curtailing the level of public expenditure in some social services, and probably increasing unemployment. Some people on the left (as well as sizable numbers in other wings of the Party) were also disenchanted by the Government's shift on the question of immigration controls. These controversial policies sometimes had a stinging impact upon potential dissidents, but, if they carried their grievances to the division lobbies, they risked bringing down their own Government. So long as Labour had to function with a minuscule majority, the dissenters realized that without solidarity and discipline in their organization, they could lose everything.

In looking back over the troubled months from October 1964 through February 1966, one can fairly portray the Government as expending most of its energy in a troubleshooting role. Problems which had been festering for some time under previous governments broke open into serious crises, first in one place and then in another. As crisis piled upon crisis, Wilson and his colleagues sought to control them in the short run by conventional ameliorative measures, at the same time taking a few cautious steps toward long-term solutions. This was all they could do until an appropriate time arrived for a new election, when they could be reasonably confident that they would be returned with a bigger majority.

From the clues available to the Prime Minister, the spring of 1966 seemed an appropriate time to go to the country for a new mandate. His majority in the House had gradually dwindled and additional casualties through death were an ever-present danger. Moreover, in the autumn of 1965 the Labour Party had moved comfortably ahead of the Conservatives in the public opinion polls, and its margin continued to hold up during the winter months. The pleasant news delivered by the polls was reinforced in January 1966 by the results of the by-election in Hull North. Although most press reporters had predicted that Labour would lose the seat, the Party actually increased its majority by more than 4,000 votes. In light of these favorable portents, Wilson called the election for March 31.

The 1966 Election

In some respects the 1966 campaign was a re-run of the battle seventeen months earlier.[8] Most of the candidates stood again, many for the same seats, and the Party leaders expounded upon several issues that had been prominent in 1964. The Labour people recognized that their victory in 1964 had been more a protest vote against the Tories than a vote of confidence in them. This time they were suing for a full mandate to carry out the program they had begun to push through.

Assuming a role that seemed to place him above the political struggle, Wilson—together with his Party strategists—was interested in making a simple appeal to the voters. After thirteen years of Tory rule, the Labour Government had inherited serious problems. It had done its best to wrestle with them, making substantial progress in putting through its policies. But the small parliamentary majority had made the going rough, and now it was necessary to appeal to the electorate again. Labour's accomplishments under trying circumstances had demonstrated its ability to govern responsibly and therefore it deserved a solid mandate and a full five-year term in order to put its entire program into operation and give it a chance to take effect. Wilson's Party campaigned with the slogan, "You *know* Labour Government Works!"

The Conservatives, under an untried leader, wanted to avoid being put on the defensive by the "thirteen wasted years of Tory rule" argument, which had damaged them during the 1964 campaign. They sought to present a positive, alternative program to resolve the problems of contemporary Britain. Their slogan was "Action not Words."

THE ISSUES. The Labour and Conservative platforms agreed fundamentally on many issues; their disagreements were less upon goals than upon the means by which the goals could be realized. Both parties gave priority to two clusters of issues: (1) how to improve the operation of the economy so as to strengthen Britain's competitive position in world markets; and (2) how to upgrade the social services.

The question of how to deal with Britain's economic problems was the most important national issue in the campaign. Since the economic objectives of the two major parties were essentially the same, contentious rhetoric centered upon how the goals could best be achieved and which party was more likely to do the job. Both sides promised to attack restrictive practices in management and the trade unions, to plan industrial development for the poorer sections of the country, and to provide incentives to encourage increases in productivity. In addition, each of the parties recognized the need for a prices and incomes policy. The Tories, however, took issue with Labour on two aspects of economic policy: they opposed nationalization of the steel industry, and they advocated gradual elimination of agricultural subsidies (which Labour wanted to retain) and substitution of a system of import controls. With Labour defending the Government's economic program and the Conservatives attacking it, spokesmen for each side virtually smothered the voters with statistics on currency balances, trade patterns, and industrial productivity. But on the public platform and in the mass media, the Tories suffered from the indictment that they had had their chance and had largely failed to resolve Britain's economic problems when they were in office.

The Common Market did not emerge as an issue until half way through the campaign. In their manifesto, the Conservatives enthusiastically supported Britain's entry, but Labour remained hesitant, following the policy laid down by Hugh Gaitskell in 1962. According to this policy, certain conditions (such as protection for British agriculture, the Commonwealth countries, and Britain's partners in the European Free Trade Association) would have to be met before the country should take such a step.[9] The Labour Party was badly split over the Common Market question, and differing viewpoints were held by members of Wilson's Ministry.

The issue began to smolder in mid-March when, after a meeting of foreign ministers from the Western European Union countries in London, France was reported to be willing to support Britain's membership. Noting that Labour's resistance to a common agricultural policy would make negotiations for entry difficult and that several Cabinet ministers opposed entry, the Tory leaders charged that the Government was capable of no more than a "paralytic response" to this new development.[10] Stung by this challenge, the Prime Minister proceeded to deal with it in a speech at Bristol on March 18.[11] In a carefully worded statement, he welcomed the change in the French attitude, and indicated the Government's willingness to lead the country into the Market, provided that safeguards for "vital British and Commonwealth interests" could be negotiated. This issue gave the Tories an opportunity to force their opponents into a more resolute stand which might have had a divisive impact upon the Labour Party. But the Conservatives failed to pursue the attack energetically, and the Common Market did not catch hold as a prominent issue.

Some political experts anticipated that defense policy would provoke a few punches and counter-punches by competing politicians. Shorty before the campaign started, the Defense White Paper had stirred up controversy with the admirals over the effective role of aircraft carriers. This dispute led to the retirement of the Chief of Naval Staff and the resignation of Christopher Mayhew, Minister of Naval Defense, who objected to the curtailment of the carrier program while Britain was still committed to a presence East of Suez. In cities that were affected by the Government's defense policy, Wilson defended the reduction of the carrier program and the cancellation of some aircraft contracts. The Conservatives, in their manifesto and occasionally in their speeches, promised to build a new carrier and to fulfill Britain's treaty obligations in the Middle East and in Asia. Defense, however, did not loom large in the campaign, partly because the Tories had studied their opinion surveys and concluded that they could not get much mileage out of the issue.

A problem as serious as housing was bound to be given an airing on the hustings. Both parties committed themselves to the building of homes, financial relief to local councils that were faced with burdens of slum clearance, protection to leaseholders, and lower mortgage rates. However, in order to insure that resources would be available for housing construction, Labour proposed to control the building of private office premises and to attack the problem of speculation in land through taxation and through the establishment of a Land Commission which would purchase, in behalf of the community, the land on which building and re-building were to take place.

While the housing question received general mention by national speakers, some local campaigns gave it much more importance. In these constituencies Labour candidates devoted considerable time to attacks upon the 1957 Rent Act, calling attention to specific local housing problems and indicating what their Party had done to improve conditions during its short tenure. The housing issue, however, became most crucial in those districts where the local councils—especially those that were Labour-controlled—had been forced to increase the rents for council properties or were contemplating such action. In some of these constituencies, the local Labour leaders worried lest their traditional supporters stage a protest by staying away from the polls on election day.

Other features of the welfare state brought both agreement and disagreement between the two parties. Both sides promised to make pension rights transferable when workers change jobs, to relax the earnings rule for retired people, and to expand educational facilities. Labour, of course, wanted to go much farther than their opponents, advocating the retraining of workers who lose their jobs through redundancy, provision for funds to tide them over, and an earnings-related pensions scheme. The Conservative position that council housing should be reserved for people who really need such accommodation reflected the Party's general philosophy that welfare benefits should be distributed so as "to concentrate better care and the biggest benefits on those in need." Labour, on the other hand, argued that to designate "those most in need" would require the application of a means test. In line with their view, the Conservatives proposed to restore fees for prescription drugs (with some provision being made for the needy) —a policy that Labour vehemently opposed. In the field of education, Labour advocated the extension of the system of comprehensive schools, to which the Conservatives took exception.

Political leaders in both parties sought to keep the immigration issue out of the campaign. This had been an explosive question in some constituencies during the 1964 encounter, but it was less openly articulated in 1966 and was probably of less political consequence. Nearly all of the constituencies that had been afflicted with the issue earlier produced a bigger swing to Labour than was characteristic of their regions.

Although to many reporters the campaign lacked sparkle, with opposing leaders conducting exercises in arithmetic and condemning each other for their past records rather than grappling with each other on crucial issues, the hecklers had a field day, and the public meetings drew larger audiences than they had in 1964. According to the Gallup Poll, 82 per cent of the sample had watched the political broadcasts on television, a result that was 11 percentage points higher than in the previous election.[12]

As is usually the case, the British voters were much more interested in economic, "bread and butter" issues than in questions of defense and foreign policy. As the campaign moved into high gear, the Gallup Poll listed the issues of most concern to the voters as follows:[13]

Prices and the cost of living	65%
Pensions and welfare of old people	58
Full employment	56
National Health Service	55
Increasing production, prosperity	51
Satisfactory educational system	49
Housing and rents	49
Income tax and other taxes	47
Maintaining value of the pound	43
Increasing export trade	42
Strikes and trade disputes	32
Foreign affairs	31
Nationalization, private enterprise	31
Colored immigration	31
Armaments and national defense	28
H-bomb	24

THE OUTCOME. British voters trooped to the polling stations on March 31 and Labour's victory was assured early the next morning. Although winning by a smaller margin than the polls had predicted, the Labour Party secured an impressive mandate for a full five-year term. Its strength in the House of Commons jumped from 317 to 363, giving the Party a clear majority of 97. On the opposite side of the political fence, the Conservatives sustained a catastrophic defeat, failing to gain a single seat and suffering a decline in representation from 303 to 253. Among the Tory casualties were five former senior ministers, six junior ministers, six other frontbench spokesmen, the chief whip and three junior whips, and the chairman of the 1922 Committee, as well as a number of promising younger M.P.s.

With a few exceptions, the movement of voters to Labour, which produced a national swing of 3.5 per cent, followed a much more even pattern throughout the various regions of the country than in 1964.[14] The swing to Labour was somewhat larger in those districts where it had been below the average in 1964, and somewhat smaller where the 1964 swing had been more sweeping. The proportionate increase in Labour support was especially marked in nearly all the industrial cities.

Although the turnout of voters in most marginal constituencies was higher than in the previous election, the size of the poll was down for the country as a whole—75.8 per cent, compared with 77.1 per cent in 1964. In fact, proportionately fewer voters went to the polling stations in this election than at any time since 1945. The decline in turnout was most pronounced in the impregnable Labour constituencies in the large industrial cities and in the mining areas.

With a strong mandate to carry on, the Wilson Government was now in a position to turn once again to the problems that were afflicting the country. However, the Prime Minister and his colleagues also faced the problem of maintaining cohesion within the Labour Party ranks. Now that Labour had been returned by a large majority, potentially dissident groups within the organization which had restrained themselves after 1964 no longer had to worry about bringing their Government down by rebellious behavior. Now, let us turn to the policies introduced by Wilson's new Cabinet in response to Britain's continuing problems, and to the impact of some of these policies upon the internal cohesion of the Parliamentary Labour Party.

The Economy

The aggregate statistics at the end of the first full calendar year of Labour government forecast difficulties for the future. The balance of payments deficit in 1965 ran to almost $1 billion; the index of industrial production in January 1966 stood about where it had been a year earlier, while wages were up 5½ per cent and prices had risen by 5 per cent.[15] If the Government hoped, as it entered office again, that it would be freed from crisis so that it could concentrate upon long-range solutions, its hopes were denied. It may be a "law" of politics that when long-range remedies are needed most urgently, immediate crises tend to impinge most heavily upon a nation's leaders. Whether "law" or not, the new Labour Government did not have to wait very long for a crisis to divert it from its main course. The crisis appeared on May 16 in the form of a maritime strike. An event of this sort illustrates in a dramatic way the dilemmas that face a Labour government which tries to deal responsibly with stubborn economic problems but which has emotional and organizational ties with the trade unions.

No government could be unsympathetic with the plight of the seamen. Compared with their comrades on the continent and in the United States, their wages were abysmally low and their basic work week was 56 hours.[16] Moreover, they were tied to some antiquated conditions of employment which had been laid down by statute in the 1890s. More surprisingly, the National Union of Seamen had not been out on strike for more than half a century. In 1966, however, the union leaders demanded a reduction in work week from 56 to 40 hours, with no reduction in pay. When the Shipping Federation rejected this claim, the Minister of Labour tried to bring the two parties to agreement, and the Prime Minister himself met with union officials in an effort to avert a walkout. But these negotiations were not fruitful, and a strike was called. Before very long 800 British ships were lying idle in the harbors.

The impact of a maritime strike upon an island economy which was trying to bolster its export trade was damaging, to say the least. The volume of exports declined rapidly, the automobile industry threatened to reduce its work shifts, and the price of fruits and vegetables rose in the shops. Even more serious, the pound sterling began to suffer in the foreign exchange markets. Although the effect of the strike was softened through the use of air transport and foreign ships by some export firms, the stoppage was estimated to have cost the seamen about $70 million in lost pay before it had run its course.[17]

The maritime strike placed the Labour Government in a thorny spot. It could ill afford to let the dispute drag on, endangering the currency reserves and causing exporters to miss their targets. But neither could it afford to encourage concessions to the seamen's claims, for this would jeopardize its prices and incomes policy, a central part of its economic program which had already been chipped away by the doctors. While still trying to effect a settlement, the Government declared a state of emergency to insure the flow of essential supplies and the performance of essential services. It also established a special Court of Inquiry to examine the claims and to recommend a solution. The Court suggested a compromise which the Government accepted but the union rejected. As the strike wore on, talks were scheduled in Downing Street with the union and management, including at times leaders of the Trades Union Congress. Eventually, on June 27—47 days after the commencement of the strike—the leaders of the seamen voted to end the walkout, accepting the basic recommendations of the inquiry with an additional concession for a longer period of annual leave.

To ride out the maritime strike, resisting the demands of the seamen, was not an easy decision for the Labour Government. The Government represented a party that is cast in the role of defending the workers against injustice and the seamen clearly fell into this category. But the Government had to weigh the justice of the union's claims against wider obligations—the need to secure the pound, to control inflation, and to safeguard its policy of linking wage increases to productivity. Against these priorities, the legitimate demands of a trade union had to take second place. The handling of the dispute demonstrated three things: (1) that a voluntary system of wage restraint was not likely to be effective; (2) that some extremists in certain unions would seek to press short-run demands, even at the cost of wrecking the Government's economic program; and (3) that the Wilson Government would not yield to all of the demands of organized labor if those demands threatened to undermine its projected solutions to Britain's economic problems.

PRICES AND INCOMES. While the Government was coping with difficulties like the maritime strike, it also tried to level a long-range attack on Britain's economic problems. This was evident in the 1966 budget, which was unveiled on May 3. Basically deflationary in character, it increased taxes and appealed for voluntary restraints in certain types of expenditure, such as overseas investment. The budget, however, provided an important regulatory device in the form of a new selective employment tax. All employers—ranging from the giant automobile company to the young widow who hired a full-time baby-sitter while at work—had to pay a tax of 25 shillings ($3.50) per week for each person on the pay roll. (The tax rates for women and teen-age employees were lower.) Every employer, however, would receive a rebate of 32½ shillings for every man employed directly in manufacturing. (Again, lower rebates were applied to women and teen-agers.)

The intent of the new tax was clear. Service industries like hairdressing, restaurants, and entertainment, as well as banking and insurance, were to receive no kickbacks. Employers in these industries would thus be encouraged to reduce their staffs to avoid the tax and thereby force additional workers into the manufacturing sector. Manufacturing industries would also be prompted to adjust the ratio of service employees to "manufacturing" employees. By increasing the cost of "frivolous" activities, the Government hoped that manpower would be released for work in enterprises that were more productive. The doorman at a hotel might lose his job and become a truck driver; the croupier, a welder; and the chorus girl, a riveter. More generally, in the words of the Prime Minister, the tax could be looked upon as a switch away from levies on personal incomes and profits to an assessment on the *costs* of production.

In theory, this was a good idea. Producers would have a sizable tax incentive to decrease their costs of production and thus, hopefully, increase their efficiency. Its weakness, however, was the weakness of any remedy that applies grossly to large aggregate categories in an economy in which the difficulties are encountered selectively. For example, the high cost, labor-intensive firm in manufacturing or construction would receive a huge subsidy which could be used to hire more and more workers to use inefficient tools. By the same token, the manufacturer of mink coats made by hand for the domestic market would receive a subsidy. Difficulties inherent in the new tax were brought to the attention of the Government by a number of M.P.s, including some Socialists, but the ministers held fast to their belief that the net results would be positive. Certainly in the short run its effect would be deflation-ary, because tax payments would run ahead of the subsidies, thus helping to cool off the economy. However, since the kick-back feature of the selective employment tax was rescinded in 1967 (except for the underdeveloped regions), it is impossible to deter-mine the long-term impact of the differential taxation scheme.

For some months the Labour Government had followed the voluntary approach to wage and price restraints. By June 1966, however, it was apparent that voluntary methods were not a smashing success. Powerful unions which felt that they had a strong case for exceptional treatment drove home their demands for wage increases. At the same time, the pound continued to be under heavy pressure in the international money markets.

On July 4, the Government unveiled a new Prices and Incomes Bill which gave the National Board for Prices and Incomes statu-tory powers and provided for compulsory notification of proposed price increases, dividend increments, and wage claims and settle-ments. Considering the nature of the existing crisis, this was a relatively mild remedy which still relied extensively on voluntary cooperation from labor and management to hold prices and wages in line. The bill nevertheless provoked controversy in the Cabinet and the Labour backbenches. The day before it was published, Mr. Frank Cousins, who was on temporary leave of absence from his post as general secretary of Britain's largest union, resigned as Minister of Technology and joined some rank-and-file Labour M.P.s in opposition to the Government's policy.

Even opposition from a powerful trade unionist like Cousins did not deter the Prime Minister from pushing ahead with his plan. In mid-July, he announced that the Cabinet had undertaken a comprehensive review of the economic situation and that an interim budget was imminent. The Government quickly put to-gether an emergency package which was introduced on July 20. Mr. George Brown, Deputy Prime Minister and Minister for Eco-nomic Affairs, had resisted some of its contents and had punctu-ated his opposition by offering to resign and then withdrawing his resignation.

The "mini-budget," as it was soon labeled, aimed to curb do-mestic demand even further and to cut overseas spending. Among the measures announced were a cut of at least $280 million in overseas civil and military expenditures, a reduction in tourist travel allowances, a petrol surcharge, tighter restrictions on bank lending, and stiffer terms for installment buying. At the same time, the Government announced that a new "Part IV" would be included in the Prices and Incomes Bill which had already been published. Under this provision, prices and wages would be frozen for six months and, during the following six months, increases would be allowed only in exceptional circumstances. The Government, however, still hoped to control wages and prices by voluntary action. Part IV laid down the norms by which the Government expected the unions and management to govern their behavior, but these norms would not have the force of law (and hence their violation would not involve penalties) unless Part IV were activated by an Order in Council, which would require approval by the House of Commons within twenty-eight days.

Understandably, Part IV provoked immediate displeasure from many trade-union leaders, especially those who had already negotiated wage increases which would now be deferred for at least six months. They found in Frank Cousins a new spokesman on the backbenches. Freed from the constraints imposed upon him by the convention of collective Cabinet responsibility, he joined Mr. Michael Foot to fight the measure on the floor of the House. Nevertheless, on August 10 the Prices and Incomes legislation— described by the London *Times* as "one of the most unloved measures ever to be lashed through Parliament at the end of a three-line whip"—was passed by a vote of 272 to 214. The Government's majority was reduced by the abstention of 22 Labour M.P.s.

But the opposition was not ready to admit defeat. Any hope that Wilson had for universal voluntary compliance was quickly shattered—such strong medicine is rarely taken simply for altruistic reasons. Just four days after the final vote on the Bill, the general secretary of the Association of Supervisory Staffs, Executives, and Technicians (ASSET) announced that test actions would be brought in the courts, demanding that companies be required to pay wage increases already negotiated. On September 29, a court handed down a judgment that an employer was legally bound to pay wage increments that he had previously contracted.[18] The same day, the Morganite Carbon Company informed the

Ministry of Labour that it would not defer the implementation of a productivity increase agreement with 2,000 workers. And the next day the Newspaper Proprietors' Association decided to pay 25,000 workers a weekly cost-of-living bonus under a 1964 sliding-scale contract.

After almost two years of unsuccessful effort to work out a voluntary scheme to hold prices and incomes down, the Government was forced to turn to punitive measures. On October 25, 1966, it reluctantly asked the House to activate Part IV by approving an Order in Council. The House voted to approve the Government's request, but 28 Labour members abstained.[19] As we shall see, however, the bulk of the opposition did not come from the working-class M.P.s with trade-union backgrounds.

Even though this strong medicine was poured down the throat of the kicking and screaming patient, it soon began to show desirable effects. By the end of 1966, inflationary pressures appeared to be coming under control.[20] Whereas, prior to July, hourly wages had been rising at an annual rate of seven per cent, they remained virtually constant from July to December. Manufacturers' prices did not rise at all, and retail prices rose only 1.5 per cent. Moreover, in the last quarter of the year, there was a balance of payments surplus of nearly $339 million, even after the installments on the American loan had been paid.

When the import surcharges were removed in the spring of 1967, however, the stubborn deficits began to show up again on the international ledger. The Government concluded that the doses of medicine would have to be continued beyond the one-year period provided by existing statutes. In March 1967, it issued a White Paper on the economic situation, indicating its intention to renew prices and incomes controls, and to strengthen some of the restrictions even further. The new legislation was introduced into the House in July. It provided for advance notification of price and wage increases and authorized the Government to delay them for as long as four months. The bill also lengthened to a maximum of six months the period of wage standstills recommended by the National Board and gave the Board power to suspend temporarily any wage or price increases that were implemented before it had had opportunity to consider them. This second Prices and Incomes Bill was approved on July 17, with 22 Labour M.P.s abstaining again.

Strong medicine often has undesirable side-effects. The tightened controls over prices and incomes were no exception. As demand dropped owing to the deflationary measures, unemployment began to rise. In July 1966, nearly 265,000 people were jobless; by October the figure had jumped to more than 435,000 with no end in sight. Although this figure was still less than two per cent of the labor force—low by American standards—it was bound to have political implications because the British tend to be less tolerant of unemployment. Coupled with the rise in unemployment was a decline in production and the growth rate remained disappointingly low. Until something could be done to bring the growth rate up to the standard of the United States and the advanced Western European countries, there could be no real solution to Britain's economic problems. Some new tonic was obviously required.

THE COMMON MARKET. Most members of the Labour Government were convinced that the deflationary measures and the severe restraints on prices and incomes were not sufficient to pull and keep Britain out of the economic doldrums. Nothing short of growth rates of about 3 per cent a year would indicate that Britain's long-range problems were being solved. But thus far the Government's policies provided little confidence that growth rates of this magnitude would be realized without some additional stimulus.

Since the late 1950s a number of prominent British figures— especially in the Liberal and Conservative parties and some leaders in the industrial community—had argued that the problem had no long-term solution if Britain remained outside the Common Market. As we have already seen, the Labour Party was divided over the issue when the Macmillan Government sought entry, and its leaders set down certain conditions that had to be met. Shortly after Wilson became Prime Minister, however, there were some indications that his Government was growing more favorably inclined toward the idea. Some Cabinet members had been strong advocates of British membership for several years and they were able to score some gains over their colleagues who held opposing views. The Party's election manifesto said nothing new about the Common Market, but, near the end of the campaign as we have seen, Wilson held out a few faint hopes for negotiating an agreement with the Six. Late in 1966 and early in 1967, Wilson and some of his leading ministers held discussions with officials of the Common Market countries, the EFTA nations, and the Commonwealth members. In March, the Prime Minister presented a report to the members of the Cabinet which served as the basis for a series of discussions about whether Britain should submit a formal application for membership. Finally, on May 2, Wilson announced that the Government would attempt to secure Britain's entry into the Market.

The most enthusiastic reaction to the announcement came from Liberals and Conservatives. On the Labour side, a sizable group of right-wing backbenchers had grown alarmed by the economic situation. At the time of the "July crisis" in 1966, they had argued for strong measures by the Government, and when the Common Market emerged as a possibility, an even larger group of them began to exert pressure for a favorable decision on application for admission. Their position, however, was countered by other segments of the Party, especially some working-class members and some middle-class leftists, who vigorously opposed it. A manifesto drawn up by Socialist dissenters carried the signatures of 73 backbenchers.[21] As the date approached for the Commons debate on the motion, the Labour whips became aware that they had a large-scale rebellion on their hands. At the appropriate time, 43 rebels tabled an amendment to the Government's motion, pointing out that it failed to adhere to the specific pre-conditions for entry which had been adopted by the Party and affirmed in the election manifesto.[22]

When the strategic division was taken on May 10, 36 Labour M.P.s voted against their government, and 51 other members abstained.[23] The vote in support of the Government was 426 to 62. More than half the opposition was registered by Labour members, many of them from the trade-union group. This was a blow to the discipline of the Party, and the reaction was swift. Seven parliamentary private secretaries who had abstained were immediately dismissed, and the Chief Whip dispatched a letter of rebuke to each of the dissidents. The admonition from the whips'

office stressed the difference between an act of "conscience" and
an act of "hostility." [24] Note, for purposes of later analysis, that
on this occasion 36 Labour members actually voted against the
Government, whereas on the other issues—such as the "wage
freeze" and the defense review—the dissidents had not ventured
so far.

Defense and Foreign Policy

We have already pointed out that the economic problems
which Britain has faced since the war have been aggravated by
her defense and foreign policy commitments. The balance of
payments difficulties, for example, would be greatly eased if defense expenditures overseas could be reduced. Much of the
dissension within the Labour Party over defense questions grows
out of the belief that the Labour's welfare schemes would be
more secure and more effective if defense expenditures were cut.

Britain's commitments abroad have been—and still are—extensive and costly. Her postwar foreign policy has aimed at maintaining her position as a world power. As British political leaders view
the problem, this involves close cooperation with the United States,
the nations of Western Europe, and the other members of the
Commonwealth. Over the years, this cooperation has been expressed in a series of treaties: the Brussels Treaty (1948), the
North Atlantic Treaty Organization (1949), the Southeast Asia
Collective Defense Treaty (1954), the Central Treaty Organization, formerly the Baghdad Pact (1955), and the Malaya Defense Agreement (1957). Most of these agreements were more
than just declarations of intent; since deterrence was the main
objective, the British were obligated to establish military bases
in distant lands and to man them with British forces.

In Europe, the British contribution to NATO consisted of an
army on the Rhine, the maintenance of which cost about $229
million annually; a semi-independent nuclear deterrent in the
form of approximately seventy "V-bombers"; and a small number
of Polaris submarines. In early 1966, nearly 27,000 service men
were stationed in the Middle East, most of them in Aden and
the general area of the Persian Gulf, and an additional 3,000
men served on British ships in the region. British land forces
numbered 54,000, in the Far East, and 9,500 more were with the

fleet. The total annual cost of the troops, equipment, and installations in the Middle and Far East amounted to $92 million. This represents a formidable military commitment for any nation to carry, and it is not surprising that it put a strain on Britain's limited resources.

Debates on defense in the House of Commons do not arise from the introduction of specific enabling legislation, as with economic issues. Many defense debates are based upon White Papers issued by the government. Shortly after taking office in 1964, the Wilson Cabinet began to review the nation's defense needs and the state of its military establishment. It issued its first appraisal in February 1966.[25] The review proposed a continuing reduction of defense expenditures overseas and a gradual diminution of Britain's military commitments, placing primary emphasis upon her Western European rather than Middle Eastern and Asian interests. The Government promised to carry out Britain's treaty obligations and to maintain a military presence outside Europe, but this capability was to be limited in three respects. First, major military operations would be undertaken only in collaboration with allies. Second, Britain would provide another country with military assistance only if that country would supply the facilities needed to make the assistance effective. Third, defense facilities would not be maintained in an independent country against its will. The Government indicated its intention to reduce the overseas forces by about one-third over a four-year period and to build no new carriers. The review indicated in detail how Britain could continue to play a major role in Europe and a limited role in the Middle East and the Far East, even with reduced military expenditures.

The Conservatives blasted the Government's policy as being tantamount to having Britain relinquish her place as a world power, but a small group of Labour backbenchers charged that the cutbacks were not extensive enough and would not be carried out fast enough. They protested that even this reduced role was beyond British resources and that social programs at home were suffering because of unreasonable defense expenditures. However, with Labour's tiny majority and a general election impending, the rebels had to be cautious about supporting their words with action.

These constraints did not apply in February 1967, when the Government issued a White Paper, setting out in detail the proposals for defense spending in 1967–68. The Government's statement reaffirmed its position that, while the armed forces East of Suez would be cut back, a military capability still would be maintained, with Singapore as its center. Most of the Labour critics aimed their blows, as before, at what they believed to be excessive expenditures. A few, including a former Minister of Naval Defense who had resigned in protest against the first White Paper, argued that it was "sheer lunacy" to try to maintain a presence outside Europe with the resources proposed. At the close of the debate, 62 Labour M.P.s refrained from entering the division lobbies.[26] This angered the Prime Minister. At a meeting of the Parliamentary Labour Party a few days later, he chastised those backbenchers who had failed to support their Government on the defense question and other issues.[27] He threatened to impose harsher discipline upon his legislative troops or even call a new election if too many Labour members failed to recognize their obligation to sustain the ministry in power.

The difficulty of breaking old ties and commitments which were also a heritage from Britain's past status in the world became evident to the Labour Government as it dealt with some of its problems in foreign policy—the rebel regime in Rhodesia, the political unrest in the Eastern Mediterranean and South Arabia, and the problems in Gibraltar and Malta. Opinions in the PLP differed over how the Government should handle each of these issues, but they did not create major discipline problems for the whips.

The same evaluation cannot be made of the Government's policy of supporting the American position in Vietnam. The issue came up for major debate in the House of Commons in July 1966. More than 90 Labour backbenchers, supported by eight Liberals, had tabled a motion calling upon the Government to dissociate itself from American military intervention completely.[28] On July 6, the day before the division, Wilson issued a stern warning to his Party members, indicating that he expected full support for the Government.[29] His admonition undoubtedly had some effect, probably because his second ministry had barely been installed. Only 32 Labour members abstained.[30] This group, however, was merely the visible part of the iceberg; a sizable number of M.P.s who strongly dissented on the Vietnam issue and who were less discreet in the division lobbies later, nevertheless voted with the Government on this occasion.

NATURE OF THE LABOUR PARTY

Thus far in our discussion we have drawn attention to the major economic, defense, and foreign policy problems that Great Britain has faced since the end of World War II, the salience of these issues in the 1966 election, and the major policies and programs pursued by the Wilson Governments since 1964. On certain crucial issues—support of American action in Vietnam, prices and incomes policy, defense, and Britain's entry into the Common Market—there were indications of some displeasure within the ranks of the PLP. In 1966, two ministers resigned and another threatened to do so. When the controversial issues were voted upon in the 1966–67 session, significant numbers of Labour M.P.s abstained, and, on the Common Market issue, some of them actually voted against their Government.

Anyone who had followed developments in the Labour Party during the years before the 1964 victory could hardly be surprised that sharp differences of opinion over some of Wilson's policies would arise within the Parliamentary Labour Party. Following its defeat in 1959, the Labour Party entered what might be termed its "time of troubles." Different Party factions analyzed the causes of the defeat differently and advanced incompatible suggestions for strengthening the organization and improving its electoral image. The Party leader, Hugh Gaitskell, and some of his closest associates felt that the Party reflected the socialist mentality of the depression years which did not appeal to the middle-class and younger voters. More particularly, they believed that the traditional emphasis on nationalization was both an economic anachronism and an electoral liability. But the goal of public ownership was listed in Clause IV of the Party's constitution, which had to be amended to change the policy. Gaitskell proposed that this be done. To many people on the left, as well as to some trade unionists and other "traditional Socialists," public ownership was the essence of Labour's program, and they vigorously fought Gaitskell's proposal. When this emotional struggle simmered down,

Gaitskell found himself leading an organization which supported Clause IV as a "valuable expression" of the Party's aims for the rest of the century.

This contest was no sooner over when another issue arose to split the Party into warring factions. The Campaign for Nuclear Disarmament (CND) began to dig its way into the constituency parties and trade unions. Its simple program—that Britain should dispense with her nuclear weapons unilaterally— had great appeal to those Labour people who, for whatever reason, were opposed to heavy military expenditures. At the Party Conference in 1960, the delegates, over the strenuous objection of their leader, voted to support unilateralism as the official position of the Party.

In the aftermath of this defeat, Gaitskell was challenged for the leadership by Harold Wilson, but he had little difficulty in retaining his post. He then launched a determined campaign to reverse the Conference decision on nuclear disarmament, taking his case directly to people in the local areas. With the help of a new organization called the Campaign for Democratic Socialism, Gaitskell gradually won back the support of many constituency parties, and in October 1961 the Party Conference renounced unilateralism.

After the nuclear defense controversy had begun to subside the Labour Party was threatened by another policy dispute, this time over the Common Market. An influential group of Labour M.P.s supported Britain's entry, but, because some national Party leaders, a number of influential trade unionists, and many activists in the local constituencies expressed strong opposition, the issue was not pressed, especially after General de Gaulle decided to veto admission. The issue continued to smolder, however, and it burst into the open again in 1966, when the prognosis for Britain's getting into the Market suddenly improved.

Policy differences within the Party, as well as the nature of its recruitment patterns, manifest themselves in the Parliamentary Labour Party. For this reason, the job of keeping his parliamentary troops marching enthusiastically in step with the government is somewhat more difficult for a Labour Prime Minister than it is for his Tory counterpart. The Conservative Party in the House of Commons, which draws heavily from the professional and managerial classes, is socially cohesive—a characteristic that facilitates communication and interaction among it members. Moreover, the organization is rarely hit by tides of ideological disputation; reflecting a strong empirical tradition, its programs are designed to answer specific problems and appeal to target voters. The Conservative members of parliament, universally interested in winning elections, are very much oriented toward their Party leaders, and a Tory Prime Minister will ordinarily command their support so long as his policies are effective and do not provoke antagonism among segments of the electorate.

The Parliamentary Labour Party, by contrast, is a highly pluralist organization. The reasons for this are partly historical. Protesting the harshness of British capitalism and the gross inequalities in the social system, the trade unions, cooperatives, socialist societies, and (after 1918) individual members in local constituency parties merged into a federated structure whose democratic processes enabled each component to be represented and to compete in the give-and-take of policy-making. This alliance is reflected in the PLP, where many members have had careers in the trade unions, others have had long association with the cooperative movement, and still others have worked primarily in local constituency parties. Of the 363 Labour M.P.s elected in 1966, 132 were sponsored officially by the unions, 18 were supported by the Cooperative movement, and 214 were sponsored entirely by the local parties.[31]

Compared with its Tory counterpart, the Parliamentary Labour Party is heterogeneous in its social composition. The Party outside parliament recruits from a wide base; far from being rooted in the industrial working class alone, it strives for a clientele of "workers by hand or by brain." The multi-class base of the larger movement is reflected in the distinctive socio-economic groupings in the PLP.[32] First, there is a cluster of "working-class" members— M.P.s who were engaged in manual employment or were officers in the long-established unions before embarking upon parliamentary careers. A second grouping includes those of middle-class background who have had the advantage of quality education and who entered the professions before coming to Westminster; many of these people continue their professional work on a part-time basis while they serve in the House of Commons. Another category of Labour members is comprised of individuals with a working-class background who managed to secure advanced education and then enter the professional world of law, medicine, teaching, and journalism. By superior ability they won scholarships to good secondary schools and universities, some at Oxford and Cambridge, others at redbrick universities; a few secured their degrees through extra-mural study while they held regular jobs; and some prepared themselves for professional employment by attending specialized educational establishments or by being articled in a professional office. Although the "business" category is small compared with the Conservative side, a few Labour M.P.s were businessmen before they stood for parliament. Some of these men started work on the shop floor and gradually advanced to the board room; others were employed in family businesses and later took them over. A final grouping of Labour members embraces those employed in non-manual jobs that are usually not classified as "professional." These include clerks, salesmen, lower-grade civil servants, welfare workers, and the like. Most of these people have had more than an elementary education but have been denied the advantage of university training; for the most part, they tend to identify themselves with the working class.

In terms of occupational attainment, then, the Parliamentary Labour Party has at least three different clusters: (1) the working-class group whose members have risen through the trade-union movement; (2) the "intellectual" wing of the Party composed of the M.P.s in professional occupations—both those of middle-class lineage with traditional middle-class education and those of working-class background who attended grammar schools and redbrick universities; and (3) M.P.s who emerged from the working class into non-manual jobs intermediate between the workers and the professionals but who tend to maintain strong linkages with the working class. Although the middle-class, professional component in the PLP has been noticeable ever since the Labour Party became competitive in parliament, its numbers swelled in the 1945 parliament, and, as we shall note soon, this trend was greatly accelerated in the 1964 and 1966 elections. In 1966 particularly, the "intake" of new Labour M.P.s included a large number of school teachers and university lecturers and only a handful of manual workers. As one observer put it, there were "too many mortar boards and not enough cloth caps."

Whatever their class, Labour Party M.P.s tend to be politically conscious and deeply concerned about issues and the points of view they represent are scattered over a wide "ideological" spectrum. Unlike many socialist parties elsewhere, the British Labour Party was born and matured in a political culture that emphasizes pragmatism, toleration, and compromise through the democratic process, and has never developed a coherent and rigid doctrine. Since few "tests of orthodoxy" were applied, the organization welcomed people with many different points of view into its ranks. Although the Party had never hammered out a general theoretical position, its members were nevertheless in basic agreement on a set of policies designed to improve the lot of the disadvantaged and to remove the glaring forms of social injustice—public ownership of certain industries, the development of welfare services, full employment, etc. The trouble was that, once its basic platform had been written into law by the Attlee Government, disagreement broke out over the meaning of socialism and the "proper order of priorities."

Rather than subscribing to an all-inclusive, systematic philosophy, Labour members tend to equate socialism with the particular policies or doctrinal tenets to which they are attached emotionally or intellectually. Some believe that socialism requires extension of public ownership; some are anti-military; some devote most of their attention to the social services and some emphasize "Socialist foreign policy." In other words, the Parliamentary Labour Party contains various "subcultures" of attitudes, outlooks, and postures which are likely to influence the behavior of members when specific issues are being considered at their private meetings in the House. Some of these currents of opinion linger from the Party's evangelical past. Even though some clusters of attitudes are not influential, all are respected and tolerated in the democratically-organized Party. Indeed, the existence of "ginger groups" is widely regarded as desirable, since they serve as "conscience prickers" and as a check upon the leadership.

For the most part, the smaller subcultures represent the earlier romantic phases of Labour as a protest movement. There are, for example, a few Christian Socialists and a tiny band of orthodox Marxists.[33] The Parliamentary Labour Party also includes a small group that was influenced by the syndicalist movement which once swept over the coalfields of South Wales and parts of Scotland. Included, too, are some survivors of the old Independent Labour Party (ILP), which used to combine dramatic forms of protest with a burning faith in the brotherhood of man.

Overlapping these outlooks but extending to other groups, depending upon the specific policy under consideration, is an attitude of distrust of military force. The PLP has always had a core of sincere pacifists who reject violence, preferring to rely upon the weapons of the angels. But when conscription or a heavy defense budget is being discussed, the pacifists may be joined by other groups of Labour M.P.s: those who feel that the military burden strains Britain's limited resources, those who believe that the social services will be jeopardized, or those who are convinced for whatever reason that Britain should play a neutralist role in world affairs. Here, the shading and overlapping of attitudes tend to create complex patterns. Often the M.P. who supports a "neutralist" foreign policy also enunciates a commitment to "traditional socialism," including public ownership. When military questions arise, it is difficult to separate them from issues of foreign policy. This was true in the cases of NATO, the Korean War, and, in the 1966 parliament, Vietnam. Even the unilateralist M.P.s in the early 1960s displayed a variety of moods. Some, of course, were pacifists by conviction, while others favored unilateralism so that the Party could swing to the left, domestically and in foreign policy.

The dominant clusters of attitudes in the PLP support attempts to provide a new theoretical framework for the Party as it copes with contemporary problems. According to Labour members who have this "revisionist" outlook, traditional moods and policies are no longer adequate for present-day needs. They feel that the loose theoretical framework which was thrown together in piecemeal fashion when Labour was in the political wilderness did not envisage the problems that Britain now faces and does not provide clear-cut answers to them. Britain in the 1960s, they assert, is much different than it was before the war, and the Party must develop a forward-looking program which is relevant to the country's needs in order to have an impact upon the electorate. In other words, the Party must get rid of its "cloth cap" image and make itself more attractive to middle-class voters and to workers who have never experienced the dole. As one Labour member saw the dilemma as early as 1955, "you cannot secure votes from an intelligent and informed electorate by policies and methods which may have sounded attractive from a soapbox fifty years ago!"

To the Labour members on the left who harbor traditional attitudes and are eager to press on to "full-blooded" socialism, the revisionist position represents a heretical betrayal of doctrinal principles. In their view, the Party ought to be markedly distinctive from its competitors in character, outlook, and program. Without clearly defined Socialist goals, the organization would lose much of its dynamism. As Aneurin Bevan once said, ". . . we should not forget that the main road to Socialist advance is open to us if we have the courage to tread it. But there is a grave danger of being seduced down side roads or stopping to pick flowers on the way." [34] Delaying the journey to the New Jerusalem by trying to "consolidate gains" or to woo middle-class voters is like stopping along the sidepaths to pick flowers. Too much concern for the views of segments of the electorate tends to make the Labour Party a carbon-copy of the Tories. Labour's job is not merely to govern, but to lead and to experiment with new ideas. Rather than try to convert middle-class people to the Labour point of view, the members of the left would sound the evangelical trumpets of Kier Hardie and George Lansbury in an effort to rally working-class people who now stay at home on polling day or even vote Conservative. Instead of running the risk of having the Labour Party become merely an "alternative to government" by picking up the mistakes of the other side, some left-wing crusaders would prefer to sojourn in the political marshland until the electorate becomes wise enough to support a wholesale renovation of the social order.

It stands to reason that the Parliamentary Labour Party—representing a federated organization that recruits politically conscious people from more than one class, that has never hammered out a consistent theoretical position but tolerates a wide range of views and provides democratic machinery through which they can be expressed—would occasionally be torn by dissension. A party that prides itself on being distinctive must continually re-examine itself to see where it is going, and arguments about the direction it should take are bound to erupt. Disagreements over which tenets of the program should be emphasized at any given time will arise inevitably. As an organization of keen minds that is continually dredging up new ideas, heat is invariably generated as the new formulations are examined and refined at the conference table and in public discussions. The Labour Party long ago became accustomed to the rough and tumble of debate over contentious issues through its trade-union experience and the intra-organizational disputes in the 1920s and the 1930s. As Nye Bevan once pointed out, "When we have differences of opinion, we sometimes express them rather roughly. If we did not, nobody would hear them."

The existence of these subgroups within the Parliamentary Labour Party sets the stage for complex patterns of interaction among them. As important and controversial issues arise, the dissident Labour members tend to merge into *ad hoc* coalitions to oppose the dominant faction which supports the leadership. These coalitions change in composition as the issues change, although there is a core of rebels who tend to be chronically discontented. It is hardly surprising, therefore, that visible opposition to the leadership is likely to show up in the tally of the divisions which are taken on crucial issues when the crises are most immediate.

In calling attention to the problems a Labour government faces as it seeks to keep its parliamentary forces intact, it is important to point out that the Labour Party, in the postwar period, has always been summoned to power when Britain was in the throes of economic crisis, compounded by dramatic international events. This was true for the Attlee Government of 1945 and for the Wilson governments of 1964 and 1966. Sobered by the grave responsibilities of office, the Labour ministries have had to take steps to rejuvenate the economy, as well as to deal with the harsh realities in international affairs. The compromises and postponements which government leaders have found necessary at various times have understandably created frustration and tensions, especially among a minority of Labour M.P.s who cling to past orthodoxies and who had hopes both in the 1940s and in the 1960s that the new government would usher in the "Socialist Commonwealth." For some of these people, the summons to stand by a Labour ministry that is merely "making capitalism work," that knuckles under the United States in foreign policy, and that delays expansion of the social services by pushing heavy defense budgets, produces an agonizing clash of loyalties. We can get a better view of the problems that Harold Wilson faces in holding the Labour members in line if we pause for a moment to examine some of the problems that the Attlee Government wrestled with in the 1945 parliament and look at two of the issues that precipitated rebellion against his regime. This brief excursion into the past will be useful for two reasons: (1) it will indicate that some of the basic problems of the first postwar Labour Government bear a resemblance to Wilson's difficulties and that a few of the proposed remedies, including a voluntary wage freeze, offer interesting parallels; and (2) an analysis of the composition of the PLP at that time will establish a base point against which to assess the changing nature of the organization.

THE ATTLEE GOVERNMENT: SUPPORT AND OPPOSITION
ON FOREIGN POLICY AND CONSCRIPTION

When Labour won its huge majority in 1945, Britain faced economic collapse. Much of her food and most of the materials needed for reconstruction had to be imported, and her import bills were difficult to meet until war industries were converted to peacetime production and a supply of manpower became available for factory work. Britain needed credit as a stopgap measure, until she could get on her economic feet and, when she was suddenly cut off from Lend-Lease aid in August 1945, she was forced to turn to the United States for emergency funds. With a view toward long-term development, the Government sought to attract manpower into essential—especially export—industries, at the same time reducing non-essential imports and expenditures overseas in an attempt to achieve a healthy balance of payments. It aimed to increase productivity so that scarcities would disappear and inflation could be avoided. With these objectives clearly marked out, the Government kept many wartime controls in force and made a valiant effort to resolve the problems it had inherited.

The economic crisis, aggravated by a severe winter in 1946–47, grew more serious during the next twelve months. Forced to combat the pressures of inflation, the Government soon introduced a stricter austerity program—the budgets of Sir Stafford Cripps were more than legend in those days—and it saw the compelling need to hold wages in line. During 1946 and 1947, the trade unions had not been especially sensitive to the economic danger. They had been interested in the forty-hour week, which would have played havoc with the official campaign to increase productivity, and they tended to resist any suggestion of a wage policy that would interfere with their hard-won right to bargain collectively. They were especially opposed to an official program of differential remuneration designed to attract workers to undermanned industries. But in 1948, after several months of conferences and negotiations, the union leaders made belated but noteworthy concessions to the Labour Government. In August 1947 they accepted the Control of Engagement Order, which provided for some direction of labor.[35] They began to urge their workers to work harder and to increase their productivity. "We cannot run twentieth-century industry," asserted one trade unionist, "by looking up nineteenth-century rule books." [36] And after they were assured that businessmen would voluntarily limit dividends and that the Government would take steps to keep the lid on prices, the union leaders agreed to a program of wage restraint. Prices, however, began to rise after the pound was devalued in 1949 and by 1951 the union leaders could no longer ignore rank-and-file pressures for wage adjustments arising out of increases in the cost of living.[37]

As Labour implemented its election platform and wrestled with unanticipated problems, the Government commanded overwhelming support from its backbenchers in the vast majority of trips into the division lobbies. Yet, on some crucial issues the Government battled on two fronts—the Opposition and the "purists" in its own organization, who were joined by other types of dissidents, depending upon the issue. Despite the high degree of Party cohesion on most questions, ministers in the Attlee Government were nevertheless called upon from time to time to extinguish the fires of rebellion on the Labour backbenches. A sample of the division lists in the 1945 parliament misses crucial instances of floor rebellions and suggests a distorted conclusion of "virtually perfect" cohesion. In actuality, as some Labour backbenchers began to feel that certain Cabinet policies were hostile to the "Socialist principles" for which they had always struggled, they raised the flag of revolt and either abstained or voted against the Government.

The frequency of these floor rebellions was greater than many students of party cohesion realize, but, given the nature of the Party and the problems with which the Government had to wrestle, they are understandable. Some Labour M.P.s, especially from the intellectual wing of the Party, were extremely critical of their Government's foreign policy and exhibited their displeasure either by willfully abstaining or by casting negative votes on such issues as: the American Loan (1945), the Bretton Woods Agreement (1945), the Foreign Policy Amendment to the King's Address (1946), the administration of Germany (1947), Palestine (1947–49), and the Atlantic Pact (1949). Some of these foreign policy critics joined anti-militarist groups to oppose peacetime conscription (1946–48). A number of trade-union M.P.s also objected to conscription. However, the Labour members of working-class background tended to be more concerned about certain domestic questions: giving immediate relief to old-age pensioners (1945); keeping a "means test" out of the National Insurance Act and supporting an increase in workers' benefits under the Industrial Injuries Bill (1946); opposing the direction of labor (1947), the serving of liquor in civic restaurants (1947), and the granting of a large annuity to Princess Elizabeth when she was to be married (1947–48); and supporting the establishment of a commission to study the adequacy of war pensions (1949). Other issues that produced unorthodox behavior in the voting lobbies on the part of various types of critics included the Civil Aviation Bill (1946), the inclusion of friendly societies in the National Insurance Act (1946), an inquiry into the monopolistic practices of the press (1946–47), the basic petrol allowance (1946–47), the Polish Resettlement Bill (1947), the Town and Country Planning Act (1947), Capital Punishment (1947–48), the Representation of the People Act (1948), and the Ireland Bill (1949).

From these twenty-two issues, some of which precipitated more than one floor rebellion, two can be taken for illustration to see what types of M.P.s supported the Government and what types were overcome by the heady spirit of rebellion. We shall examine (1) the Foreign Policy Amendment on the King's Address in November 1946, which represents the first full-scale rebellion against the Government, and (2) the Conscription Bill of April 1947, against which no fewer than 72 Labour M.P.s protested by marching into the opposition lobby. The conscription question is of special interest as the issue most likely to precipitate a clash of loyalties among the working-class M.P.s.

During 1946, the backbenches produced rumbles of discontent over the *foreign policy* of the Labour Government—for which the Foreign Secretary, Ernest Bevin, was the spokesman. The dissidents, however, were not united; various clusters of M.P.s were displeased for different reasons, whether based upon emotion or intellectual analysis. A handful were sympathetic toward the Soviet Union. More were displeased with the handling of the situation in Greece and Palestine. Many felt that Britain had drifted into a position of subordination to "capitalist" America, and that this tieup was alienating the Government from the democratic-socialist parties on the continent which were expecting British Labour to provide a lead in international affairs. Some M.P.s were alarmed that Bevin's foreign policy required a burdensome military force and they wanted more men brought home from the army to relieve the manpower shortage.

These clusters of opposition were eventually welded together in November 1946.[38] A letter from 21 Labour backbenchers to the Prime Minister warned of a drift away from Socialist principles and urged that Britain choose a "middle road" between the Soviet Union and the United States. Shortly thereafter some of the signatories, without bringing the matter to a meeting of the Parliamentary Labour Party, tabled an amendment to the King's Address, expressing the "urgent hope" that the Government would recast its foreign policy so as to encourage and collaborate with all nations and groups "striving to secure full Socialist planning and control of the world's resources" and thus provide a "democratic and Socialist alternative to an otherwise inevitable conflict between American Capitalism and Soviet Communism . . ." This motion was signed by 57 Labour M.P.s from the backbenches.[39]

This was a planned, disciplined rebellion to bring the rebels' views to the floor of the House. They wanted to stage a "public demonstration to show the leaders of the Party that there was a number of honest, moderately-minded Socialists concerned about foreign policy." If they did not succeed in changing the policy, at least they might prompt their leaders to reexamine it.[40]

At a meeting of the Parliamentary Labour Party, Attlee rebuked them for instituting a virtual motion of censure against their own Government, at a time when Bevin was conducting delicate negotiations in the United States. The PLP voted to request the signatories to withdraw their Amendment, but they decided to stand their ground. They assumed that their motion would not be put to a division, but if it were, they were prepared to abstain on their own motion.

On November 18, the Speaker called the Amendment—an unusual event in the circumstances—and a heated debate ensued. Having aired their views to the embarrassment of their leaders, the dissidents wanted to stop short of a division, but their hand was forced by two ILP members. The leader of the rebels, Richard Crossman, then sought to withdraw the Amendment, but a chorus of "Noes" from the Opposition benches prevented it. In voting, 233 Labour backbenchers supported the Government on a three-line whip, but more than 90 abstained. The Party leaders were disturbed that the number of abstentions was so unexpectedly high, and Attlee affirmed that he could not tolerate such organized opposition within the PLP.[41] A group of 44 Labour M.P.s, mostly trade-union members, called for the restoration of the Standing Orders, but for the moment this form of discipline was rejected.[42]

Before we examine the voting patterns on the foreign policy amendment, we need to explain briefly the methods employed in our analysis. To determine who in the majority party opposes the government is not an easy matter. For members to march into the opposition lobby is a striking act of defiance, and is an unusual occurrence when the whips are on. Abstaining on an important vote, if it is done deliberately, is probably a stronger signal of opposition than is a negative vote against the party leadership in the American Congress. The abstainers, however, can be separated into two different varieties—those who are excused from voting by the whips (these abstainers may be ill, out of the country, or "paired"), and those who willfully abstain in order to exhibit their opposition to the government. The official records, of course, do not indicate this distinction; the division lists contain only the names of the M.P.s who vote for or against. The whips' files have information on the willful abstainers, but it is not disclosed to the public.

We have used four different methods to distinguish between abstainers who support and abstainers who oppose the government. Three of these methods are fairly simple: (1) Journalists carefully observe the important votes in the House, and they usually list the names of members who were in the chamber shortly before the division but who did not record their votes with the whips. These M.P.s probably opposed the government, and we listed them as dissenters. (2) Often the vote on a substantive issue is preceded by a procedural vote. If an individual voted on the procedural question but not on the substantive issue, we recorded him as a dissenter. (3) Some M.P.s indicate their opposition to government policy during the debate. If an M.P. spoke against a measure on the floor and then abstained in the voting, we assigned him to the dissenter category.

By using these three methods we were able to identify many of the dissidents. Usually, however, there was a residual number of M.P.s who abstained and we had no information about whether they did so as an act of defiance. In order to assign these "unknowns" to the supporter or dissident categories, we employed a fourth method. We separated the backbenchers into groups on the basis of objective criteria, such as occupation, education, age, and years of parliamentary service. In these groups we had some M.P.s who supported the government, some who were dissenters, and some who were "unknown." We then assigned the unknowns to the supporter or dissident categories in the same proportion as the knowns in the respective matched socio-economic groupings. Assume, for example, that fifteen M.P.s were railway clerks by occupation, had had elementary education, were in the 40–50 age bracket, and were newcomers to parliament. If nine of these members supported the government, three were dissidents, and three were unknown, we assigned two of the unknowns to the supporter category and one to the dissident category. In the tables in this chapter, we report two sets of data on each issue—one that shows the remaining "unknown" category after we applied the first three methods, and one that assigns the unknowns proportionately to the supporter and dissident categories according to the fourth method.

In the tables that deal with parliamentary divisions, we are concerned primarily with two columns—the one that lists supporters and the one that lists dissidents. We have formed an "index" by subtracting the percentage of dissidents from the percentage of supporters. The purpose of this is to enable us to read the data in the two columns at the same time and to minimize the problem of the unknowns. Theoretically, the index scores could range from $+100$ to -100. The higher the score, the less the dissidence. As a score approaches either $+100$ or -100, it would indicate increasing cohesion among the backbenchers. In the former case, however, the backbench M.P.s would be cohesive supporters of the government, while in the latter case there would be a wider split between the relatively unified backbenchers and the Party leadership. A "zero" score would indicate minimal cohesion among the backbenchers. This is not a precise measure, since the unknowns are not included, although they do have an impact upon the figure. But it is a convenient way of reading the data in the columns at the same time, thus enabling us to see the relative magnitude and direction of the differences among the several categories. In this chapter we use the index scores as a rough measure for comparing cohesion and dissidence among Labour backbenchers in the 1945 and 1966 parliaments on selected issues.

One other feature of our analysis remains to be discussed: the particular groupings of Labour members whose voting behavior we wish to study. We have grouped the Labour backbenchers into three main clusters. Group I, the "working class" component, is comprised of members who were trade-union officials and manual workers prior to entering parliament. A large proportion of this group was sponsored by the unions, although professional men who were given such sponsorship are excluded from the category. A majority of this group left school at an early age to commence work. Some managed to secure secondary education, but only a handful, all of them trade-union officials, went beyond that, some of them by enrolling in extra-mural programs at universities.

At the other end of the continuum is Group III, which includes those M.P.s with university training—and, in a few instances, public school education without going on to the university—and who had been engaged in professional, managerial, and technical employment. We shall call this "professional/managerial/consultative" group by the shorthand designation "Professional." Group II is the "Intermediate" category. It embraces those backbenchers who were employed in various types of non-manual work but who had no higher education. These three groupings are an attempt to link occupation and educational attainment. Besides looking at the voting patterns of these three groups, we examine the behavior of "incumbents" and "newcomers" in the working-class category and in the combined intermediate and professional group.

We are now ready to return to the voting on the foreign policy amendment on November 18, 1946. This is analyzed in Table 1.[43]

TABLE 1

*Socio-Economic Groupings on Foreign Policy**

Voting group	Working class		Intermediate		Professional	
	No.	%	No.	%	No.	%
Govt. supporters	(93)	68.4	(43)	58.9	(47)	43.1
Known abstainers	(12)	8.8	(20)	27.4	(42)	38.5
Unknown	(31)	22.8	(10)	13.7	(20)	18.4
TOTAL	(136)	100.0	(73)	100.0	(109)	100.0
INDEX		60		32		5

* When, in any of the tables in this chapter, the total percentage does not add up to 100.0, the slight discrepancy is accounted for by the rounding out of numbers.

These data indicate the tendency for Labour backbenchers from the working-class/trade-union segment of the Party to support the Government's foreign policy more strongly than the lower-middle-class and professional groups. This finding is hardly sensational, but the data take on added interest if we distinguish between M.P.s with previous parliamentary experience and those who

were elected for the first time in the general election of 1945 or
in by-elections shortly thereafter. In making this comparison we
have pulled the intermediate and professional groups into a
single category. The results can be seen in Table 2.

TABLE 2

*Socio-Economic Groupings and Parliamentary Service:
Foreign Policy*

Voting group	Working Class				Intermediate/Professional			
	Prior service		Elected in 1945–1946		Prior service		Elected in 1945–1946	
	No.	%	No.	%	No.	%	No.	%
Gov't. supporters	(29)	56.9	(64)	75.3	(18)	51.4	(72)	49.0
Known abstainers	(3)	5.9	(9)	10.6	(10)	28.6	(52)	35.4
Unknown	(19)	37.3	(12)	14.1	(7)	20.0	(23)	15.7
TOTAL	(51)	100.1	(85)	100.0	(35)	100.0	(147)	100.1
INDEX		51		65		23		14

The important thing to note in this breakdown is that the strongest support for the Government came from the new working-class
M.P.s. Although those with prior service manifested greater discipline than the two groups of intermediate/professional members,
the manual workers and trade unionists who were elected in 1945
and 1946 provided the strongest support for the Government on
this issue. The strong working-class support for the Government
still held up after the distribution of the unknowns. However, the
difference between the working-class incumbents and the working-
class newcomers was less significant.

The voting results on the foreign policy issue after the unknowns
have been assigned proportionately can be seen in Table 3.

Although the working-class M.P.s were willing to support the
Cabinet's foreign policy, they were less enthusiastic about military
expenditures. A back-bench rebellion against peacetime conscription had occurred on the same day the dissenters on foreign policy
had tabled their amendment, but this was merely a premonitory
outburst compared with the breach of discipline on April 1, 1947.

In its Defense White Paper, the Government anticipated a cut in the size of the armed forces from about 1,400,000 men to 1,087,000 men by the end of March 1948, and the bill it brought

TABLE 3

Socio-Economic Groupings on Foreign Policy*
(with "unknowns" apportioned)

Voting group	Supporters No. %	Dissidents No. %	Total No. %	Index
Working class	(121) 89.0	(15) 11.0	(136) 100.0	78
Intermediate	(51) 69.9	(22) 30.1	(73) 100.0	40
Professional	(59) 54.1	(50) 45.9	(109) 100.0	8
Incumbent working class	(45) 88.2	(6) 11.8	(51) 100.0	76
Newcomer working class	(76) 89.4	(9) 10.6	(85) 100.0	79
Incumbent middle class	(24) 68.6	(11) 31.4	(35) 100.0	37
Newcomer middle class	(86) 58.5	(61) 41.5	(147) 100.0	27

* The figures in parentheses indicate the number of backbench M.P.s in each category.

into parliament provided for a conscription term of eighteen months. This proposal served as a catalyst to bring a number of dissident groups into common cause against the Ministry. Spearheading the movement were the pacifists, who continued to reflect Labour's traditional hatred of war, distrust of the military, and disdain for compulsion, and who had entertained the utopian hope that a Socialist government would end the need for armed might. They laid down a motion, signed by 74 backbenchers, to reject the Cabinet measure. Supporting this move were some M.P.s who were not opposed to conscription but were convinced that Britain's commitments abroad were straining the economy, and others who had rebelled on foreign policy in 1946 and wanted another crack at Bevin. Other critics of foreign policy, however, were mainly concerned with the manpower question and showed some willingness to support the Government if it would grant some concessions. This group, under Crossman's leadership, was disturbed that more than a million men would be retained in the forces during a labor shortage. After combing through the Army estimates, they concluded that 250,000 men could be demobilized safely within the next twelve months. In their view, industry would be disrupted less if the period of service were reduced to twelve months. Crossman and his colleagues tabled an amendment to the Government motion urging a review of military commitments, "so as to reduce the burden on [Britain's] manpower and financial resources." This dissenting motion attracted 44 Labour signatures.[44] All these dissenting elements thought they might be able to modify the Government's policy, for they knew that some trade-union members of the Cabinet had not been enamored with conscription in the past, and they had heard that one or two other Cabinet ministers were inclined toward twelve-month service.

The Government leaders tolerated the views of the pacifists, but they hoped to keep the number of dissidents down to about 30 or 40. At a PLP meeting they tried to dissuade the rebels from pushing their motion, and they advised members who were taking refuge under the "conscience clause" to abstain rather than vote against the Government.[45] Crossman and the "manpower group," however, threatened to join the rebels unless the ministers were prepared to reduce the length of army service.[46]

When the division was called on the second reading of the bill, 72 Labour backbenchers trudged into the opposition lobby and at least 18 others abstained. This was the biggest rebellion in the 1945 parliament. The jolt was serious enough to prompt the Government to introduce an amendment during the committee stage reducing the period of service from eighteen months to twelve months. At a subsequent meeting of the PLP, a group of M.P.s— mostly trade unionists—moved to reimpose the Standing Orders. The motion was defeated, but the Party decided to try to iron out its differences in the future by debating them in caucus rather than taking them to the floor of the House.

The patterns of Government support and opposition among the Labour backbenchers on this conscription issue can be seen in Table 4. These data suggest that the working-class backbenchers supported the Government's defense program less than its foreign policy. The M.P.s in the middle category were even more critical, however, about half of them being listed as dissidents. On the other hand, the members with professional backgrounds who had been conspicuous in their opposition to foreign policy were more

TABLE 4

Socio-Economic Groupings on Conscription

| | Working Class | | Intermediate | | Professional | |
Voting group	No.	%	No.	%	No.	%
Gov't. supporters	(73)	52.9	(32)	44.4	(72)	65.5
Dissidents*	(34)	24.6	(31)	43.1	(24)	21.8
Unknown	(31)	22.5	(9)	12.5	(14)	12.7
TOTAL	(138)	100.0	(72)	100.0	(110)	100.0
INDEX		28		1		44

* The dissidents in the tables on this issue include both the Labour members who voted against the second reading and those who are known to have abstained.

willing to go along with the Government in its defense requests, especially when the ministers showed signs of flexibility on the period of service. The pattern that emerges when the groups are separated on the basis of previous parliamentary experience is presented in Table 5.

Both groups of members with prior service were relatively weaker in their support of the Government on the conscription question, an issue about which many M.P.s with working-class background felt strongly. It should also be noted that, while the intermediate/ professional group gave the Government a comparatively high proportion of supporting votes, the smallest percentage of dissident voices were in the working-class group that had recently entered parliament. As in the case of the foreign policy division, the members of this newcomer group were more strongly inclined to support their ministers on conscription than were their working-class colleagues who had been in parliament longer.

TABLE 5

Socio-Economic Groupings and Parliamentary Service: Conscription

	Working Class		Intermediate/Professional	
	Prior service	Elected in 1945–1947	Prior service	Elected in 1945–1947
Voting group	No. %	No. %	No. %	No. %
Gov't. supporters	(24) 47.1	(49) 56.3	(17) 48.6	(87) 59.2
Dissidents	(16) 31.3	(18) 20.7	(14) 40.0	(41) 27.9
Unknown	(11) 21.6	(20) 23.0	(4) 11.4	(19) 12.9
TOTAL	(51) 100.0	(87) 100.0	(35) 100.0	(147) 100.0
INDEX	16	36	9	31

The voting picture on the conscription question after the apportionment of the unknowns is seen in Table 6.

Later, when we analyze backbench cohesion in the Wilson Government on four different issues, we treat them as a group (as well

TABLE 6

Socio-Economic Groupings on Conscription
(with "unknowns" apportioned)

Voting group	Supporters No. %	Dissidents No. %	Total No. %	Index
Working class	(95) 68.8	(43) 31.2	(138) 100.0	38
Intermediate	(34) 47.2	(38) 52.8	(72) 100.0	−6
Professional	(84) 76.4	(26) 23.6	(110) 100.0	53
Incumbent working class	(31) 60.8	(20) 39.2	(51) 100.0	22
Newcomer working class	(64) 73.6	(23) 26.4	(87) 100.0	47
Incumbent middle class	(19) 54.3	(16) 45.7	(35) 100.0	9
Newcomer middle class	(99) 67.3	(48) 32.7	(147) 100.0	35

as separately). For this reason it will be helpful now to examine the picture when we run the voting results on the foreign policy and conscription issues together. These data are reported in Table 7.

TABLE 7

Votes by Socio-Economic Groupings on the Two Issues

Category	Supporters No. %	Dissidents No. %	Unknown No. %	Index
Working class	(164) 60.7	(45) 16.7	(61) 22.6	44
Intermediate	(74) 51.4	(51) 35.4	(19) 13.2	16
Professional	(116) 53.7	(66) 30.6	(34) 15.7	23
Incumbent working class	(53) 52.0	(19) 18.6	(30) 29.4	33
Newcomer working class	(111) 66.1	(26) 15.5	(31) 18.5	51
Incumbent middle class	(35) 50.0	(24) 34.3	(11) 15.7	16
Newcomer middle class	(155) 53.4	(93) 32.1	(42) 14.5	21

Table 8 presents an analysis of the voting on the two issues with the unknowns assigned proportionately as supporters and dissidents.

A more extensive discussion would reveal that, in the 1945 parliament, the Government could ordinarily command a strong measure of loyalty from the working-class cluster on most of the important issues, including foreign policy. Some M.P.s in this group, to be sure, objected to certain Cabinet measures from time to time. But these tended to be "bread and butter" issues—wage matters, pensions, the cost of living, the direction of labor, aspects of social security—or opposition to what they felt were excessive expenditures for the royal family in a period of austerity. The biggest cause for discontent among the working-class contingent was the conscription issue. But, as we have seen, the dissenters in this category tended to be those who had had previous experience in parliament; the newcomers of similar lineage tended to support the Government much more on this controversial question.

TABLE 8

Votes by Socio-Economic Groupings on the Two Issues
(with "unknowns" apportioned)

Category	Supporters No. %	Dissidents No. %	Total No. %	Index
Working class	(213) 78.9	(57) 21.1	(270) 100.0	58
Intermediate	(84) 58.3	(60) 41.7	(144) 100.0	17
Professional	(140) 64.8	(76) 35.2	(216) 100.0	30
Incumbent working class	(76) 74.5	(26) 25.5	(102) 100.0	49
Newcomer working class	(137) 81.5	(31) 18.5	(168) 100.0	63
Incumbent middle class	(43) 61.4	(27) 38.6	(70) 100.0	23
Newcomer middle class	(181) 62.4	(109) 37.6	(290) 100.0	25

In considering reasons why the working-class M.P.s who had just entered parliament tended to be more obedient to the whips than their incumbent colleagues, one is tempted to speculate that those with previous service, including the M.P.s who had held posts in a Labour government earlier but were now backbenchers, were somewhat more disillusioned by some of the controversial policies of the Attlee regime. Moreover, they were familiar with the rules of the parliamentary game and knew how to exhibit their displeasure without going into the government lobby. The newcomers, on the other hand, had not participated in the parliamentary battles of the MacDonald era and were more cautious about engaging in floor rebellions. Furthermore, while some members of this new crop of M.P.s might have misgivings about some Government policies, other parts of the Labour program—like nationalization and social security—appealed to them strongly, and they may have been more willing to pay the price of loyalty required by giving grudging support on a few issues about which they entertained doubts.

Despite its broad support in the Parliamentary Labour Party, the main pillar of which was the working-class group, the Attlee

Government could not ignore the strains of dissidence on its back-benches. To begin with, a handful of individualists were chronically discontented, scoring their pet points against target policies and resisting the discipline of the whips. More of a problem was a small corps of M.P.s on the "left," for which the "Keep Left" group provided the intellectual direction. The leftists claimed the regular allegiance of about twenty to thirty Labour members, but on controversial questions they attracted a number of floaters from the center, depending upon the nature of the issue. The left-wing was largely leaderless until Aneurin Bevan assumed this role in 1951, when he resigned from the Cabinet. After the Labour Party returned to the Opposition later that year, the "left" became identified with the Bevanites, who usually kept the whips working overtime in the early and mid-1950s. When this movement de-clined, the left sought to reorganize through the small Victory for Socialism group, which included a few members of the old Keep Left element. At the turn of the decade, however, the VFS or-ganization was completely overshadowed by the Campaign for Nuclear Disarmament, which attracted about 45 or 50 Labour M.P.s at its peak. This organization temporarily welded together two types of dissidents—those who wanted to convert the Party to a more leftist program and those who tended to interpret So-cialism primarily in anti-military terms. Although the CND move-ment had run its course by the time the Labour Party returned to power in 1964, remnants of the 1945 left were still to be found in the PLP, as were former adherents of CND.

Changing Composition of the Backbenches, 1945–1966

In the two decades between 1945 and 1966, significant changes occurred in the socio-economic composition of the Parliamentary Labour Party—changes that, as we shall see, have implications for the maintenance of strict discipline within the organization. The long-term trend has been for the PLP to become more "middle class" in composition. This trend continued in 1964 and was noticeably accelerated in 1966. It reflects the widening educational opportunities in Britain and the growing influence of the middle class in the Labour Party itself.

The extent of the changes that have taken place are indicated in Table 9, which presents a comparison of the socio-economic features of the PLP in 1966 and in 1945 at three different levels: (1) Cabinet; (2) other ministers; and (3) the backbenchers.

TABLE 9

Socio-Economic Composition of the PLP, 1966 and 1945*

	Working class No. %	Intermediate No. %	Professional No. %
[a] Cabinet			
1966	(8) 38.1	(1) 4.8	(12) 57.1
1945	(10) 62.5	(1) 6.3	(5) 31.3
[a] Other ministers			
1966	(10) 18.2	(11) 20.0	(34) 61.8
1945	(19) 44.2	(8) 18.6	(16) 37.2
Backbenchers			
1966	(91) 33.8	(45) 16.7	(133) 49.4
1945	(138) 43.1	(72) 22.5	(110) 34.4
[b] Total Labour M.P.s			
1966	(109) 31.6	(57) 16.5	(179) 51.9
1945	(167) 44.1	(81) 21.4	(131) 34.6

* This is an analysis of the PLP immediately after each election. In 1945, three of the M.P.s were quickly elevated to the House of Lords and another died at the time of the election; their replacements are figured in the tabulations of this study. The figures in parentheses refer to the number of M.P.s in each category.

[a] Excluding ministers from the House of Lords.

[b] Excluding the whips.

These data reveal that the professional group has increased in strength at all levels, while the strength of the working-class component has clearly declined. At the Cabinet level, however, the working-class group continues to have important representation and it still constitutes about one-third of the backbenchers. As was to be expected, "professional" M.P.s scored their biggest gains in the ministerial ranks below the Cabinet level. The data indicate that, not only have the "middle-class" M.P.s increased their representation at all levels, but also that they are much more likely to rise to positions of responsibility than are their working-class colleagues.

These findings are reinforced when we examine the intake of new M.P.s—those entering parliament for the first time—in 1945 and in 1964–1966. (The intakes from the last two elections are combined into one group, since it took Labour two contests to win a majority comparable to that of 1945.) These data are presented in Table 10.

TABLE 10

Socio-Economic Composition of Intake Groups:
1945 and 1964–66

	Working class No. %	Intermediate No. %	Professional No. %
1964–66	(41) 26.3	(28) 18.0	(87) 55.8
1945	(91) 36.7	(57) 23.0	(100) 40.3

This means that the Labour Prime Minister during his second Government has a well-educated and highly competent group of backbenchers to deal with. About 50 per cent of them have had advanced education, 20 per cent at Oxford or Cambridge. In terms of previous occupation, 17 per cent of the backbenchers had been teachers, 16 per cent were barristers and solicitors, nearly 8 per cent were journalists, and there is a scattering of medical people. If the newcomers who entered parliament for the first time in 1964–66 are treated separately, the proportion of university-trained backbenchers rises to 56 per cent (in the 1966 crop it was about 70 per cent), compared with 40 per cent of the newcomers in the 1945 parliament. The new M.P.s from the 1966 election came heavily from the field of education. About 30 per cent of them were university lecturers, schoolmasters, and teachers before they won seats in the House.

These intelligent young people from the professions, especially the educators and lawyers, have been well trained for parliament. Keenly interested in public issues and very much at home in intellectual interchange, they are used to formulating and articulating their own views. They have a strong drive to participate in discussing and hammering out policy, and many of them are likely to become restive if they perceive that their main job is to take their cues from the whips and act primarily as "lobby fodder."

In discussing the characteristics of the backbenchers, we must not overlook the changes that have taken place in the group of M.P.s who were trade-union officials and manual workers before they came to Westminster. This group tended to be the one that supported the Attlee Government the most on controversial issues. This was especially true of the working-class M.P.s who entered parliament for the first time in 1945. In that parliament, nearly 20 per cent of the backbenchers had been trade-union officials, and several of them were the general secretaries of their unions. These trade-union officers, as well as the manual workers who had entered national politics through their trade-union connections, had had long experience in union work, and during the difficult years of the 1920s and 1930s they had learned the need for loyalty and solidarity from personal experience. Of the working-class M.P.s in the 1945 parliament, all but three were born before World War I (the three exceptions were born during the war). In other words, they were relatively older and had been forced to engage in industrial battles during the interwar years, before the trade unions became the recognized power that they are now. About two dozen working-class M.P.s who served in parliament right after the war, including a few who served in the Attlee Government and for a time in Wilson's Ministry, still occupy seats on the backbenches.

But the backbench working-class M.P.s in 1966 were considerably different from the group in 1945. In the first place, as we have already noted, their relative numbers have declined, being outdistanced by the non-manual and professional groups. It should also be noted that in some cases trade-union endorsement is no longer the badge of working-class identification that it once was. In recent years some unions, particularly the Transport Workers and the Municipal Workers, have sponsored some candidates with solid middle-class background. This study places these people in the professional category, despite their trade-union symbols.

Significant differences between the working-class groups of backbenchers in the 1966 and 1945 parliaments can be seen in Table 11. The picture takes on added dimensions, however, when we examine the intake of backbench working-class M.P.s in the two

TABLE 11

Backbench Working-Class M.P.s in 1945 and 1966

	(N = 139) Working-class backbenchers 1945	(N = 91) Working-class backbenchers 1966
Median age	55	57
* Elem. & Elem.+ Educ.	77.7%	60.4%
Trade union officials	36.0%	31.9%

* "Elementary+" designates those M.P.s who took work beyond elementary school in residential programs, such as that offered by Ruskin College.

parliaments. The differences are presented in Table 12. (The third column includes the working-class M.P.s in the 1966 parliament who entered the House prior to 1964.)

This table shows that the new crop of working-class M.P.s is much younger, that they have had more formal education, and that fewer trade-union officials and organizers are in their ranks. This means that they have had a much shorter span of experience in the trade-union movement than did the newcomer crop in 1945. They tended to stay in school longer and to enter parliament at

TABLE 12

Backbench Working-Class M.P.s in 1945 and 1966

	(N = 89) Entered in 1945	(N = 38) Entered in 1964–66	(N = 53) 1966 Backbenchers with service prior to 1964
Median age	50	46	63
* Elem. & Elem.+ Educ.	73.0%	47.4%	69.8%
Trade union officials	48.3%	21.1%	39.6%
Born in 1920s and 1930s	0.0%	57.9%	3.8%

* "Elementary+" designates those M.P.s who took work beyond elementary school in residential programs, such as that offered by Ruskin College.

a younger age. Moreover, since nearly two-thirds of them were born after World War I, they did not have much opportunity to engage actively in the kind of union struggles with which their predecessors were preoccupied. In other words, compared with the working-class backbenchers who entered parliament in 1945, and compared with many who came to Westminster between 1950 and 1964, the 1964–66 crop has had a different type of life experience. With more formal education, they may be more accustomed to dealing with complex social issues, including foreign policy; intelligent and keen, some of them may feel somewhat frustrated at having been denied the opportunity for advanced training and they may resent the proportionately larger intake of professional, middle-class people into the PLP. Equally important, owing to a different kind of socialization, these new working-class M.P.s may be less committed to the need for rigid discipline in the PLP than were the old trade unionists of an earlier day.

Controversial Divisions in the House of Commons, 1966–67

In light of the fact that the Wilson Government has a much different group of backbenchers to work with, compared with 1945, it will be interesting to examine the patterns of support and opposition that developed when some of the Cabinet's controversial policies were debated in the House. Members of the Government realized that elements on the left had grown restive during the period of the slender majority, and they assumed that the leftists would defy the whips sooner or later, now that possible defeat of the Ministry was no longer a restraint. But it was perceived that the left lacked effective leadership and that there was some tension between the older members and the new crop, largely over matters of parliamentary strategy. For these reasons, the Party leaders felt that with their safe majority they could treat the possibility of left-wing rebellion with calm, largely ignoring the problem. As it turned out, however, the problem of dissidence could not be cast aside so easily. It arose more frequently than the Government had anticipated and on some important issues more than just the "left" were involved.

On the vast majority of issues, of course, the Government could command overwhelming support from its backbenchers regardless of their subgroup loyalties or personal proclivities. But in attempting to wrestle with the problems it faced—Vietnam, Rhodesia, economic restraints, defense commitments, and cutbacks in public expenditures—Wilson and his senior ministers were bound to arouse hostility over the lingering question of the real meaning of Socialism and the proper order of priorities. Although floor rebellions have taken place from time to time, four of them appear to have taxed the tolerance of the whips, and, if not handled properly, could have had serious consequences for the Government's base of support on the backbenches. These rebellions were as follows: Vietnam (July 7, 1966); Prices and Incomes Bill (October 25, 1966); Defense White Paper (February 28, 1967); and the Common Market (May 10, 1967). Although some of these issues occasioned more than one outburst of dissidence, we shall confine our analysis to the votes taken on the dates indicated, for these were the rebellions that gave the Labour ministers the most concern.[47]

In an effort to identify the most supportive and the most critical socio-economic groups, it will be instructive to analyze the voting record of those backbenchers who had an opportunity to pass judgment on all four issues. Table 13 presents this information in

TABLE 13

Voting Records of Socio-Economic Groups on Four Issues Combined

Voting group	Supporters No. %	Dissidents No. %	Unknown No. %	Total No. %	Index
Working class	(258) 73.3	(72) 20.5	(22) 6.3	(352) 100.1	53
Intermediate	(124) 72.1	(39) 22.7	(9) 5.2	(172) 100.0	49
Professional	(375) 74.4	(96) 19.0	(33) 6.5	(504) 99.9	55

terms of percentages of total supporting votes and percentages of total negative votes and/or known abstentions on the four issues combined.

This table suggests that support and dissidence are fairly evenly distributed among the three groups. This may be significant in itself since the working-class group, which in the past has usually been a strong supporter of official policy, has a relatively high rate of dissidence on these four controversial issues. We are tempted, therefore, to divide the working class category into two groups— those who entered parliament prior to the 1964 election and those who began their careers later. Similarly, for the remaining M.P.s, we shall distinguish the incumbents from the 1964–66 newcomers. These data are treated in Table 14.

TABLE 14

Socio-Economic Groups and Parliamentary Service: Four Issues

Voting group*	Supporters No. %	Dissidents No. %	Unknown No. %	Total No. %	Index
Incumbent working class	(155) 76.0	(30) 14.7	(19) 9.3	(204) 100.0	61
Newcomer working class	(103) 69.6	(42) 28.4	(3) 2.0	(148) 100.0	41
Incumbent middle class	(172) 67.2	(59) 23.0	(25) 9.8	(256) 100.0	44
Newcomer middle class	(327) 77.9	(76) 18.1	(17) 4.0	(420) 100.0	60

* "Incumbent" refers to M.P.s who served in parliament prior to 1964, and "Newcomer" includes those elected in the period from 1964 to 1966. The intermediate and professional categories are combined into a "middle class" group.

Interestingly, the new M.P.s of middle-class background tended to be more loyal to the whips' commands than their counterparts with previous service. Even more interesting, however, the working-class newcomers had the highest rate of dissidence and were among the least supportive of the government on these issues. The working-class members were the most critical on the question of the Common Market, so we decided to pull that issue out and run the voting analysis on the other three issues.

Although we included the middle-class group in the three-issue run, we were especially interested in comparing the working-class M.P.s by length of parliamentary service. The results are included in Table 15.

TABLE 15

Socio-Economic Groups and Parliamentary Service: Three Issues

Voting group	Supporters No. %	Dissidents No. %	Unknown No. %	Total No. %	Index
Incumbent working class	(126) 82.9	(10) 6.6	(16) 10.5	(152) 100.0	76
Newcomer working class	(83) 74.8	(25) 22.5	(3) 2.7	(111) 100.0	52
Incumbent middle class	(130) 67.7	(41) 21.4	(21) 10.9	(192) 100.0	46
Newcomer middle class	(254) 80.6	(45) 14.3	(16) 5.1	(315) 100.0	66

This table indicates even more the weaker degree of support among the working-class newcomers. Parenthetically, all of the opposition recorded for the incumbent working-class M.P.s occurred on the defense issue.

In general, the same patterns prevail when each of these issues is treated separately, as can be seen in Table 16. Comparable analyses of the four issues (treated separately and combined) with the unknowns distributed according to the method we have employed are presented in Tables 17, 18 and 19.

On the Vietnam issue, Labour members in the three categories—working class, intermediate, and professional—exhibited roughly the same division, but the incumbent M.P.s of working-class background supported the Government's policy more than their working-class colleagues who had recently entered parliament. On the other hand, newcomers of middle-class background received the same loyalty score as the incumbents in this cate-

TABLE 16

Votes by Socio-Economic Groupings on 4 Issues Treated Separately

Category	Number	Supporters No. %	Dissidents No. %	Unknown No. %	Index
VIETNAM					
Working class	92	(69) 75.0	(10) 10.9	(13) 14.1	64
Intermediate	45	(35) 77.8	(6) 13.3	(4) 8.9	65
Professional	132	(109) 82.6	(16) 12.1	(7) 5.3	71
Incumbent working class	53	(41) 77.4	(1) 1.9	(11) 20.8	76
Newcomer working class	39	(28) 71.8	(9) 23.1	(2) 5.1	49
Incumbent middle class	68	(54) 79.4	(9) 13.2	(5) 7.4	66
Newcomer middle class	109	(90) 82.6	(13) 11.9	(6) 5.5	70
WAGE FREEZE					
Working class	92	(82) 89.1	(7) 7.6	(3) 3.3	82
Intermediate	45	(35) 77.8	(7) 15.6	(3) 6.7	62
Professional	132	(106) 80.3	(14) 10.6	(12) 9.1	71
Incumbent working class	53	(51) 96.2	(0) 0.0	(2) 3.8	96
Newcomer working class	39	(31) 79.5	(7) 17.9	(1) 2.6	62
Incumbent middle class	68	(48) 70.6	(11) 16.2	(9) 13.2	54
Newcomer middle class	109	(93) 85.3	(10) 9.2	(6) 5.5	76
DEFENSE REVIEW					
Working class	92	(68) 73.9	(19) 20.7	(5) 5.4	53
Intermediate	45	(31) 68.9	(11) 24.4	(3) 6.7	45
Professional	128	(86) 67.2	(32) 25.0	(10) 7.8	42
Incumbent working class	54	(41) 75.9	(9) 16.7	(4) 7.4	58
Newcomer working class	38	(27) 71.1	(10) 26.3	(1) 2.6	45
Incumbent middle class	68	(39) 57.4	(21) 30.9	(8) 11.8	27
Newcomer middle class	105	(78) 74.3	(22) 21.0	(5) 4.8	53
COMMON MARKET					
Working class	93	(53) 57.0	(37) 39.8	(3) 3.2	17
Intermediate	45	(30) 66.7	(15) 33.3	(0) 0.0	33
Professional	130	(90) 69.2	(35) 26.9	(5) 3.8	42
Incumbent working class	55	(32) 58.2	(20) 36.4	(3) 5.5	22
Newcomer working class	38	(21) 55.3	(17) 44.7	(0) 0.0	11
Incumbent middle class	68	(45) 66.2	(19) 27.9	(4) 5.9	38
Newcomer middle class	107	(75) 70.1	(31) 29.0	(1) 1.0	41

TABLE 17

Votes by Socio-Economic Groupings on 4 Issues Treated Separately
(with "unknowns" apportioned)

Category	Number	Supporters No.	Supporters %	Dissidents No.	Dissidents %	Index
VIETNAM						
Working class	92	(81)	88.0	(11)	12.0	76
Intermediate	45	(39)	86.7	(6)	13.3	73
Professional	132	(114)	86.4	(18)	13.6	73
Incumbent working class	53	(52)	98.1	(1)	1.9	96
Newcomer working class	39	(29)	74.4	(10)	25.6	49
Incumbent middle class	68	(58)	85.3	(10)	14.7	71
Newcomer middle class	109	(94)	86.2	(15)	13.8	72
WAGE FREEZE						
Working class	92	(85)	92.4	(7)	7.6	85
Intermediate	45	(38)	84.4	(7)	15.6	69
Professional	132	(116)	87.9	(16)	12.1	76
Incumbent working class	53	(53)	100.0	(0)	0.0	100
Newcomer working class	39	(32)	82.1	(7)	17.9	64
Incumbent middle class	68	(55)	80.9	(13)	19.1	62
Newcomer middle class	109	(99)	90.8	(10)	9.2	82
DEFENSE REVIEW						
Working class	92	(72)	78.3	(20)	21.7	57
Intermediate	45	(33)	73.3	(12)	26.7	47
Professional	128	(91)	71.1	(37)	28.9	42
Incumbent working class	54	(44)	81.5	(10)	18.5	63
Newcomer working class	38	(28)	73.7	(10)	26.3	47
Incumbent middle class	68	(44)	64.7	(24)	35.3	29
Newcomer middle class	105	(80)	76.2	(25)	23.8	52
COMMON MARKET						
Working class	93	(55)	59.1	(38)	40.9	18
Intermediate	45	(30)	66.7	(15)	33.3	33
Professional	130	(92)	70.8	(38)	29.2	42
Incumbent working class	55	(34)	61.8	(21)	38.2	24
Newcomer working class	38	(21)	55.3	(17)	44.7	11
Incumbent middle class	68	(47)	69.1	(21)	30.9	38
Newcomer middle class	107	(75)	70.1	(32)	30.5	40

TABLE 18

Voting Records of Socio-Economic Groups on Four Issues Combined (with "unknowns" apportioned)

Voting group	Number	Supporters No. %	Dissidents No. %	Index
Working class	352	(278) 79.0	(74) 21.0	58
Intermediate	172	(132) 76.7	(40) 23.3	53
Professional	504	(396) 78.6	(108) 21.4	57
Incumbent working class	204	(172) 84.3	(32) 15.7	69
Newcomer working class	148	(106) 71.6	(42) 28.4	43
Incumbent	256	(189) 73.8	(67) 26.2	48
Newcomer middle class	420	(338) 80.5	(82) 19.5	61

gory. When voting on the wage freeze, the working-class group awarded the Government the highest level of support, but here again the incumbents were more responsive to the whips than were the newcomers. The same thing was true of the middle-class newcomers, as compared with the incumbent group.

TABLE 19

Socio-Economic Groups and Parliamentary Service: Three Issues (with "unknowns" apportioned)

Voting group	Number	Supporters No. %	Dissidents No. %	Index
Incumbent working class	153	(142) 92.8	(11) 7.2	86
Newcomer working class	111	(86) 77.5	(25) 22.5	55
Incumbent middle class	192	(145) 75.5	(47) 24.5	51
Newcomer middle class	315	(265) 84.1	(50) 15.9	68

On the defense review, the working-class element gave the Government the highest support, the incumbents once again exhibiting stronger loyalty than the newcomers. This pattern becomes more pronounced if an adjustment is made for the right-wing M.P.s who abstained to protest the Government's failure to apply sanctions against the habitual rebels. A lower degree of support was registered by the intermediate and professional groups, each of which contains a sizable cluster of M.P.s who were once associated with the CND movement. The newcomers in the intermediate/professional group were still slightly more loyal than the incumbents, but they tended to support the Government less on defense than on Vietnam and the wage freeze, reflecting the opposition of former CND members as well as criticism from some otherwise loyal M.P.s who worry about the effect of defense expenditure upon the social services.

As mentioned earlier, the issue that distorts the general pattern is the Common Market, and the distortion occurs in two ways. The first arises from the possibility that a large group of adamant pro-Marketeers may have exerted considerable pressure on the Government to apply for entry. Had the Party leaders refused to adopt this policy, they might have been faced with an even larger rebellion, this time from the right. The potential threat to the Government by this group was more serious than ordinary dissidence from the left because its members might have been willing to collaborate with like-minded Liberals and Conservatives to achieve their objective. The leftists, of course, can rarely find M.P.s in other parties with whom they can coalesce to strengthen their hand. It should be noted that by studying dissidence only through an examination of the division lists, one is unable to identify the dissidence that may have erupted before an issue comes to the floor of the House. Through their fervent support for stringent economic measures in 1966 and for the Common Market in 1967, a significant right-wing faction posed a problem for the Party leaders who could hardly ignore its demands. These demands may have been reflected in the policies that the Government brought into the chamber.

The second way in which the Common Market distorts the general pattern is in the behavior of the working-class M.P.s. On this issue they gave the Government their weakest support, with about

40 per cent voting negatively or abstaining. On this question, the incumbent support was once again higher than that of the newcomers. Although the professional category tended to be more loyal than the intermediate group, the difference between the incumbents and the newcomers was slight.

Considering the changing composition of the Labour back-benches and the voting behavior of the various groups on these issues, we should keep under observation the following tendencies:

1. As in the past, there is a small core of left-wing dissenters who opposed the Government on every (or nearly every) issue. A total of fifteen M.P.s, for example, were known to be in the dissidence column on all four issues, and sixteen others exhibited their displeasure on three of the four issues. The membership of these core groups can be broken down as follows:

	Dissidents on Four Issues	Dissidents on Three Issues
Working Class	4	5
Intermediate	5	1
Professional	6	10
Incumbent Working Class	0	0
Newcomer Working Class	4	5
Incumbent Middle Class	6	5
Newcomer Middle Class	5	6

2. The working-class group is now proportionately smaller, and the newcomer group is not as supportive of the Government as was the comparable group in the immediate postwar years.

3. The intermediate group tends to be the least responsive to the controversial policies of the Government.

4. The newcomer M.P.s of middle-class background—a group that is growing in strength—exhibits at the moment a relatively high degree of support for the Wilson Cabinet. The people in that category, however, are a highly qualified and a potentially independent lot, and for this reason they may be vulnerable to dissidence that springs from frustration. The Party's leaders will probably stand a better chance of retaining the loyalty of this group

if they are able to provide these backbenchers with challenging and constructive work in the legislative process.*

Discipline in the Parliamentary Labour Party

It should be clear by now that the problem of maintaining discipline in the Parliamentary Labour Party consists of much more than merely sending a three-line whip to the members of a presumably cohesive and unified Party on the eve of an important division. Different ideological predispositions, contrasting class backgrounds, and varying socialization experiences lay the basis for potential disagreements over major policy in the organization. While these elements are fairly obvious, three other factors are sometimes overlooked.

First, the PLP has never developed adequate channels of communication between the ministers and the backbenchers, especially during the preparatory stages of legislation.[48] The structures—the advisory study groups, the PLP meeting, and the Liaison Committee —and the organizational procedures do not lend themselves readily to the handling of backbench criticism in its initial phase. This often means that by the time the dissidence has become organized, the policy has already been hammered out and the ministers have committed themselves publicly, making reversals of position more difficult. This helps explain why dissenters sometimes take their case to the floor of the House. A second and related factor is that the institutional procedures in the House of Commons itself do not permit the rank-and-file members to play much of a constructive role in policy making.

The third factor arises from the high levels of political aspiration of some—but by no means all—Labour backbenchers. The disappointments of Tory M.P.s at not being appointed to a ministry may be assuaged by the awarding of "honors," but this type of reward is not so attractive to aspiring Labour backbenchers. They are more intent upon securing positions as junior ministers and in moving upward to more senior posts later. Probably more than a few of these people become discouraged when a Prime Minister appoints to junior ministerial positions some colleagues whom they perceive as not so deserving as themselves.

* We have discussed some of these matters with Mr. Samuel Brittan.

All these factors can contribute to general feelings of frustration, particularly among the most talented and articulate Labour members who are denied a real outlet for their energy. While lounging in the social rooms waiting for the division bell, they have plenty of time to interact with their associates, to discuss policy matters, to develop alternative solutions, and to "cook up" legislative strategies. The fomenting of a rebellion enables many dissidents to join with colleagues who feel as they do in expressing views on an issue about which they have strong beliefs; for others, it may be a way of protesting, not only on a given issue, but also against the structures and procedures of their Party and the House, which, they feel, tend to isolate them from their leaders and to block their influence over policies; and for some, it may simply provide relief from boredom. In other words, individual M.P.s may defy the whips for a number of quite different motives. The leaders of the rebellion, however, invariably oppose the policy of the government strongly, either on grounds of ideology or self-interest.

What strategy the rebels decide to follow depends upon a number of considerations. When a general election or a series of by-elections are to be held, the dissidents may postpone action to foster the image of a united Party. Similarly, when the Party holds power by a slim majority, its members will probably forego the luxury of any strong and open forms of opposition (unless they can be certain that the Tories will abstain on the issue in question). In this case, however, their private, informal communications with ministers are likely to induce the Government to keep the most controversial issues off the floor. Note that no steel nationalization bill was presented to the House during the 1964 parliament.

Potential rebels will be inclined to be most open and forceful under the following circumstances: (1) when the Cabinet is split on an issue: (2) when an issue has not been included in the election manifesto; (3) when the dissident view coincides with Party Conference decisions (as, for example, when the Conference favored unilateralism in 1960); and (4) when the Party has a comfortable majority. The rebels will be more confident, too, if the group is fairly large in size; they realize that public defiance of the whips by four or five members is an ineffective means of opposition and that such a small group is much more vulnerable to discipline by the PLP than is a band of fifty or sixty.

A group of dissidents who wish to register their unhappiness for the benefit of their ministers can adopt a number of different tactics. Often the first step occurs when one or two M.P.s who hold strong views on a matter formulate an Early Day Motion and collect for it as many signatures as possible. Actually, these motions are rarely called for debate by the Speaker, but they have been used increasingly during the past two decades to call the attention of the Party leaders to an issue that is disturbing the backbenchers. Of course, motions placed upon the Order Paper are often not accurate measures of backbench opinion. The PLP has a few habitual motion-signers, and some members sign motions because they are being circulated by their friends, even though they may not have strong beliefs about the subject matter. But, when an issue stirs anti-government feeling among M.P.s who are ordinarily loyal, the list of signatures provides the leaders with a rough gauge of the extent of dissidence. That the leaders occasionally pressure the sponsors to withdraw a motion and the signatories to remove their names suggests that such motions are not idle gestures.

Not all Labour backbenchers who sign an Early Day Motion are willing to carry their grievances to the division lobby, a much more risky act. Voting against his government is probably the most serious step a rebel can take. For this reason, it is very rare. As mentioned earlier, decisions by 33 Conservative backbenchers to oppose and by 60 to abstain tumbled the Chamberlain Government in May 1940. Even though it had a majority of 81 on the vote of confidence, the division result indicated clearly that it had lost control of the situation and could no longer carry on. When a crucial issue emerges in the House, the question of whether the Labour rebels will merely abstain or go so far as to vote against their leaders will be determined in large measure by what the Opposition does. If they can be confident that the Tories will support the Labour Government on the issue or will abstain, the dissident Labour backbenchers can go into the opposition lobby safely. We have already noted that, in the 1967 vote on the Common Market, 36 rebels voted against the Government because they knew that most Tories and probably all the Liberals would support Wilson.

But if the Tories are likely to oppose the Government, the Labour dissidents tend to express their opposition by refusing to vote. This, it should be pointed out, is no refusal to "stand up and be counted." The Government knows full well that the abstention is an act of defiance.

The Labour Party leaders, who want to preserve the unity of the parliamentary group when they take over the government, are naturally eager to avoid floor rebellions. Exhibitions of dissidence help create the image of a weak, feuding organization. If the Tories abstain on an issue, thereby permitting the Labour rebels to vote against their leaders, the division lists will portray the extent of the cleavage within the Party. Even when the Conservatives support the Labour Government, the ministers are sensitive to negative votes and abstentions by their own people because they do not want their legislation to be dependent upon the support of their opponents.

For a large majority of Labour backbenchers, of course, the question of whether to support their government is not difficult. Most of them agree with their leaders on the essential issues and do not have a compelling urge to display their dissidence publicly. Even though the rank-and-file M.P.s may be tempted to sound the tocsin of rebellion occasionally on an issue about which they nurture strong feelings, most of them succumb to subtle pressure for political conformity. The bonds of solidarity usually are tightened when Labour comes to power. Though some M.P.s may disagree on strategy and tactics, consensus exists on many issues that are linked with certain concrete objectives. Moreover, they all want the Labour government to do a good job and present a respectable image to the British public. This desire helps develop organizational cohesion. After all, when the Labour Party governs effectively, its members from the marginal constituencies encounter less difficulty in being returned to Westminster. On the other hand, if the Party does not work together as a team and is thrown out of office, the rebel M.P.s will be much more unhappy with the Tories in command than they ever were with their own leaders.

The machinery of the Parliamentary Labour Party provides another important deterrent to rebellion. M.P.s who oppose the government on a given issue have some opportunity to air their views at the PLP meetings. When the dissidents fail to persuade the majority of their colleagues in closed session, they are often viewed as having had their chance, and this places them in a somewhat weaker position when they decide to carry the dispute to the House chamber, where the schism will be exposed to the Opposition and the general public.

Torn between its desire to respect the different shadings of opinion and its need to present a respectable appearance in the division lobbies, the PLP has developed a set of norms and procedures to help resolve this dilemma. When an individual Labour member or a group of M.P.s persistently engage in rebellious behavior or even when they embarrass the Party by a single breach of discipline, its leaders may seek to enforce these rules. The stages of action which may be taken against violators of discipline are as follows:

1. Gentle persuasion, reproach, and warning by an ordinary whip.
2. Persuasion and reproach by the Chief Whip—as Morrison says, "more in sorrow than in anger."
3. In exceptional cases, a conference with the Deputy Leader or the Leader of the Party.
4. Reference of the matter to the Liaison Committee of the Parliamentary Labour Party, which may recommend to the PLP meeting that the whip be withdrawn.
5. Withdrawal of the whip by the PLP, and notification of this action to the National Executive Committee (NEC). (This sanction cuts the dissident member off from the Party parliamentary organization.)
6. Referral of the case to the National Executive Committee for its disposition.
7. Denial by the NEC of endorsement for prospective Labour candidacy in the next parliamentary election.
8. Expulsion from the Party.

The system of discipline in the Parliamentary Labour Party is based upon norms introduced in the early years by the trade unionists who had learned the need for unity from bitter experience. These rules were given form when the PLP was small, for its members had to stick together in order to make any impact at all, or even survive. Although the cohesion of the PLP rests upon deep feelings of loyalty to program and leadership rather than upon fear of sanctions for dissentient behavior, disciplinary action in exceptional cases is provided by reference to the Standing Orders. In their old form, the Orders authorized sanctions (including loss of endorsement as a Labour candidate or expulsion from the Party) for things "said or done" in the House and for outside activities contrary to the principles or decisions of the organization. "Persistent refusal to observe the decisions of the Parliamentary Party" was to be reported to the National Executive Committee for appropriate action. It was understood, however, that a Labour M.P. could *abstain* from voting on a particular issue (especially on conscription and temperance) on grounds of "conscience," though it was expected that he would not *vote against* the Party's decision. The dissidents were to give to the whips advance notice of their intended behavior.

Early in the 1945 parliament, the Labour Government decided to rely upon the loyalty and comradeship of the backbenchers and to recommend suspension of the Standing Orders for a period of time, after which the experiment would be appraised. They recognized that a certain amount of "individuality" was essential to the healthy working of the system and they were confident that, "even if at times there was a little bit of kicking over the traces," they could "take it." [49] However, even while the Orders were suspended, the PLP still retained authority to withdraw the whip in serious cases of dissidence.

The leading members of the Attlee Cabinet soon became disturbed by the frequency and size of the floor rebellions, especially over foreign policy and peacetime conscription. Herbert Morrison expressed this concern shortly after the defense debate:

> There have, however, been occasions when there has been such an excess of individualism as to involve the danger of muddle and confusion calculated to do us no good in the country, and when jumping over the traces was so pronounced that the whole apple cart was liable to be upset. That, of course, will not do, and our great Labour Party, while agreeable to that proper degree of liberty which is essential to the working of a free Parliament, will expect our members in the House not to rock the boat dangerously or to upset the apple cart.[50]

Although in the 1945 parliament a handful of Labour M.P.s were expelled for rebellious conduct and several parliamentary private secretaries were dismissed for voting against the Government on a three-line whip, the Standing Orders remained suspended while Labour was in power and for a few months when the Party entered into opposition. In March 1952, however, the PLP was embarrassed by the failure of 57 of its members to support a Party motion on defense, and the Standing Orders were reimposed, though in revised form. Under the new rules, a Labour M.P. was expected to support the decisions of PLP meetings, except that an individual might abstain "on matters of deeply-held personal conscientious conviction." The modifying clause was to apply only to *individuals,* not groups, to discourage what Arthur Henderson once called "organized conscience." Two types of discipline by the PLP were authorized: (1) Withdrawal of the whip "on account of things said or done" in the House, accused members having the right to defend themselves before the caucus; and (2) Reporting to the NEC cases of "serious or persistent breaches of Party discipline," the dissidents again having the right to be heard. The revised Standing Orders also required PLP members to consult with their officers before tabling any motions or amendments related to Party policies and decisions.[51]

On November 24, 1959, shortly after the general election, the Standing Orders were replaced by a "code of conduct" resolution which had been drawn up in a series of conferences and presented to the PLP by Hugh Gaitskell.[52] While the new code was more permissive, sanctions still might be applied in certain breaches of discipline. After the defense dispute, a new set of Standing Orders was drawn up and put into effect on December 13, 1961.[53] The sanctions authorized by the new regulations were similar to those in the old Orders. They again recognized the right of PLP members to abstain on "matters of deeply-held personal conscientious conviction," but they explicitly stated that an M.P. was not entitled to *vote against* the decisions reached in PLP meetings. These regulations have remained in effect under the Wilson regime, although discipline was relaxed during most of the 1966–67 period.

In practice, the Labour Party organization outside parliament has been extremely reluctant to impose sanctions against its members of parliament, and there are not many instances of such action being taken. The largest wave of disciplinary measures occurred during the 1945 parliament when four leftist M.P.s and one right-wing member were expelled from the Party by the National Executive Committee for voting contrary to PLP decisions. Action by the Parliamentary Party itself has been confined to withdrawing the whip and this sanction has always been applied to a tiny group of dissidents. In November 1954, for example, the whip was withdrawn from seven Labour members when they disobeyed a PLP decision to abstain on a motion supporting German rearmament. Six of them voted against the motion and one supported the Conservative Government. The rebels were readmitted to the fold later in the session upon undertaking not to disobey future whips. A year later, when the issue of Britain's manufacture of the H-bomb began to rock the Labour Party, Aneurin Bevan issued a personal challenge to Attlee in the chamber to define the Party's policy. He and about sixty other members abstained from voting for the official PLP motion. As a result, the whip was withdrawn from Bevan and the NEC nearly expelled him from the Party.[54] Shortly before the 1955 election, however, he was restored to grace. Again, when the unilateralist movement was at its peak, five Labour M.P.s voted against the service estimates, and the whip was withdrawn from them.

But, considering the number of floor rebellions, the number of cases of disciplinary action under the rules is exceedingly small. As Herbert Morrison has pointed out, Party leaders and back-benchers alike are reluctant to punish colleagues who take exception to PLP decisions, even though the dissidents have had an opportunity to influence policy and are expected to support the majority. This reluctance stems in large part from the strong tradition of toleration of dissent within the organization. Since Gaitskell's death, however, the reluctance has probably been reinforced by the fact that several of the new Party leaders were dissidents themselves earlier in their careers and resisted punitive action against fellow M.P.s before they rose to positions of responsibility in a Labour government. For example, nine members of the Wilson ministry refused to support the Attlee Government in the foreign policy dispute in November 1946.[55] In 1952, when the PLP was considering a motion to disband the Bevanite organization as a "party within a party," thirteen M.P.s who opposed that action were later to serve in the Wilson Government.[56] Again in 1961, after the Party had withdrawn the whip from the five members who had voted against the service estimates, nearly 80 Labour M.P.s representing many shades of opinion addressed a letter to Hugh Gaitskell urging that the whipless rebels be reinstated. Members who had strong convictions on the defense question, they felt, should not be subjected to disciplinary action.[57] No fewer than eighteen of the signatories took posts later in the Wilson Government, where they were faced with the problem of maintaining solidarity in Labour's parliamentary ranks.

Even though formal disciplining of M.P.s under PLP rules does not occur very often, the possibility of sanctions may deter some potential dissidents. The Party leaders, however, can employ other methods to encourage loyalty in the division lobbies, quite apart from punitive action under the Standing Orders. For one thing, when the breaches of discipline become too flagrant or too frequent, a Labour Prime Minister can threaten to request the monarch to dissolve parliament, throwing the country into a general election. If this threat is perceived as realistic, it may have some impact. The prospect of another election is not attractive to many M.P.s; some dislike campaigning, and the members from marginal constituencies, some of whom are invariably found in rebel groups, run the biggest risk of being defeated. However, if the Prime Minister threatens dissolution when conditions are not favorable to the Party, the dissidents are likely to perceive the threat as unrealistic and the stratagem loses its effectiveness.

A more subtle and more effective sanction to hold in line some types of Labour members is the leaders' control over the upward mobility of individual M.P.s. A well-educated, "intellectual" backbencher who has never experienced trade-union "solidarity" may look upon the Standing Orders as a rule book for juveniles. But he may be greatly influenced by the perception that his chances for a ministerial post are better if he supports the Party leadership fully. This factor certainly operated in the 1945 parliament. A sizable number of M.P.s realized that the cost of rebellion was lack of promotion. Only one former rebel got a Cabinet post, and few Labour members who had been involved in a serious breach of discipline during that period were elevated to ministerial position. On the contrary, several parliamentary private secretaries were sacked because of their indiscretions at division time.

Labour's New Approach:
Better Discipline through Greater Cohesion

After Richard Crossman became Leader of the House, he and the Chief Whip attempted to carry out their duties under a more relaxed system of discipline.[58] While the Standing Orders were not rescinded, there was a general understanding that dissidents would not act together in secret groups but that individual M.P.s who felt they could not support the Government from honestly-held personal conviction would be permitted to abstain without being put on the punitive carpet. It was hoped that this would produce an atmosphere of loyalty and trust among the backbenchers, that the number of rebels on controversial issues would be small, and that rebellious groups would not be organized as an embarrassment to the Ministry. Although some Labour members persisted in their opposition to Wilson's policies, Party leaders were reluctant to go so far as to withdraw the whip from any of the dissidents.

This does not mean that all backbenchers were pleased that some of their colleagues could snub the Government with impunity. A band of M.P.s, who prided themselves on being loyal at division time, urged their leaders to stop the chronic offenders from enjoying the freedom to "trail their consciences." [59] The loyalists were largely older, working-class members, most of whom carried trade-union endorsement. When they saw that their views would not prevail, some of them threatened to disobey the whips on certain issues to protest against those who did so habitually. Two of these M.P.s reportedly abstained on the defense review precisely for this reason.[60] For a time this development alarmed the whips who saw the prospect of two-way rebellions in the future—one element composed of the persistent rebels and the other comprising loyalists protesting against the persistent rebels.[61]

Government leaders, too, were disturbed by the upsurge of dissidence, especially on the part of the habitual offenders. On several occasions, the Prime Minister lectured the members of the Parliamentary Party on the need for solidarity and the importance of supporting the Government. His threat at one meeting of the PLP to call a new election was probably ineffective, for the M.P.s knew that he would never face the voters when Labour's stock was sinking. But the meeting was noteworthy because of the dramatic warning he issued to his backbenchers: "Every dog is allowed one bite, but a different view is taken of a dog that goes on biting all the time." Carrying the metaphor a bit further, he cautioned the persistent dissenters that they might lose their Labour "dog licenses" for the next campaign.[62]

In 1967–1968, the rebels taxed the patience of the whips even further, as they refused to support the Government's cuts in public expenditures, increased contributions to the national insurance scheme, and the imposition of charges on drug prescriptions. To save the Government possible embarrassment in the division lobbies, the Parliamentary Labour Party has adopted a new disciplinary code. These rules introduce an intermediate step between chastisement by the Chief Whip and the withdrawal of the whip— suspension of a rebel for a specified time from the privileges of PLP membership, including attendance at meetings and affiliation with the organization's groups. In certain cases of provocation, the Chief Whip has the authority, after consultation with Party leaders, to extend the period of suspension. Several groups of rebels have already been handed out this form of punishment.[62a] In recent months, however, the severity of the whip has been noticeably diminished, and strict attendance is being enforced mostly on votes of confidence.

In general, Wilson and his Labour colleagues have neither relied upon formal rules nor resorted to negative sanctions to hold potential rebels in line. On the whole, the Prime Minister's approach has been *political,* not legal; he has tried to create a new institutional environment to eliminate major sources of the backbench frustration which tend to nourish rebellions against authority. In the short term, his large majority has enabled him to tolerate some breaches of discipline; but for the long run he has been attempting to build within his parliamentary organization a broader consensus which, hopefully, will reduce the incidence of Labour revolts.

Recent patterns of ministerial decisions suggest that Government leaders are pursuing two main strategies: (1) they are providing a wider base of representation in the Ministry; and (2) they are seeking to reform some of the structures and procedures in parliament to make the role of the backbenchers more meaningful.

REPRESENTATION IN THE MINISTRY. Wilson has been careful to cultivate a wide basis of support in the Labour parliamentary organization. His Ministry is the largest in the history of British political parties. The noticeable increase has taken place in the number of parliamentary secretaries and ministers of state. When the Labour members in his Government appear at PLP meetings or in the division lobbies, the Prime Minister can count on more than 100 votes which are delivered under the principle of collective responsibility.

But the strategy of building consensus is more complex than this. Unlike Gaitskell, who led the Party from the right, Wilson is identified more with the center—probably a better vantage point from which to guide a party that has a strong right wing and a smaller but more vocal left wing that can draw upon the center faction on certain issues. Wilson has also gone out of his way to give various shades of ideological opinion representation in his Government. Not only were different currents of thought represented in his first Government—an astute political move, given the nature of the Party and the size of his majority at the time— but when he has reshuffled his Ministry, he has often awarded positions simultaneously to M.P.s from the right, the center, and the left. For example, the roster of ministers since the 1966 election lists Gaitskell supporters and Gaitskell opponents, "pro-Marketeers" and "anti-Marketeers," and M.P.s who have supported one defense policy and others who have fought it. The Ministry includes a sprinkling of former members of the "ginger groups" and rebel movements which sprang forth immediately after the war and during the 1950s. "Ex-rebels" who have adjusted well to the harness of office include six founders of the "Keep Left" group, nearly a dozen "Bevanites" or M.P.s who were on the fringe of the movement, and about the same number from the Campaign for Nuclear Disarmament. (Some of these members of the left moved successively from one rebel group to the next.) It is not unusual to hear right-wing Labour M.P.s express laudatory comments about the performance of these former members of the "left" in their new ministerial roles.

The elevation of a number of leftist spokesmen to positions that require them to use their talents constructively has implications for the maintenance of solidarity in the PLP. Obviously, the wider span of representation in the Ministry broadens the Prime Minister's base of support. Moreover, the cooptation of these people into the Government siphons off the natural leaders of the "back-bench left," rendering it less effective in rebellious action, at least until it develops new leadership. This strategy is the opposite from that followed by Attlee in the 1945 parliament. With the exception of Aneurin Bevan, Labour members who had recently kicked over the traces were, for the most part, denied jobs in the Ministry. This meant that many younger M.P.s who were eager to carve out successful political careers grew more cautious about linking themselves with dissident movements, especially after 1946.

By bringing former rebels into his Government, the Prime Minister prevents them from opposing Labour's program on the floor of the House, but this strategy has a negative aspect. In the first place, it displeases some Labour backbenchers on the right who have long records of loyalty in the division lobbies, When a left-wing member was selected as a junior minister, for example, some M.P.s from the same region who had served the Party faithfully in parliament for a much longer period resented the appointment and publicly complained about it.[63] Furthermore, some potential dissenters undoubtedly perceive that non-conformist behavior may no longer be the bar to political advancement that it once was. Indeed, when ministerial reshuffles elevate people from all segments of the Party, such behavior might even enhance their chances for promotion. As one disappointed Labour member portrayed the situation, ". . . it seems the best way to make the Prime Minister notice you is to make a nuisance of yourself." The weakening of this traditional sanction may have an effect upon Labour governments in the 1970s, since the backbenches have a heavy component of talented young people who are understandably anxious to make good in parliament. Possibly, as promotions come slowly owing to the oversupply of ability relative to the number of jobs, some of those who suffer from career frustrations may consider opposition to the Government as a quicker way to break into the Ministry.

REFORM OF PARLIAMENT. The Prime Minister and his senior colleagues have also concerned themselves with the reform of parliament which, in addition to making the institution more efficient, would help get the group of highly qualified backbenchers more involved in its operations so that they might be less inclined to engage in disruptive activities. Parliamentary reform has been strongly urged by some academicians and other knowledgeable observers for many years and the Wilson Government, sometimes a bit reluctantly, has taken a few steps in this direction. Although it is too early to make a judgment on the effectiveness of these measures, the Labour Party leaders are undoubtedly interested in making the role of the backbench M.P.s more challenging.

That the problem existed became clear shortly after the first Wilson Government was installed, when 65 backbenchers—86 per cent of whom were newcomers to the PLP—submitted an Early Day Motion requesting that House procedures by stream-lined, including the establishment of some "specialized commit-tees." [64] In a report issued in the autumn, the Select Committee on Procedure recommended that a system of specialized commit-tees be set up, and, as an initial step, that the existing Estimates Committee be recast so that its subcommittees would become more specialized. It also recommended that the Committee's span of jurisdiction be broadened.[65] In 1966, the Estimates Committee rearranged its subcommittees to provide for greater specialization, covering Technological and Scientific Affairs, Economic Affairs, Social Affairs, Defense and Overseas Affairs, and Building and Natural Resources.[66]

The movement to give the backbenchers freer rein and oppor-tunities for more meaningful participation gained impetus after the 1966 election. During the debate on the Queen's Address, the Prime Minister suggested that one or two new cross-bench com-mittees might be established "to review any issue which might be considered within the field of administration of some of our great social Departments . . ." [67] He indicated that a small group of backbenchers on each committee might meet informally with the appropriate ministers to discuss particular problems in domestic affairs. The subjects he had in mind were education, landlord-tenant relations, planning decisions, regional development, and the like—issues of great social concern which would excite the interest of qualified M.P.s. To illustrate, he cited the fact that many new members were former teachers whose experience would enable them to make a significant contribution to the resolution of edu-cational problems.

The Prime Minister, however, was not convinced that committees should be established to discuss questions of defense and foreign policy, which, of course, are of particular concern to some restless backbenchers. Moreover, Wilson—like most previous government leaders who have considered the issue of parliamentary reform—wanted to avoid having the proposed committees develop into powerful bodies, as in the American Congress. Their main purpose, in his view, was to provide opportunity for backbench M.P.s to become better informed about what the government was doing and thus better equipped to criticize policy in House debates.

In December 1966, two select committees were set up as pilot experiments—one for Agriculture, Fisheries, and Food and the other for Science and Technology. These were expected to operate along the lines of the Select Committee on Nationalized Industries which had been created in 1957. Shortly after the Select Committee on Agriculture was formed, its members became interested in the effect of Britain's entry into the Common Market on domestic agriculture and requested funds from the Government to travel to Brussels.[68] This request disturbed some Government leaders who were not eager to have the Committee become too involved in policy. They could hardly overlook the fact that the Committee's chairman opposed Britain's entry into the Market and had abstained when the vote was taken in the House. At first the Government rejected the request on the ground that the visit to Brussels was inappropriate at the time, since Britain was in the process of making application. Later, however, it decided to make funds available for the trip.

As Leader of the House, Crossman has taken the committee idea much further by suggesting that a "pre-legislation" committee be set up to assist in formulating some legislative proposals before the government takes them to the debating chamber.[69] If the existing committees and others that might be established begin to build strength, this development might have important implications for the operation of the House of Commons. A viable committee system might well become the channel through which frustrated backbenchers can communicate their views to the government more effectively and thus exert greater influence over official policy.

Besides taking some steps to give backbenchers a chance to participate more effectively in House affairs through committees, the Government appears to have given them unusual opportunities in the 1966 parliament to become directly involved in legislation through the introduction of private members' bills. Traditionally it has been very difficult for private members to steer their pet measures—the majority of which have not been controversial—through the complex legislative machinery to the final stage of royal assent. In his study of private members' bills, Professor Bromhead has examined the fate of such legislation under the Labour Government during the period 1949–51.[70] According to his findings, out of 53 bills introduced only 13 reached the statute books. In contrast, 81 private members' bills were introduced during 1966–67, and 24 of them received royal assent. Equally significant, some of these bills dealt with issues that would attract socially-conscious backbenchers on the Labour side. Two of them generated a great deal of controversy—the Termination of Pregnancy Bill, which was sponsored by a Liberal, in collaboration with a Labour rebel, and the Sexual Offenses Bill, which was introduced by a Labour member. These two measures were strenuously opposed all the way and were debated hotly in all-night sessions which attracted larger audiences in the chamber than private members' bills customarily draw. The spirited controversies devoured the quota of allocated time, and under ordinary circumstances the bills would have died. The Government, however, came to the rescue, making extra time available, and the two bills eventually became law.[71] Although technically non-partisan, a number of the private members' bills which were introduced in 1966–67 were of greater consequence than usual and the Labour backbenchers who were involved in getting them passed could feel a sense of real accomplishment. In the important instances in which this happened, they could also feel grateful to the Government leaders who gave them a spot on the legislative timetable. It is too early yet, however, to discern whether the Government is giving wider scope to private members' bills as a method for keeping backbenchers busy by absorbing themselves in legislative crusades. It is also too early to determine whether the Government's willingness to give support to some of these controversial measures, which interest many Labour backbenchers, can be used to reward those who are usually loyal to the Government.

By improving the chances for backbenchers to move into the Government as a result of the Ministry's increased size and by giving them a more important legislative role through the cross-bench committees and through the sponsorship of private members' bills, the Prime Minister and his colleagues have in effect augmented the supply of positive rewards which they can dispense for loyalty. If this strategy proves effective, the incidence of *persistent* rebellion may be reduced and the strong negative sanctions (such as the withdrawal of the whip and expulsion from the Party) may be reserved for a diminishing group of diehard rebels. Should this happen, the certainty that negative sanctions will be applied against those who persist in defying the whip may help to deter even the persisters. Furthermore, in shifting to a more influential role for the backbenchers, the sponsors of the reform may be introducing innovations that will profoundly change the character and functioning of the House of Commons itself. If these developments mature, the role of the backbencher may come a bit closer to the idealized treatments of the Commons in the nineteenth century, albeit through a new set of institutional arrangements.

SUMMARY

The task of welding together the diverse elements that are allied in the Parliamentary Labour Party has never been easy. In contrast with the Conservatives who have more homogeneous social backgrounds and educational experience, the PLP is recruited from both working-class and middle-class segments of British society and has a wide range of formal educational attainment. Moreover, the Party has always embraced and tolerated a broad spectrum of political thought and its democratic machinery permits these differing viewpoints to find easy expression. The organization includes members with a high degree of ideological commitment, but, because the Party lacks a coherent doctrine, many of them tend to define Socialism in accordance with the set of priorities in which they have a devoted interest. This means that on certain issues which, to some M.P.s, involve the basic principles of Socialism—for some, the issue may be defense and for others, it may be foreign policy or the social services—compromise policies acceptable to all are extremely difficult to hammer out.

The problem of achieving harmony within the PLP has been greatly exacerbated since the war because of the enormous difficulties that have confronted the British people in the domestic

economy and in the international sphere. In 1945–50 and again
in 1964–66, the electorate has placed the Labour Party in command when Britain was in great distress, faced with problems that
would have challenged the genius of any political organization.
Determined leadership and innovative policies were called for, but,
especially after 1949, when Labour had placed on the statute
books nearly all the program it had formulated during the previous three decades, the Party's traditional doctrines had few answers to Britain's current problems. Whether Fabian or Marxian,
the classical analyses seemed more appropriate to the evils of
capitalism as portrayed by Charles Dickens than to the problems
of Britain in the 1950s and the 1960s. While most of the policies
introduced by a Labour Government commanded the support of
its backbenchers, it was to be expected that some Labour members
who believed that the "proper order of priorities" was being
violated would oppose certain components of its program.

The task of maintaining widespread PLP support for a Labour
Government has also been rendered more challenging by the
changing composition of the Labour backbenches. During the
immediate postwar years, the backbenchers included a large group
of M.P.s with working-class backgrounds, many of whom were
officials of the long-established trade unions and most of whom
had had union experience during the difficult times. In fighting
for the rights of the workers, they had perceived the need for
solidarity, and they carried over into parliament the feeling that
they should support their leaders, especially when they had to
deal with issues they were not accustomed to handling. These
working-class backbenchers, to be sure, were not always pleased
with the Government's policies. But its overall program was so
appealing that many of them were often willing to go along on
those issues to which they objected. This meant that on many
controversial questions the Government could rely upon a strong
base of support in the working-class group, especially among those
working-class M.P.s who entered parliament for the first time
in 1945.

In the 1960s, however, the situation has changed considerably.
The relative size of the working-class contingent has been noticeably reduced, and the newer crop of M.P.s in this category—
younger, more sophisticated, and with less trade-union experience

in rigorous industrial combat—has tended to be less loyal. Again
in contrast with the situation in 1945, the Wilson Government,
understandably, has not been able to offer these potential dissidents a program of broad social reform to offset the more contentious issues they are expected to support.

Accompanying the decline in the number of working-class backbenchers is the increase in the number of M.P.s who have had
advanced education and who have been engaged in professional
and other middle-class employment. Far from having experienced
the virtues of solidarity and loyalty to leadership in trade-union
work, many of these people have been trained to think through
problems on their own and to stand up for their independent views.
As free-wheeling individualists, their policy positions are somewhat unpredictable. A small group of them, of course, usually
can be expected to take a left-wing posture on crucial issues. But
many of them may be inclined to support the official position on
one issue and oppose it on another. In other words, a large number
of these M.P.s are increasingly difficult to type-cast as being left,
right, or center. Under these circumstances, the formation and
regrouping of coalitions in support of or against particular policies
may be even more complex than in the past.

In any event, the new flock of M.P.s in the non-manual and
professional categories, along with some of the more independent
members in the working-class group, are not likely to perform for
very long as lobby sheep, blindly following the whips under the
guise of shepherds. Although they recognize the importance of
Party cohesion and the need to sustain their Government, many
of them feel that this cohesion can be achieved best when the
backbenchers are given more opportunity to discuss policy at
PLP meetings and to play a larger part in the legislative affairs of
the House before the important decisions are made. In their view,
the old style of discipline reflected in the Standing Orders is inappropriate for the present group of Labour backbenchers. Moreover, some of the talented and articulate M.P.s who have entered
the House in recent years and have thus far been loyal to the
Government are eager to succeed in their parliamentary work and
the longer they are denied ministerial appointments or opportunities for other constructive work in the legislative process, the
more likely they are to be provoked into defying the whips.

These attitudes betray certain weaknesses in existing arrangements within the Party and in the House of Commons. In the first place, the organizational machinery of the PLP does not facilitate adequate communication between the front benches and the back-benches, with the result that some rank-and-file M.P.s feel that their views are often not given a proper hearing. They believe that the advisory discussion groups and even the PLP meetings do not afford them sufficient opportunity to present their thoughts on important policy matters. In the second place, the organization and procedures of the House of Commons itself tend to cut the backbenchers off from meaningful participation in the policy-making process.

In addressing themselves to the problem of controlling dissidence and maintaining Party cohesion in parliament, Prime Minister Wilson and his colleagues have followed a political rather than a legal approach. Although provoked by the behavior of the persistent rebels, they have refrained from taking punitive action against the offenders by withdrawing the whip or by having them expelled from the Party. Cognizant of the basic problem, the Wilson Government has sought to attack it from three different directions: (1) the size of the Ministry has been increased, and hence the chances for upward mobility have been improved; (2) representation in the Ministry has been broadened to include differing shades of Socialist belief, and, since some prominent members of the left have been appointed to Government posts, the dissidents in that wing of the Party have been deprived of their leadership; and (3) initial steps have been taken to establish a system of cross-bench committees, which, along with more favorable treatment of private members' bills, may enable frustrated backbenchers to play a more constructive role in the House.

In light of the changing composition of the Labour backbenches, Wilson's general approach to the problem of cohesion, especially his efforts to involve them more deeply in legislative affairs, seems to have a better chance to succeed than would reliance entirely upon the rules and sanctions of the Standing Orders. Such a system was more appropriate a generation ago, when it commanded wider support in the backbenches, although, as we have seen, the Party leaders have usually been hesitant about applying it at all. With the large intake of professional people and a different generation of working-class M.P.s, the backbenches are different now and new solutions to the problem of discipline are required.

While tackling the problems that Britain faces in the 1960s, Prime Minister Wilson has pursued within the PLP the politics of consensus-building. With the base he has managed to establish, he has been able to push extremely controversial policies through the Party machinery and the legislative processes of the House. In attempting to build a wider consensual base within his own organization, however, Wilson has supported some structural and procedural changes which may have ramifications far beyond the organizational boundaries of the PLP. These reform measures may precipitate important changes in the role and functioning of the House of Commons which will outlive the Wilson Government.

NOTES

1. W. Beckerman and Associates, *The British Economy in 1975,* London: Cambridge University Press, 1965, p. 12.
2. See chart in *New York Times,* June 14, 1966.
3. *Ibid.*
4. *Report of the Committee on Housing in Greater London,* Comnd. 2605, London: H. M. Stationery Office, March 1965, p. 101.
5. *The Times,* March 5, 1965.
6. *The Times,* February 1, 15, 1966.
7. *Notices of Questions and Motions,* February 14, 1966, EDM No. 408.
8. For the most detailed analysis of the election, the reader is referred to D. E. Butler and Anthony King, *The British General Election of 1966,* New York: St. Martin's Press, 1966.
9. For the official Labour position, see *Report of the Sixty-First Annual Conference of the Labour Party,* 1962, pp. 245–251.
10. *The Guardian,* March 17, 1966; *Daily Telegraph,* March 18, 1966.
11. The text of the speech is printed in *The Guardian,* March 19, 1966.
12. *Gallup Political Index,* Report No. 71, p. 41.
13. *Gallup Political Index,* Report No. 71, p. 35. Six of the issues listed in the interview schedule are not included in our list.
14. See Butler and King, *op. cit.,* pp. 261–64, 275–77, 299–310.
15. *The Guardian,* May 16, 1966.
16. *The Times,* April 16, 1966; May 3, 1966.
17. *The Guardian,* June 30, 1966.
18. *The Times,* October 1, 5, 1966.

19. See below, pp. 85, 88–89.

20. See British Information Service, *British Record*, April 14, 1967; Ann D. Monroe, "The British Economy," *Current History*, May 1967, pp. 270–75, 308.

21. *The Guardian*, May 4, 1967.

22. *Notices of Questions and Motions*, May 9, 1967.

23. See below, pp. 85, 88–89.

24. *The Times*, June 3, 1967.

25. *Statement on the Defense Estimates*, Comnd. 3203, London: H. M. Stationery Office, February 1966.

26. See below, pp. 85, 88–89.

27. See below, pp. 102–103.

28. *Notices of Questions and Motions*, June 30–July 6, 1966, EDM No. 111.

29. *The Times*, July 7, 1966.

30. See below, pp. 85, 88–89.

31. *Report of the Sixty-Fifth Annual Conference of the Labour Party*, 1966, p. 5.

32. For an excellent analysis of the Parliamentary Labour Party in the 1950s, see S. E. Finer, H. B. Berrington, and D. J. Bartholemew, *Backbench Opinion in the House of Commons, 1955–59*, New York: Pergamon Press, 1961, especially pp. 14–23.

33. Although the PLP contains a few orthodox Marxists, it is important to remember that the Labour Party takes a strong stand against Communism. The Communist Party and Communist-front organizations are on the list of proscribed organizations.

34. *Glasgow Herald*, June 18, 1951.

35. See *Daily Herald*, August 7, 1947.

36. *News Chronicle*, September 23, 1949.

37. See *Financial Times*, October 18, 1951.

38. For accounts of this rebellion, see *The Times*, November 14–20, 1946; *Daily Telegraph*, November 14–18, 1946; Richard Crossman, in *Sunday Pictorial*, April 6, 1947. For the debate, see *House of Commons Debates*, November 18, 1946, Vol. 430, Col. 526–94.

39. *House of Commons Notices of Motions, Questions and Orders of the Day*, November 13–18, 1946.

40. J. P. W. Mallalieu, in *Huddersfield Examiner*, December 2, 1946.

41. *News Chronicle*, November 29, 1946.

42. *Observer*, November 24, 1946.

43. Biographical information on Labour M.P.s has been drawn from a wide variety of sources: *The Times Guide to the House of Commons; Labour's Election Who's Who; Dod's Parliamentary Companion; Who's Who;* Frank Illingworth, *British Political Yearbook, 1947;* Carol Bunker, *Who's Who in Parliament; The Catholic Who's Who; Scottish Biographies; The Jewish Yearbook; Who's Who in Local Government; The Labour Who's Who;* and *Reports of the*

Annual Conference of the Labour Party. Use has also been made of clippings in newspaper "morgues," obituaries, election addresses, and interviews.

44. *House of Commons Notices of Motions, Questions and Orders of the Day*, March 17–28, 1947.

45. *Observer*, March 30, 1947; *The Times*, April 1, 1947.

46. *News Chronicle*, May 9, 1947; *The Times*, April 6, 1947.

47. The references for the debates, division lists, and newspaper reports of negative votes and abstentions on the four issues are as follows: (1) Vietnam—*House of Commons Debates*, July 7, 1966, Vol. 731, Col. 679–819; *The Guardian*, July 9, 1966. (2) Prices and Incomes—*House of Commons Debates*, October 25, 1966, Vol. 734, Col. 842–970; *The Times*, October 26, 1966. (3) Defense Review—*House of Commons Debates*, February 27–28, 1967, Vol. 742, Col. 97–224, 281–404; *The Times*, March 1, 1967. (4) Common Market —*House of Commons Debates*, May 8–10, 1967, Vol. 746, Col. 1061–1184, 1281–1414, 1504–1656; *The Times*, May 11–12, 1967.

48. James J. Lynskey, *The Role of British Backbenchers in the Modification of Government Policy*, unpublished Ph.D. dissertation, University of Minnesota, 1966, especially Chapter 4.

49. Herbert Morrison, Speech at Labour Party demonstration in Margate, reported in *The Times*, May 26, 1947.

50. *Ibid*.

51. For a copy of the revised Orders, see *Report of the Fifty-First Annual Conference of the Labour Party*, 1952, p. 201.

52. See *The Times*, November 23–25, 1959.

53. See *The Times*, December 13, 1961; *Report of the Sixty-First Annual Conference of the Labour Party*, 1962, p. 85.

54. See *The Times*, March 17, 1955; April 21, 1955.

55. See below, pp. *000*.

56. See *Oldham Evening Chronicle*, October 24, 1952.

57. *Daily Telegraph*, March 21–24, 1961.

58. See *The Guardian*, May 6, 1967.

59. *Daily Telegraph*, March 8, 1967.

60. *The Guardian*, March 6, 1967.

61. *Daily Telegraph*, March 8, 1967; *The Times*, January 27, February 27–29, 1968.

62. See *The Times*, March 3, 1967.

62a. See *The Times*, January 19, 22, and February 28–29, and May 30, 1968.

63. See *Daily Telegraph*, March 8, 1967.

64. *Notices of Questions and Motions*, June 22–28, 1965, EDM No. 257.

65. See *House of Commons Debates*, October 25, 1965, Vol. 718, Col. 172–291.

66. Peter Bromhead, "The British Constitution, in 1966," *Parliamentary Affairs*, Spring 1967, pp. 112–113.

67. *House of Commons Debates*, April 21, 1966, Vol. 727, Col. 75–81.

68. See *Manchester Guardian Weekly*, June 29, July 13, 1967.

69. *Manchester Guardian Weekly*, July 20, 1967.

70. P. A. Bromhead, *Private Members' Bills in the British Parliament*, London: Routledge and Kegan Paul, 1956, p. 190.

71. See *Manchester Guardian Weekly*, June 29, July 13, 1967.

Change in French Politics after the 1965 Presidential Elections

by William G. Andrews

I. INTRODUCTION

THE WORLD RUBBED ITS EYES IN WONDER ON DECEMBER 6, 1965. The mighty Charles de Gaulle had been slapped in the face humiliatingly—by his own people. Using the system of direct popular election he had given them, they had refused to re-elect him to the Presidency he had created. His opponents had polled 55.4 per cent of the vote, depriving him of the majority required for first-round election. Two weeks later, however, he won the runoff election with 54.5 per cent of the vote.

De Gaulle's second-round victory did not erase the psychological shock of the earlier setback. The king had been seen naked. De Gaulle was vincible, perhaps even mortal. Playing his game by his rules, the opposition had nearly defeated him.[1] Playing better, it might win.

That inference opened a third phase in the political history of the Fifth French Republic. During the first phase, 1958–62, non-Gaullists had held a majority of the National Assembly seats, but had been so cowed by the fear that de Gaulle might dump the Algerian problem back in their laps and by his use of referenda that they had not dared defy him. Furthermore, the hermaphrodite constitutional structure (neither parliamentary nor presidential) limited their opportunities to express their opposition effectively. During the second phase, 1962–65, the opposition regained its opportunities because the Algerian problem had been settled, the regime had become clearly presidential, and the high tide of de Gaulle's popular-

117

ity had passed. Yet, throughout the second phase, Gaullism seemed invincible. Gaullists dominated the Assembly and de Gaulle seemed impregnable in the Presidency. The third phase opened with presidentialism firmly in place in the institutions, but with the Gaullist hold on political power shaken. The signal was given by the Presidential elections in December 1965. Competitiveness was returning to French politics. Presidential institutions were available to give it point, force, and focus.

The essay that follows will examine the stimulus that inaugurated the third phase and the responses it evoked from candidates, voters, deputies, and political parties. Especially, it will consider the extent to which bipartism was stimulated by the 1965 elections and, even more specifically, the impact those elections had on the agonized struggle for unity on the French political Left. It will show that bipartism increased, that the Left advanced toward unity, that France became more democratic, but that the road ahead was still long.

II. STIMULUS: THE PRESIDENTIAL ELECTIONS OF 1965

A. Round One

THE CAMPAIGN. The December 5 poll shocked de Gaulle as much as anyone. He had stage managed it with the consummate skill of the greatest showman since P. T. Barnum in order to demonstrate beyond doubt that de Gaulle needed no "intermediaries," that his bond with the French people required no adhesive from parties or parliaments, that he could win re-election to the nation's highest office without effort.

To prove his point, he had cast himself as sole actor in the Gaullist election campaign and then refrained from performing. He forbade local campaigning in his behalf and interdicted campaign addresses by ministers. The principal Gaullist political party, the Union for the New Republic (UNR), was muzzled and a private, non-party "civic association" waged what little Gaullist campaign was planned.[2]

De Gaulle intended to campaign very little himself. He used the text of an eight-minute speech he delivered two weeks before the campaign as his election address (a statement sent postage-free to all voters) and, superimposed over a misty portrait of himself, as his principal, official campaign poster. Smaller, unofficial posters used the closing lines of that speech as their sole text. Another misty portrait of the candidate dominated large billboard posters that had the tricolor for background and "for the Success of France" as their only inscription.[3] De Gaulle disdained to use his air time during the first round of addresses and planned to speak "only a limited number of minutes" for the entire campaign instead of the four hours allotted him.[4] By unofficial report, he intended to speak only once, late in the campaign.[5]

Then, the first shock hit. Press reports, Gaullist leaders, prefects, and public opinion surveys indicated that the Opposition broadcasting campaigns were having effect. After seven years of Gaullist monopoly, the Opposition appeared on radio and television. Frenchmen could see for the first time that it offered attractive candidates and arguments. De Gaulle's support fell from 61 to 57 per cent between November 6–16 and November 17–24 and to 51 per cent in November 17–27. Jean Lecanuet, de Gaulle's center-right opponent, increased his support from about 3 to 13 per cent and support for François Mitterrand, center-left candidate endorsed by the French Communist Party (PCF), jumped from 23 to 27 per cent.[6] Even more startling was a telephone survey which disclosed that every respondent had followed the television campaign and 29 per cent had changed their opinions about the candidates as a result.[7]

The Gaullists' reaction to this unsettling information was swift and unmistakable. Their leaders held a crucial strategy meeting on November 24, the sixth day of the campaign. Afterward, a minister announced, "We are joining the dance." They launched a real campaign effort. The UNR went into action at the local level. Ministers swarmed like locusts across the landscape to address campaign meetings. De Gaulle was urged to enter the fray. At first, he held back. Then, on November 26, he capitulated, announcing that he would add a fifteen minute campaign broadcast on November 30 to the December 3 broadcast already planned.[8]

This Gaullist reaction reflected the general realization that the Fifth Republic had turned a corner. Politics in France had become genuinely competitive again, but the situation differed from the pre-1962 period in that the struggle took place in a presidential arena now. De Gaulle discovered he had to descend into the arena he had constructed.

THE RESULTS. De Gaulle's discovery was too late. The extra Gaullist effort was vain. King Lear failed to stem the tide. His support continued to fall. By November 30–December 3, it had dropped to 43 per cent.[9] The first-round balloting on December 5 gave de Gaulle 43.7 per cent of the vote, far short of the majority required for first-round election. (See Table 1.)

TABLE 1

Election Results, December 5, 1965

	Number	%
Registered voters	28,235,002	100.0
Valid ballots cast,	23,757,672	84.1
De Gaulle	10,386,734	43.7
Mitterrand, left-center	7,658,752	32.2
Lecanuet, right-center	3,767,408	15.9
Tixier-Vignancour, extreme right	1,253,959	5.3
Marcilhacy, right-center	413,125	1.7
Barbu, non-political	277,644	1.2

Source: L'Année politique 1965, p. 114, from official returns of the Ministry of the Interior. Overseas results are not included.

Public opinion surveys indicated that de Gaulle's lead on the first round was largely the result of his appeal to French women. (See Table 2.) They also showed that political party identification correlated highly with presidential electoral behavior. (See Table 3.) Most strikingly, they showed that the split between the "clericals" (MRP and Independents) and the "anti-clericals" (Radicals and Socialists) remained profound.

SIGNIFICANCE. "I was wrong." With that startling and unprecedented admission to his Council of Ministers on December 8, de Gaulle acknowledged that the Fifth Republic had entered a new, more democractic phase.[10] He had thought the French electorate would behave in presidential elections as it did in referenda. Instead, it had behaved as in parliamentary elections. "The French have returned to their traditional families," he said,

TABLE 2

Distribution of Support by Sex, Presidential Election,
December 5, 1965
(by per cent)

	De Gaulle	Mitterrand	Others
Men, SOFRES	40	35	25
Men, IFOP	43	36	21
Women, SOFRES	53	21	26
Women, IFOP	50	26	24

Sources: SOFRES public opinion survey, *L'Express*, December 6–12, 1965, p. 44; IFOP public opinion survey, *Le Nouvel Observateur*, December 22, 1965, p. 10.

with reference to the ideological currents that have kept French politics swirling for so long.

Presidential elections do, indeed, differ from referenda, but the difference lies less in ideology than in electoral instrumentalities.

TABLE 3

Distribution of Support by Party Identification,
Presidential Election, December 5, 1965 (by per cent)

	De Gaulle	Mitterrand	Others
UNR, SOFRES	98	—	—
UNR and Independent Republicans, IFOP	92	4	96
MRP and Independents, SOFRES	31	6	37
MRP and Independents, IFOP	56	23	21
Radicals and Socialists, SOFRES	24	55	21
Radicals, Socialists, and Communists, IFOP	15	74	11
Communists, SOFRES	7	87	6

Sources: Same as Table 2. MRP = The Christian democratic Popular Republican Movement.

De Gaulle's referenda always functioned, in effect, as plebiscites. He always threatened to resign if he lost a referendum, but no alternative President was clearly visible to the French electorate. The French voters knew the meaning of a "yes" vote: de Gaulle would remain President. They could not know the meaning of a "no" vote for they knew not who would replace de Gaulle. Confronted by a choice between de Gaulle and the Great Unknown, they voted "yes" quite naturally. The presidential election, however, gave them viable and visible alternatives. They could choose de Gaulle, Mitterrand, or Lecanuet. They knew that one of two men would fill the Presidency if it were vacated by de Gaulle.

Viable democracy requires that the people be able to choose their government. The key branch of contemporary government is the executive. Because of the multiparty, parliamentary system of the Third and Fourth Republics and the undemocratic presidential electoral college of the Fifth Republic before 1962, the French never, before 1965, had had the opportunity to elect their chief executive democratically. In the 1965 election they did. Therefore, the principal significance of the 1965 election was that it introduced modern democracy into France, perhaps in spite of de Gaulle's intentions, as he seems to have admitted when he said he had been wrong.

B. Round Two

THE CAMPAIGN. As no candidate had won a majority of first-round votes, a runoff election two weeks later was necessary. The constitution (Art. 6) permitted only de Gaulle and Mitterrand to compete.[11] The contrast between the first and second round Gaullist campaigns marks vividly the change that had occurred in French politics.

De Gaulle strode into the second-round campaign a changed man. He commanded all Gaullists, from top to bottom to go forth and sing his praises. Local campaigns were mounted. De Gaulle used every minute of broadcast time to which he was entitled. Moreover, he submitted to unprecedented public indignities. For the first time since his return to power, he was interviewed by a journalist—and the interview was televised. The authoritarian monarch of the first round descended from his olympian heights to campaign as a democrat in the second round.

RESULTS. De Gaulle's campaign had the intended effect. All four of the candidates who had been eliminated from the second-round ballot endorsed de Gaulle's remaining opponent, Mitterrand, more or less openly, but he gained only 2,898,628 of their 5,712,136 first-round votes while de Gaulle picked up 2,258,581. As de Gaulle had led Mitterrand by 2,727,982 votes on the first round, he won easily December 19 on the second round, 12,645,315 (54.49%) to 10,557,480 (45.50%).[12]

The value of de Gaulle's feminine support increased for the second round. A public opinion survey, December 14–16, gave Mitterrand a 42 to 40 edge among male respondents but a 29 to 47 deficit among women.[13] Clearly, de Gaulle was saved by the women to whom he had given the suffrage immediately after World War II.

SIGNIFICANCE. De Gaulle still was firmly in office, though the political situation was no longer the same. De Gaulle, the Opposition, and the French people discovered that de Gaulle did not win every election automatically. His opposition on the Left learned that it could work together supporting a common candidate in an election campaign. Those two discoveries dominated the consciousness of the French political public over the next two years and more. The following sections of this study will consider the responses elicited by those discoveries.

III. THE RESPONSE

A. The Problem

Electoral democracy requires that the people be offered a choice between authentic candidates. Less well understood is a second requisite: that the choice be limited to two candidates having reasonable prospects of victory. The availability of more than two candidates with significant popular strength prevents the voter from predicting the effect of his vote. If he prefers A over B and B over C and votes for A and if the distribution of votes gives C fewer than half the votes but more votes than B and gives B more votes than A, his vote will help permit the election of the candidate he preferred least.[14]

The French presidential runoff election system avoids the problem described above by permitting only two candidates to contest the second round. The parliamentary electoral system encourages, but does not require, the reduction of candidacies to two for the second round. Those mechanisms assume some prior process by which the political currents in the electorate are channeled into support for the two finalists. The first-round election performs that function in part. It gives the voters a chance to express their preferences among several candidates in order to identify the two most popular. However, it, too, assumes some prior simplification of opinion patterns. If all currents of political opinion, or even all organized currents of opinion were to put forth candidates for the first round, the candidate lineup would be so confusing that the voters, once again, would be unable to predict the effects of their ballots.

This study portrays the events following the 1965 elections to ascertain the extent to which French political forces adjusted to the situation created by those elections, especially the extent to which a more simplified pattern of forces developed. The first section below considers the patterns of candidacies in the 1967 parliamentary and cantonal elections (the only general elections held during the period being studied) comparatively with their earlier counterparts. The second section will study voting patterns in those elections to discover if they moved compatibly with any changes in candidacy patterns. Next, the behavior of deputies will be scrutinized to see how well it fits with trends in candidacies and voting. Finally, developments in extra-parliamentary party organizations and alliances since 1965 will be examined for indications that new patterns are appearing in them. The final section will concentrate heavily on leftwing parties, both because changes there have been more important and interesting than elsewhere and because the movements themselves affect a larger portion of the electorate.

B. Candidates

THE 1967 PARLIAMENTARY ELECTIONS. The number of candidates who contested the first round of the 1967 parliamentary elections rose slightly from the 1962 figure. (See table 4.) This was entirely the result of an increase in the number of parliamentary constituencies from 465 to 470. The number of candidates per seat fell microscopically from 4.67 to 4.66.

Candidacies had fallen from 6.45 per seat in 1958. If the 1965

TABLE 4

Seats, Candidates, Voters in Parliamentary Elections, 1962 and 1967

	1st-Round Balloting		2nd-Round Balloting	
	1962	1967	1962	1967
Seats contested	465	470	369	398
Candidates, number	2,172	2,190	889	783
Candidates per seat	4.67	4.66	2.4	2.0
Registered voters (millions)	27.5	28.3	22.0	24.2
Registered voters per candidate	12,673	12,919	24,699	30,864
Bipartite contests, number	3	0	223	337
Bipartite contests (percentage)	0.6	—	60.4	85.1

Source: Le Monde.

election had any effect, then, it retarded a trend toward concentration.[15] Even taking the growth of the electorate into account, the picture hardly changes. In 1962, the ratio of candidates to registered voters was 1 to 12,673. In 1967, it was 1 to 12,919, a change of 1.1 per cent. Between 1958 and 1962, the change had amounted to 39.4 per cent.

Candidacies on the first round in 1967 hardly responded to the stimulus of the presidential elections. Given the nature of the French electoral system, however, the crucial test is the second round. Any number of frivolous candidates on the first round can obscure the true trends. A provision of the electoral law, however, eliminates from the second round all candidates who received the votes of fewer than ten per cent of the registered voters.

The number of candidates contesting the second round fell from 889 in 1962 to 783 in 1967. As the number of seats being contested on the second ballot increased from 369 to 398, the average number of candidates per seat fell from 2.4 to 2.0, a decline of 16.6 per cent. This continued the trend from 1958 when an average of 2.9 candidates had contested each seat. The 1958–62 decline had amounted to 17.2 per cent.

Close inspection of the returns suggests that the change from

1962 to 1967 was even greater than the averages indicate. In 1962, two-way contests occurred in three constituencies on the first round and in 223 constituencies on the second round for a total of 226 of the 465 seats (48.6%). In 1967, such contests took place in no districts on the first round but in 337 districts on the second round for a 71.7 percentage.

Thus, bipartite contests increased in number by 47.6 per cent in the five years and the amount of democracy in French parliamentary elections increased proportionately. In 1967, in half again as many election districts as in 1962, Frenchmen were able to cast their votes with confident knowledge of the effect they would have.

THE CANTONAL ELECTIONS OF 1967. The only other general election held in France during the period under review was the cantonal election of 1967.[16] Data from these elections are not as useful for purposes of this study. First, detailed data are extremely difficult to obtain, being available at no single location in France. Second, the councils serve six-year terms, one-half coming due for election each triennium. Thus, only half the departments held cantonal elections during the period under study. Third, voter turnout is much lower for cantonal than for parliamentary or presidential elections, the abstention rate regularly exceeding 40 per cent. Those limitations notwithstanding, the cantonal elections of 1967 may give us some indication of trends in candidacies.

In 1961, 5,691 candidates contested 1,504 general council seats in the first round.[17] In 1967, 6,000 candidates contested 1,709 seats.[18] Thus, the average number of candidates per seat declined from 3.8 in 1961 to 3.5 in 1967. (See Table 5.)

The number of registered voters increased in the relevant districts from 11,803,127 in 1961 to 14,750,499 in 1967. Thus, the number of registered voters per candidate rose from 2,074 to 2,458, a concentration increase of nearly 20 per cent.

In the second round of the 1961 elections, 1,321 candidates contested 469 seats.[19] In 1967, the comparable figures were 1,349 and 597.[20] Thus, the average number of candidates per seat declined on the second round from 2.8 in 1961 to 2.3 in 1967, a drop of 17.9 per cent.

Data on cantonal elections comparable to those used to calculate the number of bipartite parliamentary contests are not available for the first ballot. However, in second balloting 210 of 469 con-

TABLE 5

Seats, Candidates, Voters in Cantonal Elections, 1961 and 1967

	1st-Round Balloting		2nd-Round Balloting	
	1961	1967	1961	1967
Seats contested	1,504	1,709	469	597
Candidates, number	5,691	6,000	1,321	1,349
Candidates per seat	3.8	3.5	2.8	2.3
Registered votes (millions)	11.8	14.8	—	—
Registered votes per candidate	2,074	2,458	2,458	—
Bipartite contests, number	—	—	210	425
Bipartite contests (percentage)	—	—	44.8	71.2

Source: Le Monde.

tests (44.8%) were bipartite in 1961 and 425 of 597 (71.2%) in 1967, a dramatic increase.

SIGNIFICANCE. Political leaders and prospective candidates in both the parliamentary and cantonal elections of 1967 responded to the stimulus of the presidential elections by reducing the number of candidacies, especially on the second round. The first ballot operated increasingly like an American primary election. On the first ballot, both the Left and the Right selected their candidates for the second round. Then, Left and Right confronted one another in largely bipartite contests to determine the final winner.

The trend apparent in the cantonal elections may be especially important in assessing the evolution of French politics. De Gaulle had less personal influence on cantonal than on parliamentary elections. Therefore, any changes at that level were less likely to be temporary mutations created by the presence of a charismatic, but mortal, man and more likely to reflect basic shifts in political behavior. The evident concentration of candidacies in the 1967 cantonal elections suggests that the stimulus of the presidential elections of 1965 penetrated forcefully to the local political elite.

C. Voters

THE 1967 PARLIAMENTARY ELECTIONS. Consolidation and consequent democratization at the level of party leaders and candidates does not reflect popular attitudes and behavior necessarily. The leaders, being closer to de Gaulle in the political hierarchy, might be more susceptible to his influence than are the voters in general. Working within the governmental institutions of the Fifth Republic, they might adjust more fully to its presidentialism than do the average citizens whose contacts with the State are more occasional and less profound.

If that is the case, French presidentialism is resting on a very fragile foundation. The disappearance of de Gaulle could cause the whole structure to collapse. A look at voting behavior, therefore, may be useful in assessing the extent to which presidentialism has penetrated the French polity.

Examination of the overall results suggests, most strikingly, that the electoral behavior of the French was remarkably stable from 1962 to 1967. (See Table 6.) On the first round, the Gaullists and the Communists increased their shares of the vote very slightly,

TABLE 6

Distribution of Votes and Seats by Party, First Round of National Assembly Elections, 1962 and 1967

NOVEMBER 18, 1962				MARCH 5, 1967			
Party	Votes	%	Seats	Party	Votes	%	Seats
Communist	3,992,431	21.8	9	Communist	4,980,690	22.6	8
Extreme Left	449,743	2.5	—	Extreme Left	506,592	2.3	—
Socialist	2,319,662	12.7	1	FGDS[1]	4,197,117	19.0	1
Radical, allies	1,384,998	7.6	8				
UNR-UDT	5,847,403	31.9	46	5th Republic	8,256,411	37.4	51
Indep. Repub.	798,092	4.4	12				
MRP	1,635,452	8.9	14	Dem. Center	2,864,272	13.0	3
Independent	1,660,896	9.1	6				
Others	241,309	1.3	—	Others	1,254,971	5.7	—
	18,329,986	100.2	96		22,060,053	100.0	63

[1] Federation of the Democratic and Socialist Left.

Sources: L'Année politique 1962, pp. 126, 129, and *LM*, March 7, 1967, recomputed to omit French overseas territories. Total percentage for 1962 reaches 100.2 by rounding official statistics.

the Federation parties declined a bit, the Democratic Center parties lost more heavily, and miscellaneous candidates gained. A modest global movement of votes toward concentration was evident. The two largest parties (UNR-UDT and PCF in 1962, 5th Republic and PCF in 1967) increased their share of the vote from 53.7 per cent to 60.0 per cent. The three largest parties gained from 66.4 per cent to 79.0 per cent. The four largest parties gained from 75.5 per cent to 92.0 per cent.

The first-round trends were carried forward on the second round. (See Table 7.) The two largest parties in 1962 had won 61.8 per cent of the vote. In 1967, they won 66.8 per cent, with the Federation supplanting the PCF for second place. The three top parties gained from 82.0 to 88.0 per cent and the four leaders rose from 89.4 to 95.2 per cent.

Looking behind the global returns to the constituency results, we find the same trends evident. The percentage of votes cast for the two leading candidates in each constituency on the first ballot in 1962 was 71.1 per cent. That figure climbed by 8.1 percentage points to 79.2 per cent on the second round in 1967. The corre-

TABLE 7

Distribution of Votes and Seats by Party, Second Round of National Assembly Elections, 1962 and 1967

NOVEMBER 25, 1962				MARCH 12, 1967			
Party	Votes	%	Seats	Party	Votes	%	Seats
Communist	3,243,041	21.3	32	Communist	3,931,768	21.2	64
Extreme Left	183,844	1.2	2	Extreme Left	173,466	0.9	4
Socialist	2,304,330	15.2	64	FGDS	4,501,226	24.2	114
Radical, allies	1,068,101	7.0	34				
UNR-UDT	6,165,929	40.5	183	5th Republic	7,899,961	42.6	186
Indep. Repub.	241,853	1.6	8				
MRP	806,908	5.3	22	Dem. Center	1,328,777	7.2	24
Independent	1,125,988	7.4	22				
Others	68,107	0.5	2	Others	730,789	3.9	15
	15,208,101	100.0	369		18,565,987	100.0	407

Sources: L'Année politique 1962, p. 129 (slightly corrected) and (LM,) March 14 and 15, 1967, recomputed to omit French overseas territories.

sponding second-ballot figure rose from 92.3 per cent in 1962 to 96.6 per cent, closing nearly half (44.2%) the distance to perfect bipartism.

THE 1967 CANTONAL ELECTIONS. The same general trend toward voting concentration can be discerned by comparing the 1961 and 1967 cantonal election results. (See Tables 8 and 9.) In first-round balloting, the two largest parties in 1961 (PCF and the Socialist "French Section of the Workers' International," SFIO) won an aggregate 35.4 per cent and in 1967 (PCF and FGDS) 46.7 per cent. With the third largest parties (Radicals in 1961, 5th Republic in 1967), they won 51.2 per cent in 1961 and 64.9 per cent in 1967. In second-round balloting, the aggregate two-party vote climbed from 43.9 per cent in 1961 (PCF and Independents) to 48.6 per cent in 1967 (FGDS and PCF) and the three-party vote (adding the SFIO in 1961 and the 5th Republic in 1967) went from 62.3 per cent in 1961 to 70.6 per cent in 1967.

Detailed constituency returns from first-round balloting in cantonal elections are not available. Trends with respect to voting for the two leading candidates in each constituency cannot, therefore, be determined. However, changes in second-round balloting between 1961 and 1967 reflect the same trends that were discerned in the parliamentary elections. Indeed, the shifts were even greater.

TABLE 8

Distribution of Votes and Seats by Party, First Round
of Cantonal Elections, 1961 and 1967

JUNE 4, 1961				SEPTEMBER 24, 1967			
Party	Votes	%	Seats	Party	Votes	%	Seats
Communist	1,206,712	18.6	21	Communist	1,838,770	24.5	68
Extreme Left	177,665	2.7	17	Extreme Left	154,727	2.1	11
Socialist	1,090,648	16.8	173	FGDS	1,667,315	22.2	287
Radical, allies	1,023,668	15.8	398	Other Left	504,412	6.7	127
UNR	831,170	12.8	102	5th Republic, allies	1,369,674	18.2	190
MRP	634,380	9.8	97	Dem. Center, MRP	607,644	8.1	114
Independent	660,610	10.2	154	Independent	809,967	10.8	164
Others	859,955	13.3	173	Others	554,810	7.4	107
	5,279,302	100.0	1,135		7,507,319	100.0	1,068

Source: Le Monde. For 1967, new constituencies created from the Seine department after 1961 were omitted, as they had not voted in 1961.

TABLE 9

*Distribution of Votes and Seats by Party, Second Round
of Cantonal Elections, 1961 and 1967*

JUNE 11, 1961				OCTOBER 1, 1967			
Party	Votes	%	Seats	Party	Votes	%	Seats
Communist	729,947	24.4	31	Communist	800,964	23.2	70
Extreme Left	35,757	1.2	11	Extreme Left	39,007	1.1	14
Socialist	550,236	18.4	98	FGDS	953,982	26.4	173
Radical, allies	337,502	11.3	111	Other Left	98,811	2.7	49
UNR	397,864	13.3	64	5th Republic, allies	792,259	22.0	106
MRP	277,047	9.3	45	Dem. Center, MRP	274,525	7.6	35
Independent	582,888	19.5	58	Independent	371,197	10.3	72
Others	80,409	2.7	51	Others	277,204	7.7	51
	2,991,650	100.1	469		3,607,949	100.0	570

Source: Le Monde. As no official totals were published, these figures were compiled from the constituency returns. For 1967, new constituencies created from the Seine department have been omitted.

In 1961, 85.0 per cent of the second-round ballots were cast for the two top candidates. In 1967, that figure had reached 95.4 per cent, a rise of a 10.4 percentage points, closing more than two-thirds the gap to bipartite perfection.

SIGNIFICANCE. Close inspection of returns for the 1961, 1962, and 1967 elections discloses concordant evidence indicating clearly that the French electorate has followed the political leaders in their adjustment to presidentialism. The relevant trends are no less striking in local than in parliamentary elections, suggesting that the tradition of fragmented "parish pump" politics may have been dislodged by the rearrangement of forces higher in the political and governmental hierarchies.

Obviously, much of this change resulted from the formation of the FGDS and its durability will depend heavily on the ability of the FGDS to survive. A section of this study (see pp. 194–220 below) is devoted primarily to a discussion of the formation and the development of the FGDS. It may contribute to an understanding of the survival prospects of the FGDS and, hence, of the patterns of voting concentration.

Changing patterns of candidacies and voting indicate more

general trends in politics. In order to have full and direct effect, however, they must be projected into the governmental structure, especially parliament. The next section will carry our exploration into that area.

D. Deputies

Voting affects most immediately the composition of parliament. Yet, votes are not translated automatically into seats. Some mode of electoral system must define the rules for that translation. The same distribution of votes may produce different distributions of seats with different electoral systems. The effect does not end, however, once the seats have been allotted. Parliament must be organized politically and the attitudes of the deputies determine the form of that organization. Finally, after they organize parliament, the deputies vote on matters of public policy. Their voting, especially the extent to which they vote in disciplined groups, is very important in discerning the effectiveness with which extra-parliamentary changes have penetrated the walls of the Palais Bourbon. In this section, therefore, we shall look successively at the operation of the electoral system, at the organization of parliament, and at the voting behavior of the deputies to see what light they can shed on changes in French politics flowing from the presidential elections.

THE ELECTORAL SYSTEM. The Fifth Republic uses the single-member constituency, majority-ballot system for both cantonal and National Assembly elections.[21] This system provides that each district elect one representative. If no candidate in a given district receives the ballots of more than one-quarter of the registered votes and one-half the voters casting valid ballots, a runoff election is held one week later. A plurality suffices for election on the second round.

An alternative electoral system principle is proportional representation (PR). PR, in principle, assigns seats to parties directly proportionate to their share of the popular vote. Hence, a party winning 10 per cent of the votes receives 10 per cent of the seats and another winning 60 per cent of the votes receives 60 per cent of the seats. The PR principle cannot be applied integrally, for a large electorate fractionates almost infinitely while a deputy resists fractionation. Many electoral systems have been devised to apply the PR principle. Perfect integrity is most nearly achieved when the political system is treated as a single electoral constituency.

If national PR had been used in the 1967 National Assembly elections, the two largest parties on the first ballot would have received 17 fewer seats than they did with the existing system. (See Table 10.) On the other hand, if PR had been used in the 1967 cantonal elections, the top two parties would have won 180 more seats than, in fact, they received.

TABLE 10

Distribution of National Assembly and General Council Seats after 1967 Elections Compared to Hypothetical Distribution Using PR

Party	National Assembly			General Councils		
	%, 1st Round Ballots	Actual Seats	PR Seats	%, 1st Round Ballots	Actual Seats	PR Seats
Communist	22.6	72	106	26.4	175	451
Extreme Left	2.3	4	11	2.0	25	35
FGDS	19.0	115	89	21.6	465	369
5th Republic	37.4	237	176	18.5	313	316
Dem. Center	13.0	27	61	8.1	155	138
Others	5.7	15	27	23.4	576	400
TOTAL	100.0	470	470	100.0	1,709	1,709

Source: Le Monde. One Corsican General Council seat was omitted because the results were invalidated.

The disparity between the comparisons in the two types of elections may result from the large residual category of votes in the cantonal elections. Nearly one-quarter of the votes were cast for candidates who did not bear the label of any of the five main electoral organizations. This was true of only 5.7 per cent of the votes in the parliamentary elections. Although, as we have seen, the trend toward concentration had been great at the local as well as the national level, it had not yet proceeded as far and this may have prevented the electoral system from having its full effect.

Parties and candidates are not, however, mere passive spectators to the operation of the electoral system. They may respond to its characteristics in such a way as to maximize the advantages they may derive from it. One form of response is the formation of electoral coalitions. If parties believe that an electoral system pays a premium for candidate concentration, they may form electoral coalitions to exploit that advantage. Conversely, if concentration takes place primarily for other reasons, it may be encouraged and rendered more durable if it also receives an electoral premium.

This occurred in the French general elections after the presidential elections of 1965. As the two largest parties gained in voting strength they also gained disproportionately in seats. This was true in all four forms of balloting: both first and second rounds in both National Assembly and cantonal elections. The aggregate percentage of the seats won by the two largest parties as a percentage of the aggregate percentage of the votes they won increased significantly in all four categories. (See Table 11.) Thus, by award-

TABLE 11

The Percentage of Seats Won by the Two Largest Parties as a Percentage of the Percentage of Votes They Won, 1961, 1962, 1967

Election	2 Largest Parties, 1961 and 1962			2 Largest Parties, 1967		
	% of Votes A	% of Seats B	Col. B as a % of Col. A	% of Votes A	% of Seats B	Col. B as a % of Col. A
1st Rd., Nat. Ass.	53.7	57.3	106.7	60.0	93.7	156.2
2nd Rd., Nat. Ass.	61.8	58.3	94.3	66.8	74.2	111.1
1st Rd., Cantonals	35.4	17.1	48.3	48.0	34.9	72.7
2nd Rd., Cantonals	43.9	19.0	43.3	47.8	42.1	88.7

Source: Computed from returns reported in *Le Monde* and *L'Année politique 1961.*

ing an electoral premium for concentration, the electoral system encouraged the trend toward concentration and rendered its continuance more likely. Whether its effect has been as great as would be the effect of PR is probable but uncertain, but the existence of substantial effect seems clear.

No discussion of the relationship between electoral systems and partisan configurations is complete without a word of caution.

Just as parties respond dynamically to the influence of electoral systems, so do voters. The fact that voters line up in a given way with one system is no assurance that they would have lined up the same way if they had been acting within the framework of a different electoral system. For instance, voters in sympathy with a point of view that is known generally to have the support of 20 to 25 per cent of the electorate spread evenly across an area entitled to ten deputies will be more likely to vote for candidates representing that view if the area is organized as one 10-member PR district than if it is organized as ten single-member districts. In the former case, they would elect two or three deputies. In the latter, none. Our hypothetical comparison, therefore, has very limited indicative value. Another change in the electoral system might alter voting behavior again, leaving nothing from the concentration except memories. As far as it goes, however, our comparison suggests that the electoral system at least did not retard the trend toward concentration and probably encouraged it.

GROUPS. The political process does not conclude, of course, with elections. Deputies are important politically primarily as participants in the activities of the National Assembly. They organize themselves politically to participate in those activities by forming party caucuses they call "parliamentary groups." Until certain reforms were introduced in 1968, no deputy who did not belong to a group of at least thirty deputies could participate fully in the work of the Assembly. Groups accept associate members who may not subscribe fully to their statements of principles but wish to gain the organizational advantages that derive from group membership.

Changes in the configuration and behavior of the groups are further indications of current trends in French politics. The concentration of candidacies and voters can have full effect only if it is projected into parliament. One form such projection may take is the formation of larger groups.

Groups declined in members from six to five from the 1962 to the 1967 legislature. (See Table 12.) Their average size increased from 73.2 to 88.8 members. A small part of that increase came from the addition of five seats to the Assembly. Mainly, however, it came from the consolidation of the Socialist and Democratic Rally (Radical) groups into the FGDS group. As a result, even though the Gaullist group declined in size because of electoral attrition, the two largest groups increased their share of the seats from 62.0 to 66.0 per cent (including associates).

TABLE 12

Groups in the National Assembly, 1963 and 1967

1963			1967		
Group	Members	Associates	Group	Members	Associates
UNR-UDT	216[1]	17	U.D.-V[e][2]	179[1]	22
Independent Republicans	32	5	Independent Republicans	41	3
Socialist	64	3	FGDS	116	5
Democratic Rally (Radicals)	35	4	—	—	—
Democratic Center	51	4	PDM[3]	38	3
Communist	41	—	Communist	71	2
Unaffiliated	10	—	Unaffiliated	7	—
TOTAL	449	33	TOTAL	452	35

[1] M. Jacques Chaban-Delmas, President of the National Assembly and, as such, unable to vote except in case of a tie, was among these members.
[2] "Democratic Union for the Fifth Republic" (Gaullist).
[3] "Progress and Modern Democracy."
Sources: L'Année politique 1963, p. 2; *LM*, May 13, 1967. Elections for seven seats were annulled by the Constitutional Council in decisions handed down from February 5, 1963, to March 12, 1963. The vacancies so created were filled by special elections from March 31, 1963, to May 12, 1963. The fluctuations in the composition of the groups that resulted from those changes have been taken into account in the calculations used to measure cohesion.

The Gaullists were divided into two groups in the 1962 legislature. Both before and after the 1967 elections great pressure was brought to bear upon the Independent Republicans to join the UNR in a single Gaullist group. They refused, however, and formed a separate group again. If they yield and parliamentary

Gaullism unites organizationally, the two largest parliamentary groups will hold 74.7 per cent of the seats.

Parliamentary groups may be no more than organizational devices without real identity or cohesion. This was often the case in the Fourth Republic.[22] Deputies belonging to one group often split into two or three more or less equal voting blocs. On the other hand, groups might be devices by which the greater cohesion in candidacies and voting is projected into parliament and brought to bear effectively on public policy decisions. The paragraphs below will present research evidence tending to show whether the latter has been the case.

VOTING. One might expect reasonably that the growth in the size of the groups would cause them to become less cohesive. The merger of the Socialists and Radicals, for instance, might have simply transferred the cleavage from between the older, smaller groups to within the newer, larger one.

Examination of a sample of roll call votes in the National Assembly indicates that this was not the case. Cohesion increased rather than decreased.[23] In 1963, an average of 91.4 per cent of the 481 deputies (excluding the non-voting presiding officer) voted in agreement with the majority of the groups to which they belonged. In 1967, that percentage rose to 94.6 of the 485 eligible deputies, an increase of 3.2 percentage points. Nearly half the statistical distance to perfect discipline was covered in that four-year period. (See Table 13.)

Furthermore, most of the remaining incohesion was located in two groups, the non-affiliated (who, by definition, were 100 per cent incohesive) and the Gaullist Independent Republicans, who were torn between their loyalty to de Gaulle and their desire to avoid absorption into or complete identification with the main Gaullist group, the UD-V[e]. The cohesion index for the Independent Republicans was 83.5. The other four groups had an average cohesion index of 97.4.

The 94.5 index figure for the PDM is especially remarkable. The PDM is the lineal descendant of the Democratic Center, which had a cohesion index of only 79.8. It drew its members from a great variety of traditional French political "families." The 28 PDM deputies whose origins can be traced through election returns and directories of the National Assembly had these backgrounds: Christian democrat 9, Radical or UDSR (Democratic and Socialist Union of the Resistance) or both 8, traditional conservative (Independents) 9, Gaullist (UNR) 2. That so diverse a group votes with such cohesion is a truly astonishing development if viewed in perspective with the voting behavior of the deputies in the Fourth Republic.

TABLE 13

Voting Cohesion by Parliamentary Groups, 1963 and 1967

1963				1967		
Group	Vote Oppor- tunities	Disci- plined Votes	Co- hesion Index	Group	Vote Oppor- tunities	Disci- plined Votes	Co- hesion Index
UNR-UDT	2,790	2,675	95.8	U.D.-Ve	3,600	3,435	95.4
Ind. Rep.	437	351	80.3	Ind. Rep.	792	662	83.5
Socialist	804	800	99.5	FGDS	2,178	2,173	99.7
Dem. Rally	468	439	93.8	—	—	—	—
Dem. Center	660	527	79.8	PDM	738	698	94.5
Communist	483	479	99.1	Communist	1,314	1,313	99.9
Unaffiliated	—	—	—	Unaffiliated	—	—	—
TOTAL	5,642	5,271	91.4		8,622	8,281	94.6

Source: Computed from roll call votes reported in *Le Monde*.

Perhaps even more important, however, was the success of the fusion of Socialists and Radicals. The FGDS had greater cohesion in 1967 than had, in 1963, either the Socialist group or the Democratic Rally, from which most of its members had come.[24] That the Socialist and Radical traditions could be fused into so cohesive a group is another measure of the impact of Gaullism and the 1965 elections on French politics. Furthermore, whereas the PDM is a more-or-less direct successor to the Democratic Center and, therefore, is only extending into the 1967 legislature with greater solidity a coalescence that had already occurred in the 1962 legislature, the FGDS was wholly new, at the parliamentary level, in 1967.

SIGNIFICANCE. The trend toward consolidation and effective democracy that was evident outside parliament after the presidential elections also has been found within it. Comparisons of the configuration of the parliamentary groups and the voting behavior of the deputies between 1963 and 1967 reflect this.

Whether these changes—and, indeed, the even more dramatic changes that occurred between 1958 and 1963—result from the peculiarities of de Gaulle's charisma or represent more fundamental changes cannot be determined now, of course. Additional light may be cast on the situation, however, by scrutinizing developments in partisan organization that have occurred concurrently with the changes described in this section and, indeed, are most directly responsible for most of them. To this topic we turn in the next section.

E. Political Party Regroupment

BACKGROUND. Political parties, in France as elsewhere, are the fundamental organizations of political life: The organizational form they take and the relations they establish among themselves, therefore, are key indicators of the character of politics in a country. In order to understand better the evolution of French politics since the 1965 presidential elections we will examine certain major events in the lives of the parties.

Three of the four principal political "families" undertook major reorganizational efforts after the presidential elections. The leading Gaullists tried to bring all their followers under one organizational tent. The center-right clericals sought to amalgamate the MRP with the old National Center of Independents (CNI) and several other fragments of similar affinity. By far the most interesting and important development in party organization, however, has been the formation by the SFIO, Radical-Socialists, the Convention of Republican Institutions (CIR), and UDSR of the Federation of the Democratic and Socialist Left (FGDS). As a result, the non-Communist Left achieved an unprecedented degree of unity. The effort that produced the FGDS and its impact on the French Left and on French politics in general will occupy most of our attention in this section.[25]

Multipartism had been one of the most striking features of French political life in the Third and Fourth Republics (1870–1958). From six to ten major parties, some so riven by factionalism that they resembled coalitions of cliques, vied for power. No party ever won as many as 30 per cent of the vote and the largest party usually polled 20 to 25 per cent. Nor was any trend away from multipartism evident toward the end of that period. The three largest parties in 1945 had won 74.5 per cent of the votes and 71.3 per cent of the parliamentary seats. By the 1956 elections the comparable percentages were 56.3 and 60.7.

Yet, the French public disliked multipartism. Late in the Fourth Republic, a survey disclosed that 97 per cent of its respondents thought France had too many parties.[26] Much thought and effort had been directed toward simplifying the party system, but little had been accomplished.

The establishment of the Fifth Republic gave fresh breath to the efforts. The creation of a powerful presidency that could give new focus to political activity, the adoption of a more congenial electoral system, the decline in power of the fragmented National Assembly, the use of referenda, with the bipolar responses they necessarily evoked all contributed toward developing a more favorable atmosphere for bipartism.

From 1958 to 1965, a number of efforts to exploit these conditions were made.[27] The most ambitious of these was the presidential candidacy of Socialist Gaston Defferre.[28] That attempt collapsed in June 1965. By September 1965, therefore, very little had been accomplished in the simplification of the party system. A presidential election virtually requiring wide cooperation among the anti-Gaullists was three months away and they were as divided as ever. The pages that follow will describe the response of the Left to that challenge and the consequences that flowed from that response.

MITTERRAND'S CANDIDACY. Defferre's abandonment of his presidential campaign had deprived the Left of its only candidate. During the remainder of the summer possible candidates were discussed much but little was done. Then, on September 9, François Mitterrand announced that he would challenge de Gaulle's bid for a second term as president.[29]

Mitterrand, who had supported Defferre's candidacy to the very end, had been a somewhat shadowy figure in Fourth Republic politics. After flirting briefly with the wartime Vichy regime, he had played an important and heroic role in the Resistance movement and in de Gaulle's Free French. After the war, he helped found and lead the Democratic and Socialist Union of the Resistance (UDSR), a small party allied with the Radicals that was noted especially for its leaders' virtuosity at ministerial "musical chairs."

Mitterrand had been elected to the Assembly in November 1946 when he was two weeks past his thirtieth birthday and became Minister of Veterans Affairs less than three months later. He retained his parliamentary seat throughout the Fourth Republic and held ministerial office in eleven different governments. His public record was somewhat smudged by several scandals but he was never proven culpable personally. He opposed de Gaulle's return to power and lost his Assembly seat in 1958. After taking refuge in the Senate, 1959–62, he was returned to the Assembly by the 1962 elections.

As the UDSR had never become a major party, Mitterrand's role had been largely that of a "loner" in politics without a substantial organization or personal following. However, this increased his opportunities to play the "honest broker" among the Communist, Socialist, and Radical machines, each of which distrusted its major rivals.

For his candidacy to have any prospect of success he had to win the support of all three of those parties. He did not, however, regard his candidacy as an end in itself. He thought of it mainly as an instrument to promote greater unity on the French Left. For its relevance both to the Mitterrand candidacy and to his longer term aims, we may now turn to an event that occurred on the day following the announcement of his candidacy.

THE FORMATION OF THE FGDS. Defferre had founded his presidential campaign on an attempt to form a "Democratic Socialist Federation," uniting the MRP, Radicals, UDSR, Socialists, and the CIR clubs. When his bid failed, the SFIO and the CIR proposed that the Radicals and UDSR form with them a "small federation." Representatives of those organizations negotiated an agreement for such a federation during the summer. On September 10, 1965, they presented publicly a provisional charter for a Federation of the Democratic and Socialist Left (FGDS) subject to ratification by their organizations.[30]

The charter provided that the member organizations would transfer to the FGDS authority to define policy for them in the vital areas of individual and public liberties, political and governmental institutions, foreign affairs, social and economic matters, and electoral questions. It set forth the principles which, they agreed, should serve as the foundation for those policies and listed the main policy aims of the FGDS.[31]

The initial structure of the Federation consisted of a 39-member "federal executive committee" and a secretariat. Below that pinnacle the constituent organizations would maintain their separate structures. Regional, departmental, and local units of the Federation were authorized but not provided for by the charter. The federal executive was to include representatives of the member organizations in the following numbers: SFIO 13, Radical party 8, UDSR 3, CIR 6, other clubs 6, Cercle Jean Jaurès 3. Each participating organization was to designate one of its members to serve, in turn, as chairman of the executive committee for a three-month term. The secretariat would include a "general delegate" and six assistants, all to be designated for renewable two-year terms by the executive committee from among its members. The Federation could receive individual associate members directly but full membership was possible only through membership in one of the constituent organizations. Member organizations would pay FGDS dues in proportion to their membership on the executive committee.[32]

Structural changes could be made by a three-fourths vote of the executive committee. Other decisions required a two-thirds majority. The executive committee membership and voting provisions were designed to insure that no two organizations in concert could impose their will and that no single organization could obstruct.

By early December, the SFIO, Radicals, and the CIR had ratified the agreement by unanimous or near-unanimous votes of their annual conventions. The only significant qualification had resulted from the Radicals' insistence on parity of the parties on the executive committee which was increased in size thereby to 44 with another seven seats being held in readiness for other political clubs that were expected to join later. Also, the secretariat was enlarged to ten members. Top leaders from the member organizations were named to the executive committee. The executive committee first met December 9; elected Mitterrand its president; picked Charles Hernu, animator of the CIR, to be General Delegate; chose nine other members of the secretariat; and decided to meet monthly.[33]

Thus, by mid-December the Federation had come into existence and had begun to function. The French non-Communist Left that had been in complete disarray in mid-summer was closer to unity than ever before in its history.

SIGNIFICANCE OF THE FORMATION OF THE FGDS. The formation of the Federation was, indeed, a very long step toward regroupment of the French Left. The long decades of fierce rivalry between the Socialists and Radicals, however, were not forgotten overnight. Rightwing Radicals such as former party presidents Félix Gaillard and Maurice Faure were especially reluctant to join the long march. Furthermore, the FGDS at the time of its formation was a mere skeleton. The principles on which the member organizations had agreed were broad and vague. The Federation's structure was hardly more than a cork bobbing along atop its parent groups. Many observers believed that the centrifugal forces within them would cast it ashore, high and dry, at any moment. Nevertheless, December 9, 1965, was a key date in recent French political history. It marked the first time the constituent organizations of the FGDS had found it possible to come together under the same organizational tent, even if, for the moment, only their heads were inside.

Of perhaps equal significance, however, was the immediate reason for their coalescence. Theirs was a shotgun marriage. De Gaulle, perhaps unwittingly, wielded the firearm in the form of the presidential elections. Although Mitterrand had dissociated his candidacy explicitly from the fate of the FGDS and the latter did not, in fact, come into existence formally until after the first ballot of the elections, the two events were inextricably linked. The founders of the Federation had seen clearly that the impending dominance of presidential politics would accord an immense premium for united action. The election certainly had been the catalyst in the process.

Further insight into the bowels of contemporary French politics can be derived from comparing the Defferre and Mitterrand federations. Why did Mitterrand succeed so easily where Defferre had expended so much effort in vain?

At the final session of the organizers of Defferre's federation, three issues proved insoluble. On all three, the SFIO and the MRP were irreconcilable:[34]

1. The SFIO insisted that the Federation take a clear stand opposing increased State aid to Church schools. The MRP refused.
2. The SFIO insisted that the Federation form electoral alliances exclusively or at least by strong preference with the Communists. The MRP refused.
3. The SFIO insisted that the name of the Federation include the word "Socialist." The MRP refused.

In each case, each party felt that if its condition were not met, the electoral disadvantages of participating in the Federation would outweigh, perhaps fatally, the advantages. In short, clericalism and Marxism remained the oil and water of French politics.

The Mitterrand Federation avoided Differre's dilemma by excluding the MRP. It took a strongly anti-clerical stand in its charter,[35] developed a close electoral alliance with the PCF, and gave "Socialist" a place of honor in its name. The Radicals insisted, however, that "Democratic" and "Socialist" be conjoined by "and" and that "Left" be inserted in order to make clear that the Federation was composed of both Socialists and Democrats of the Left.[36]

The groundwork for the Federation was laid on the favorable soil of a presidential election campaign which was bipolar naturally because only one office was at stake. No proportionality was possible in the distribution of rewards. The builders of the Federation realized that, even though the need for united action in the parliamentary elections scheduled for 1967 would not be so obvious, it would be none the less real. On the 1965 foundations they had to build a sturdy structure by 1967 if it were to survive the buffeting it would receive from individual candidates called upon at that time to sacrifice their personal ambitions to the common good. To that effort we turn our attention now.

BUILDING OF THE FGDS. The founders of the FGDS regarded it openly as no more than a first step toward eventual fusion of the member organizations and the absorption of still other political organizations of the Left. The charter itself called it only "a first decisive step in the direction of a profound and irreversible unity" and explicitly envisaged structural changes to tighten the bonds. It also opened the way for admission of "all organizations" willing to accept the charter and structures. The lower echelons in the member organizations retained exclusive initiative to form Federation units at the regional, departmental, and local levels, but all such units required executive committee approval.

The animators of the Federation began at once after ratification of the charter to put flesh and blood on the skeleton. On January 11, 1966, the executive committee authorized formation of a "delegation of the parliamentary Left" to "harmonize the activities" of the deputies and senators belonging to Federation member organizations.[37] It accomplished little, however, before the 1967 elections. In the meantime, the main work in building the FGDS took place outside parliament.

The Federation developed well-articulated national leadership organs quickly. The first meeting of the executive committee set up three "working groups" in the secretariat to study (1) FGDS relations with other political formations; (2) policy, program, and doctrine; and (3) internal organizational matters, especially membership recruitment and local and intermediate-level organizations.[38] Other committees were formed later to prepare an electoral statement and to devise electoral strategy.[39] Also, the executive committee added three members, enlarged the secretariat to 13 members, and appointed two deputies to Hernu.[40]

The biggest splash, however, was made by the formation of an FGDS *"contre-gouvernement"* in obvious imitation of the British "shadow government." The executive committee gave Mitterrand the title of "leader of the left" (in effect, shadow prime minister) and authorized him to appoint a team of prospective ministers. He made clear that the choices were his rather than the executive committee's and assigned each member responsibility for a policy area. Although SFIO general secretary Mollet and Radical president Billères had been very cool to the project initially, they accepted key posts in it. Apparently to demonstrate the importance of the shadow cabinet it was given an elaborate set of appendages, including six "permanent rapporteurs," four "provisional rapporteurs," a general secretary and two deputies, two special assistants to Mitterrand, and a representative to "French and European parliamentary assemblies." [41]

Despite an initial burst of publicity and enthusiasm, the shadow cabinet had more symbolic than practical importance. It met occasionally and issued a few policy statements but these declined in frequence with the passage of time. Its principal importance lay in its clear recognition of Mitterrand's pre-eminence. It was set up in a presidential manner as in the United States and contemporary Britain rather than as a true collective executive in the French manner before 1958 or the British in the 19th century.

Less information is available on the development of the Federation's infra-structure than on the leadership organs. One measure of its success, however, was its attractiveness to other clubs. Several important clubs, including the prestigious Club Jean Moulin, joined during the year. As early as February 1966, the Federation claimed 200,000 members and by October departmental federations had been formed in 86 of the 93 departments.[42]

By the March 1967 legislative elections, then, the FGDS was well-established and functioning. Its various units met regularly and frequently, especially at the national level and it had developed all the apparatus of a viable political organism. Still, the real test of a partisan organization, be it unitary or federal, is its ability to win electoral office. The next section will review the FGDS's preparations for its first real test on that critical matter: the parliamentary elections of March 1967.

PREPARATIONS FOR THE 1967 PARLIAMENTARY ELECTIONS. The Federation was an electoral instrument from its conception. In its founding charter the member organizations committed themselves to present collectively only one parliamentary candidate per seat.[43] Disputes were to be arbitrated by the executive committee which "will accord only one investiture per constituency." Mitterrand reaffirmed this intention publicly in February 1966 and proposed seven principles to guide the selection process in March. The Federation identified its "14th of July Program" expressly as a sort of election platform to be endorsed by all its candidates as a prerequisite to investiture.[44]

In December, the executive committee began to publish lists of endorsed candidates. Its first rule was that all incumbent deputies of Federation parties would be invested automatically. Next, it required the local units of its sponsor organizations to negotiate agreement on a single candidate per seat. In a few cases where they failed, the executive committee arbitrated. All candidates were required to sign a pledge to (1) withdraw from second-round balloting if a Communist or Unified Socialist Party (PSU) candidate were "better placed"; [45] (2) join, if elected, the FGDS group in the National Assembly; (3) accept voting discipline in the Assembly on all questions covered by the Federation charter; and (4) work for union among all French "democrats" after the election.[46]

By campaign time, the Federation had put its imprimatur on 412 candidates, endorsing no more than one per seat, but not contesting 58 seats. In a few cases, local party or Federation committees or candidates defied the executive committee, resigned from the Federation in protest, or renounced candidacies, but more than 95 per cent of the time, the local organizations and candidates swallowed their unification medicine even when they thought it poisonous.[47]

At least as delicate as the task of composing a single list of Federation candidates was the negotiation of electoral agreements with the Communists and the PSU, a Marxist splinter party. No such agreement had been formed since 1936 and a great deal of bitter quarreling had divided the relevant parties since then.

Radicals and Socialists did not agree entirely on alliance strategy for the elections. The majority in the SFIO felt that the Federation should enter electoral alliances only with the Communists and the PSU. Many Radicals favored a more flexible arrangement, leaving local federations free to make agreements with any "authentic republican" defeat of Gaullism being the only consideration.

To resolve that discord, the executive committee appointed a 16-member "blue ribbon" committee, including Mitterrand, Billères, and Mollet, to report by October 6, 1966. After some difficulty and delay, the committee recommended a compromise plan that was accepted: 1. If a Federation candidate were outdistanced on the first round by a PCF or PSU candidate who seemed able to win on the second round, he should withdraw in his favor. 2. If no Federation, PCF, or PSU candidate seemed capable of winning, the Federation candidate should withdraw in favor of any anti-Gaullist centrist who was a possible winner. 3. If no anti-Gaullist of the Left or Center were able to win, the Federation candidate should withdraw without endorsing another candidate. Thus, the PCF and PSU became preferred, but not exclusive, electoral allies.[48]

With its own house in order, the Federation opened negotiations with the PCF and PSU. The executive committee appointed a nine-man team headed by Mitterrand, Mollet, Billères, and Hernu. It met three times in December with a similar PCF team. On December 21, the teams announced agreement. Even though their joint communiqué contained a lengthy résumé of the "important convergences between the [policy] objectives of their organizations," the Communists expressed regret that the two formations had failed to write a common program, which they had always regarded as a necessary condition for an effective and honorable alliance, and both parties reaffirmed their previous programs. The Federation reaffirmed its earlier decision on alliances and the Communists proclaimed its continued refusal to withdraw in favor of centrist candidates, no matter how well placed. The heart of the agreement provided that both parties would support "the candidate of the Left who was best placed" in all constituencies where "the Left was in a position to win." In cases of conflicting interpretations of the agreement, the parties promised to "examine the situation together on the day after the first round." [49] The PSU agreed with the PCF and the FGDS on terms virtually the same as the FGDS-PCF pact.[50]

The agreement provided for substantial, but not complete, cooperation between the FGDS and PCF. Apart from their discord on the suitability of centrists as second-choice allies, the words "best-placed" left room for conflicting interpretation. To the Communists this meant the candidate with the largest number of votes on the first ballot. To the Federation it could mean the candidate who had the best prospects of assembling all leftwing votes under his banner on the second ballot. Because Communist votes were regarded generally as more readily transferable to a Federation candidate than were Federation votes to a Communist, a Federation candidate who had slightly fewer first-round votes than a Communist might appear "best placed" to the Federation.

With a solid phalanx of internal unity and broad but incomplete accord with the PCF and PSU, the Federation entered its first real test: the March 1967 parliamentary elections. We turn to see how they affected the drive toward simplification of French politics.

THE TEST OF MARCH 5. The National Assembly elections of March 5 and 12, 1967, were, in the words of a leading French journalist, a "great date." [51] For one thing, for the first time in the history of French democratic parliamentary elections, truly national campaigns were conducted. Consolidated national lists with one candidate per list per department were compiled centrally by all the major parties, an operation conducted previously only by the parties of the Left. The leaders of the national parties traveled across the country speaking on behalf of their parties' candidates in all regions. Previously, the national leaders did no more than make an occasional foray into constituencies adjoining their own.

The main reason March 5, 1967, was a great date, however, was because the new cohesion of the non-Communist Left passed its first major test with flying colors. On March 5, the unity of the Federation stood firm. The national Federation agreements came unstuck in only 2.3 per cent of the 470 constituencies (2.7 per cent of the 412 for which the FGDS invested candidates). That is, only eleven local-Federation or Federation-party candidates ran against official FGDS candidates.[52] Seven of those cases occurred in the "hillbilly" country of south-central France.[53] In only four of them did the presence of the conflicting Federation candidates affect the outcome palpably,[54] each time causing the Federation to lose a seat it probably would have won if it had been united.

The impact of the Federation may be seen vividly in districts 1 and 2 of the rural, hillbilly department of Lot.[55] The incumbents were rightwing Radicals, Maurice Faure and Georges Juskiewenski. Faure, a native of a small town in the region, had been his party's national president, its parliamentary group leader, and a minister in the last two governments before de Gaulle's return to power. He had represented Lot 1 since 1951, having been re-elected on the first ballot in 1962 with 63.1 per cent of the vote. In short, he was the archetype of the well-entrenched local notable who had made good nationally also. Juskiewenski was a close political associate of Faure but had much less standing nationally. He had been re-elected on the first ballot in 1962 with 65.9 per cent of the vote.

Faure had been a prominent supporter of Lecanuet in the 1965 presidential elections and had belonged to Lecanuet's Democratic

Center until the Radical party had forbidden that affiliation to its members. He and Juskiewenski had been notoriously unsympathetic to the FGDS and had not sought its endorsement, despite the fact that as incumbent deputies, they were entitled to it automatically. The departmental FGDS had endorsed opponents to both incumbents but the national FGDS had withheld its investiture.

Balloting on March 5 produced these results:

Lot 1		Lot 2	
Gaullist	14,833	Gaullist	15,166
Faure	13,338	Juskiewenski	11,191
Local FGDS-SFIO	7,916	PCF	10,355
PCF	6,108	Local FGDS-CIR	3,611
	42,195		40,323

No candidate having received a majority in either district, runoff elections were required. In both cases, the incumbents could win the runoffs handily if they could win all the votes of the Left. To a large public meeting in his district at which he was castigated for being a "weathercock," Faure announced that he had joined the FGDS and sought and obtained its endorsement for the second ballot.

"I was wrong," he said. "I believed . . . in the strength of personal positions. All that is finished."

He had to pay dearly for his indulgence *in extremis*. To obtain PCF support on the second round, he sacrificed Juskiewenski, who withdrew. The SFIO candidate remained in the battle against Faure without the endorsement of either the departmental or national FGDS. The other departmental FGDS candidate endorsed the PCF candidate. The results were:

Lot 1		Lot 2	
Faure	20,834	Gaullist	21,594
Gaullist	18,674	PCF	18,112
SFIO	3,541	Juskiewenski	97
	43,049		39,803

The case of Lot confirms the general picture that the Federation succeeded in maintaining its unity on March 5. The March 12 balloting, however, tested its discipline still more rigorously.

THE TEST OF MARCH 12. The PCF-FGDS-PSU agreement for mutual desistments was honored and profitable almost everywhere. In 453 of the 470 districts a Communist candidate and either a Federation or a PSU candidate or both contested the first ballot. Sixty of those races were decided on the first round. In 21 of the remaining 393 contests, the ten per cent rule[56] eliminated all PCF, FGDS, and PSU candidates from the second round and in a twenty-second the Communist was eliminated by that rule and the FGDS candidate withdrew from hopelessness. In another 93 districts, only one PCF, PSU, or FGDS candidate remained after "10 per cent" eliminations. Therefore, in 278 constituencies candidates of the Left were eligible to compete against one another on the second round. In only eight (2.9%) did they do so. Loyalty to the party accords was 97.1 per cent perfect.

None of the eight violators was elected. All but one lost votes on the second ballot.[57] The outcome in no district was affected by indiscipline. The four SFIO violators were expelled from the party and from the Federation before the second round. The other violators included one CIR, two PCF, and one UDSR candidates.[58]

The PCF accepted the Federation interpretation of "best placed" in thirteen constituencies where its candidates ran ahead of Federation candidates on the first ballot but, realistically, were less likely to win on the second ballot because they were less likely to benefit from transfer votes.

Thus, the principle of "republican discipline" worked with near-perfection at the level of candidacies. Persuasive evidence indicates that it worked quite well at the level of the voters, also.

This was the finding of a multiple regression analysis made by SOFRES, a public opinion survey organization.[59] SOFRES analyzed 38 districts which had Communist, FGDS, Gaullist, and Democratic Center candidates on the first-round ballot but only the FGDS and a Gaullist on the second. Eighty per cent of the first-round PCF voters cast Federation second-round ballots, ten per cent voted Gaullist, and ten per cent stayed home. In 115 districts where the first-ballot situation was the same, but only the FGDS and Gaullists competed on the second round, the FGDS voters split 59 per cent for the PCF, 38 per cent Gaullist, and three per cent abstentions. In the 1962 election, the comparable figures for the Socialists and Radicals were 53 per cent PCF and

47 per cent Gaullist. Therefore, in five years the percentage-point gap had widened from 6 to 21, a 350 per cent increase of preference for the PCF over Gaullism.

Another calculation shows that the Left increased its share of the vote from the first to the second round in 239 of 366 districts (65.3%).[60] It advanced in 134 of 179 cases (74.9%) when the Federation bore the banner of the Left on the second ballot, in 79 of 180 cases (55.6%) when the PCF supplied the second round candidate, and in five of the seven second-ballot races (71.4%) that the PSU fought. This suggests that, generally speaking, the candidate of the combined Left was able, not only to hold on to the first-round Left voters, but even to draw other voters from the Center or abstention for the second round. Federation candidates succeeded best at that operation, but even the PCF did very well.

The alliances seem, then, to have been profitable in terms of votes. Votes are good, however, only if they elect deputies.

The Left alliance in 1967 won its members a substantial premium in parliamentary seats. (See Table 14.) With only 0.3 per cent more votes on March 12, 1967, than on November 25, 1962, they won 9.6 per cent more seats. The alliance won 32 additional seats for the PCF and 25 to 27 more for the Federation.[61]

TABLE 14

Percentage of Votes and Percentage of National Assembly Seats Won by the Left, 1962 and 1967

	November 25, 1962		March 12, 1967	
	% Vote	% Seats	% Vote	% Seats
PCF	21.3	8.9	21.4	16.1
PSU	1.2	0.5	0.9	1.0
FGDS	19.4	26.6	19.9	28.5
TOTAL	41.9	36.0	42.2	45.6

The Federation and its alliance with the PCF had demonstrated their worth. Not only had they survived, but they had paid handsome dividends as well. The success gave it renewed impetus and encouraged the Federation leaders to move forward toward greater integration of its organization and closer cooperation with the PCF.

FGDS ORGANIZATIONAL REFORMS. During the year following the 1967 parliamentary elections, the Federation increased its integration at the parliamentary, national leadership, and local levels. The "fusion" for which some of the leaders called still remained beyond its grasp, however.

At the parliamentary level, all 116 deputies elected with Federation endorsement formed a single group. Radical, Socialist, and CIR "sub-groups" were forbidden.[62]

Only one deputy resigned from the group during its first year. He was Robert Hersant, a Radical who had been involved with assorted political movements from Far Left to Far Right and who, as an incumbent deputy, had received the Federation label without requesting it. Because of his questionable background, he had been the only better placed Federation candidate for whom the PCF had not desisted on March 12.[63]

Even while Hersant remained, however, the group had observed perfect discipline. Occasionally, a member had been absent from a vote, but the group president, Gaston Defferre, reported at the end of the first session of the 1967 legislature that not a single case of indiscipline had occurred.[64]

Within a month after the unprecedented merger of Socialists and Radicals, in a single parliamentary group, the FGDS initiated sweeping reforms in its extra-parliamentary structure.[65] Basically, the organization was to be transformed from a sort of confederation ruled by diplomatic delegations from sovereign and equal parties into a true federation with the parties represented in its executive organs proportionately to their size and the representatives voting as individuals rather than in blocs.

The executive committee appointed a committee to propose a new structure and a new doctrinal statement. Rather than await its report, however, it began at once to introduce reforms by establishing a "Political Bureau" (PB) to "put into effect the executive committee's decisions." The principle of "weighted" representation was introduced in the composition of the PB with 11 SFIO, 7 Radicals, 6 CIR, and 2 other club members.[66] The PB became at once the most active organ in the FGDS. It met two or three times a month deciding the Federation's leading issues. For instance, the PB arbitrated the disputes over Federation designations for the cantonal elections.

The committee reports on doctrine and structure were accepted by the PB and the executive committee and ratified by the member organizations, virtually unanimously in all three cases, by early February and were being implemented by late February.[67] The new statutes increased the proportionality of membership in the PB (SFIO 13, Radicals 7, CIR 6), introduced the principle into the executive committee (SFIO 33, Radicals 18, CIR 18) and the departmental federations, and provided for voting as individuals. Departmental federations were summoned to hold conventions in 1968. The parties were to count their members and make their dues schedules uniform. The reform committee remained in existence to supervise implementation of its recommendations.

At this point, Maurice Faure, whose deathbed conversion was described above, re-entered the drama. He and former Prime Minister and Radical party president Félix Gaillard, who had opposed their party's leftward drift determinedly, scrambled aboard. They campaigned frantically for seats on the reconstituted PB and executive committee and were accepted with something less than enthusiasm as symbols of the Federation's progress toward fusion and to prevent a split in the Radical party.[68]

Other organizations, too, began to clamber for space on the bandwagon. The centrist Republican Center, composed largely of former rightwing Radicals, voted to solicit FGDS membership.[69] The PSU, in its typical, amoebic way, split into five parts over the question of joining the FGDS. The majority demurred, but four different factions split off and began to wend their devious ways toward the Federation by four different routes.[70] Several "political clubs" that had remained aloof until then, decided that affiliation was the better part of valor.[71]

The long-term profits of the successful operation of March 5 and 12, 1967 and of the moves toward tighter integration were being collected as the French political public increasingly regarded the FGDS as a viable and successful enterprise. Senatorial by-elections and cantonal elections later in 1967 tested this new cohesion at its most sensitive point, local politics, with its "parish pump" traditions.

TEST OF SEPTEMBER 24. FGDS candidate discipline survived the

senatorial by-elections and the cantonal elections of June and September–October 1967, but with little or no profits. All SFIO and
Radical candidates in the five senatorial elections in June bore the
Federation label. In four of them, only one Federation candidate
contested, but in the fifth, four FGDS candidates competed for
the same seat.[72] With unity, the FGDS would have won that seat
handily on the first ballot. As it was, its best placed first-round
candidate won on the runoff.

Discipline was virtually perfect in the cantonal elections. Only
six of the 646 districts for which detailed results are available
had more than one candidate bearing the label of the Federation
or of one of its member organizations. In none of those six did
the indiscipline affect the outcome. The official Federation candidate won all six. Detailed results are not available for most of the
1,068 seats won on the first ballot. If cases of indiscipline occurred
in those districts, however, they could not have affected the outcome directly.[73]

In terms of electoral fruits, Federation discipline seems to have
fared poorly in the cantonal balloting. In 1961, the Socialists,
Radicals, and other Left won 48.6 per cent of the seats with 32.6
per cent of the first-round vote. In 1967, its first-round vote fell off
by 3.7 percentage points to 28.9 per cent but its share of the seats
fell even more, by 9.8 percentage points to 38.8 per cent.[74]

Although the 1967 cantonal elections were a real triumph for
the Federation in maintaining the discipline of its candidates, they
were a setback as far as electoral profit was concerned. Not only
the Federation did not gain extra seats by its cohesion, but it
seems actually to have lost seats thereby.

The Federation campaign was not, however, conducted in a
vacuum. The relations between the FGDS and the PCF continued
to generate much activity and controversy, as we shall see now.

NEW BONDS WITH THE PCF. As the March 1967 elections had
given renewed impetus to the Federation so also did they inspire
new moves toward closer cooperation among the FGDS, PCF, and
PSU. These moves developed in parliament and between the
national leadership organs.

The groups worked together in parliament more than at any
time in two decades. The four PSU deputies attached themselves
to the Federation group and the FGDS, PSU, and PCF deputies

established a "permanent delegation of the Left" to coordinate
their parliamentary activities. The PCF and PSU supported the
unsuccessful candidacy of FGDS group president Defferre for the
National Assembly presidency.[75] The two groups sponsored jointly
a motion of censure in May 1967 and a petition for a special
session of parliament in January 1968.[76] Neither move succeeded
nor had more than symbolic importance. The Federation and the
PCF usually sided together on roll-call votes.

Still, they did not always work together well. Much mutual
suspicion remained. For instance, the SFIO's precipitate move to
call a special session was suspected and resented widely among
its partners. Certainly, the bonds that united the Federation were
far firmer than those that linked it to the PCF.

This was even more true outside parliamont. No FGDS leader
advocated structural ties with the PCF even remotely similar to
those that bound the SFIO, Radicals, and CIR. Nevertheless, the
success of the electoral alliance in the March 1967 balloting
induced the Federation to seek closer and more permanent cooperation with the PCF. The PCF refused to respond, however, unless the FGDS would agree with it on a common doctrinal statement
or program.[77]

The two formations reconstituted the negotiating teams that
had hammered out the agreement for the parliamentary elections.[78]
After long and difficult negotiations, they presented a 7,000-word
joint doctrinal statement in February 1968.[79]

The document set forth, not only the views on which the
parties agreed, but also their views when they disagreed. About
three-fifths of the statement comprised agreement. The remainder
was divergence.

They agreed most fully on institutional questions. The FGDS
dissented from the PCF desire to restore proportional representation and to renounce the 1958 constitution and, unlike the PCF,
it balanced the dangers of "personal power" against those of "assembly government, generator of instability." It agreed, however,
that the balance of power between President and parliament
should be redressed somewhat, that de Gaulle's worst constitutional
"abuses" should be ended, that "majority contracts" binding the
parliamentary majority to a specific governmental program should

be introduced, and that parliament should be dissolved automatically if a motion of censure passes. The parties concurred in proposing a rather modest program to increase protection for civil liberties, including adoption of *habeas corpus* and the establishment of a "supreme court."

They also expressed many common views on economic and social issues. The PCF shopping list for industries to nationalize was longer, its advocacy of a rise in the minimum wage was more exigent, and its proposed tax reform more radical. The parties agreed on the seriousness of the unemployment problem, the need for greater worker participation in management, and the economic folly of the French nuclear striking force.

Foreign policy produced least agreement. Sixty per cent of that section of the statement set forth disagreements. They disagreed on NATO, European integration, East Germany, Vietnam, the Middle East, and the remaining French colonial possessions. They agreed on the Oder-Neisse line, on nuclear disarmament, and on increased aid to less developed countries.

The declaration was historic. For all its discord, vacuity, and demagogy, it went further than ever before in uniting the Left on a common doctrinal statement. Even the parties' joint discussion of their disagreements was a very substantial achievement. That they could agree on much else was unprecedented.

The statement articulated views and attitudes that found more concrete form in FGDS-PCF electoral cooperation. This had been true in March 1967 before the doctrinal negotiations. It was also true in the cantonal elections.

THE TEST OF OCTOBER 1. Both the FGDS and the PCF reaffirmed the principle of "republican discipline" for the cantonal elections of September 24 and October 1, 1967, but they disagreed on its meaning. The PCF asserted that each Left candidate should withdraw on the second ballot in favor of the candidate who was "the best placed by universal suffrage," meaning the candidate of the Left who had won the largest number of votes on the first ballot.[80] The Federation contended that all other Left candidates should withdraw in favor of the candidate of the Left who was "best placed to defeat the candidate of personal power," [81] which would include some Federation candidates who had trailed Communists on the first round but could garner more votes from non-Marxist voters on the second ballot than could the PCF.

Despite the persistent discord on that interpretation, discipline held up almost universally. In only 21 of the 605 (3.5%) contests did candidates of the Left confront one another on the second round. Federation and Communist candidates met in eleven districts, of which the Federation won six and the PCF five. The PSU defeated a PCF but lost to an FGDS candidate. Non-Federation Radicals or Socialists defeated three PCF and lost to two Federation candidates. Finally, one FGDS candidate won a seat at the expense of another.

The alliance was heavily beneficial to the PCF, but seems to have hurt both the FGDS and PSU. The PCF had won only 6.6 per cent of the second ballot races in 1961 with 24.4 per cent of the second-ballot vote. In 1967, it won 12.3 per cent with only 22.2 per cent of the vote. On the other hand, the Socialists and Radicals had won 44.6 per cent of the second ballot seats with only 29.7 per cent of the vote in 1961, but won only 38.9 per cent with a 29.1 per cent ballot in 1967. The PSU had won 2.3 per cent of the seats with 1.2 per cent of the vote in 1961 and 1.0 per cent with 2.1 per cent in 1967.

The difference in consequences of the alliance in the parliamentary and cantonal elections suggests that the new pattern of voting behavior that manifested itself so strikingly in parliamentary elections had not penetrated to the local level. Yet, the discipline of the national organizations is being honored almost universally by candidates for local office. The political elite dances to the new tune but the masses seem to be holding back when local politics are concerned.

*   *   *

The Socialists and Radicals, then, have taken substantial steps toward complete fusion of their parties with most of the political clubs of the Left. Also, they have developed more cooperative relations with the PCF than at any time in the recent past. These have been the most significant moves toward simplification of the French party system since 1965, but they haven't been the only ones. Now, we shall take a brief look at others.

Other Parties

The Center and the Gaullists made significant efforts and some progress toward greater unity during the period under study. Space limitations prevent detailed consideration of them, but they do require some mention.

As Mitterrand's presidential candidacy had placed him at the center of the unification efforts on the Left, so had Lecanuet's campaign brought upon him the burden of uniting the Center. Less than two months after the 1965 elections, he organized the Democratic Center (CD), grouping the Christian Democratic MRP, the traditional conservative National Center of Independents (CNI), and some rightwing Radicals.[82] Since then, he had struggled to make it an effective political instrument. In some respects, the Center succeeded better than the FGDS. It fused the MRP and CNI almost completely, for the former completely and the latter virtually ceased to exist as political parties.[83] It held an authentic national convention less than three months after its formation and another one eighteen months later.[84] By early 1969, the FGDS still had not managed that feat. The Center was nearly as successful as the Federation in imposing candidate discipline in the parliamentary elections though it fizzled badly in the cantonals.

Despite certain superficial appearances, however, the Center was not healthy. Many Christian democrats and non-Gaullist conservatives remained aloof from its efforts or defected later.[85] Also, the ties between the CD and the PDM parliamentary group were very tenuous. PDM leaders publicly refused to acknowledge the CD's paternity. On one crucial occasion an attempt to maintain PDM voting discipline broke down completely.[86] Worst of all, the CD was unable to confer electoral benefits on its candidates. They lost one-fourth of the MRP and CNI voters of 1962 and one-fifth of Lecanuet's 1965 supporters.[87]

Compared to the Left, therefore, the Center had been less successful. Compared to its past, on the other hand, it had made progress toward unification. Its vulnerable electoral position, however, created the danger that it might unite a smaller and smaller organization more and more closely until it would vanish as a splendid monolith.

The Gaullists were still less successful. After much gnashing of teeth, they produced a single list of candidates for the 1967 parliamentary elections, but nothing availed to force Valéry Giscard d'Estaing's Independent Republicans into the same parliamentary group as the UNR. So, the Gaullists were the only divided political "family" in the Assembly. The UNR did manage to absorb some Gaullist mini-parties and re-designated itself the Union of Democrats for the 5th Republic. Repeated efforts to render viable the extra-parliamentary structures of the movement also showed few signs of success.

Significant steps toward consolidation were taken in candidacies for the National Assembly and for the General Councils, in voting for the National Assembly, and in group formation and voting behavior in the National Assembly. The most important direct causes of the consolidation were the formation of the Federation of the Left and its alliance with the PCF. The political elite, therefore, responded to the stimulus of the 1965 elections by consolidation and movement toward bipartism and the voters followed its lead in the 1967 National Assembly election.

On the other hand, analysis of voting results suggests that the voters did not respond the same way in the 1967 cantonal elections. Those elections were least affected by de Gaulle's influence. The parties and candidates behaved in them as they had behaved in the parliamentary elections, but the voters did not.

This must raise in the minds of all students of French politics the question of whether the new spirit has really taken root in the French body politic. Have the voters, the people, really changed their fundamental political attitudes and behavior in such a way and to such an extent that they will survive the passage of de Gaulle from the scene? When de Gaulle's presence no longer dominates parliamentary elections as it did not dominate the 1967 cantonal elections will the voters behave as they did in the 1967 parliamentary elections or as they did in the 1967 cantonal elections?

If they continue the pattern they set in the parliamentary elections, the evolution toward bipartism and effective democracy will continue. If not, the whole edifice so laboriously constructed by the Left, by the Democratic Center, and by the Gaullists themselves will be undermined. Without a solid foundation in congenial popular attitudes, the Fifth Republic will stand like the

Biblical house upon the sands: "And the rain descended, and the floods came, and the winds blew and beat upon the house; and it fell: and great was the fall of it."

EPILOGUE

The essay above was completed before the "events" of May–June 1968. This brief epilogue will extend its analysis through March 1969, covering, especially, the parliamentary elections of June 1968.[88]

The student strike and seizures of buildings and the general strike of May–June 1968 cannot be discussed in the limited space available here. Suffice it to say that the disorders got so nearly out of hand that, for a moment, de Gaulle seemed ready to resign and that, when that moment passed, he called parliamentary elections as a decisive part of his counterattack. Those elections were held in such extraordinary circumstances—crisis overlaying crisis—that evidence derived from them to illuminate our central question should be regarded with caution.

The Campaign

One reason for such caution lies in the hasty organization of the campaigns. Whereas, the partisan federations—especially the FGDS —had about 15 months to prepare for the 1967 elections, they had barely ten days in 1968. At best, the national campaign machinery they had developed was fragile and rickety. In 1968, it lacked time to become its best. The haste with which the campaign was organized, however, did not affect only the FGDS. None of the parties— not even the Gaullists—were able to mount the kind of national campaigns that were so striking a feature of the 1967 campaigns.

Another reason was the chaotic prologue to the campaign and the frightened reaction it produced. The voters' decisions in such an atmosphere may not be accurate indicators of long-term trends. Furthermore, de Gaulle was peculiarly well placed to benefit from this situation. His prominence and his identification with law and order made him an obvious haven for the frightened.

The Gaullist campaign, directed by Pompidou, capitalized on these fears. As Pompidou said: "On the one hand, I stressed . . . the danger presented in recent weeks by the Communist party and its allies, which attempted to profit from the disorders to seize power. On the other hand, I emphasized equally that the unreliable candidates—that are called Center or Modern Progress and Democracy—could not represent, at a difficult moment, an adequate defense." [89]

The PCF, PDM, and FGDS reacted to the situation by competing with the Gaullists in condemning the agitators and by blaming the regime for having allowed things to come to such a pass. Only the PSU went into the campaign breathing (slightly stale) revolutionary fire.

The Candidates

The abrupt onset of the campaign did not prevent a slight increase in the number of candidates. The number rose from 2,190 in 1967 to 2,267 in 1968. However, the increase resulted entirely from the entry of 79 candidates presented by Technique and Democracy, a political club claiming only 1,000 members in all France that obviously was interested in cheap television visibility rather that parliamentary seats and averaged only 2.1 per cent of the votes in the districts it contested. Without Technique and Democracy, the 1967 figure of 4.66 candidates per seat remained constant; with it, the figure rose to 4.82. Because no special pre-election registration was permitted, the number of registered voters declined and, therefore, the average number of registered voters per candidate also fell, from 12,919 in 1967 to 12,427 in 1968.

The number of candidates contesting the second round fell from 783 in 1967 to 677 in 1968, however the number of seats being contested also declined, from 398 to 316. Therefore, the number of candidates per contested seat actually rose slightly from 2.0 to 2.1. The number of constituencies in which the voters were called upon to choose between only two candidates also declined, from 337 in 1967 to 271 in 1968—that is from 71.7 per cent of the contests to 57.7 per cent.

The Results

The first round balloting on June 23 produced a substantial gain for the Gaullists and the second-round, a week later, gave them the greatest election victory in the history of the French republic. For the first time, one party (the Gaullist UDR) won a majority of the seats in the national Assembly and exceeded 40 per cent of the first-round vote. (See Table 15.)

TABLE 15

Distribution of Votes and Seats, 1968 National Assembly Elections

Party	1st Round			2nd Round		
	Votes	%	Seats	Votes	%	Seats
PCF	4,435,357	20.0	6	2,935,775	20.1	27
PSU	874,212	3.9	—	83,777	0.6	—
FGDS	3,654,003	16.5	—	3,097,338	21.3	57
PDM	2,290,165	10.3	4	1,141,305	7.8	22
UDR	9,663,605	43.7	142	6,762,170	46.4	204
Other Gaullist[1]	424,819	1.9	—	—	—	—
Others	796,496	3.6	2	557,047	3.8	6
TOTAL	22,138,657	99.9	154	14,577,412	100.0	316

[1] These lines include only candidates who ran without UDR investiture.

Source: This table, compiled from the election issue of *Le Monde*, omits statistics for the seventeen overseas constituencies which elected fourteen UDR, one PCF, one PDM, and one unaffiliated candidates.

The Left lost ground. The PCF-PSU-FGDS coalition fell from 43.9 per cent of the first-round votes in 1967 to 40.4 per cent in 1968. The Center also slipped, from 13.0 per cent to 10.3 per cent.

Although the elections hurt the opposition, they did not halt the trend toward bipartisan. The two largest parties (UDR and PCF) increased their share of the first-round vote from 60.0 per cent to 63.7 per cent. With the third largest party (FGDS), they rose from 79.0 per cent to 80.2 per cent. Thus, the electorate continued its march from the smaller to the larger formations.

The Deputies

As in 1967, the electoral system distorted the distribution of seats to the advantage of the Gaullists. If PR had been used the Gaullists (UDR and others) would have wound up with 214 seats rather than 346. The opposition Left would have increased from 90 to 190 seats and other non-Gaullists would have won 66 seats

TABLE 16

Distribution of National Assembly Seats After 1968 Election Compared to Hypothetical PR Distribution

Party	% First Round Ballots	Actual Seats	PR Seats
Communist	20.0	33	94
Extreme Left	3.9	—	18
FGDS	16.5	57	78
PDM	10.3	26	49
UDR[1]	43.7	346	205
Other Gaullist	1.9	—	9
Other	3.6	8	17
TOTAL	99.9	470	470

[1] The principal Gaullist electoral organization changed its name to Union for the Defense of the Republic for the election.

rather than 34. (See Table 16.) Also, the system continued to award a premium to the two largest parties. (See Table 17.)[90]

When the new National Assembly formed into parliamentary groups after the elections, the Gaullists remained divided and the

TABLE 17

The Percentage of Seats Won by the Two Largest Parties as a Percentage of the Votes They Won, National Assembly 1968

	% of Votes	% of Seats	Col. B as a % of Col. A
	A	B	
1st Round	63.7	96.1	150.9
2nd Round	66.5	73.1	109.9

PCF, FGDS, and PDM remained united. Also, nine deputies again refused to affiliate with any group.[91] Thus, the number of groups and their average size remained constant. However, the percentage of seats held by the two largest groups (UDR and Independent Republicans) increased from 66.0 to 72.1 (including associates). Furthermore, for the first time the two largest groups were supporters of the government. (See Table 18.)

TABLE 18

Groups in the National Assembly, 1968

	Members	Associates
UDR	270	23
Independent Republicans	57	4
FGDS	57	—
PDM	30	3
Communist	31	1
Unaffiliated	9	—
TOTAL	456	31

Source: Le Monde, July 13, 1968.

The cohesion of the groups remained high for the Autumn 1968 parliamentary session, increasing slightly from the 1967 figures of 94.6 per cent solidarity to 94.8 per cent. The Independent Republicans were still the least cohesive. Even so, despite the increase in their numbers, they rose in the cohesion index from 83.5 in 1967 to 84.4 in 1968. Nor was the breakup of the extraparliamentary FGDS reflected in the Chamber. The cohesion of FGDS group declined only from 99.7 per cent to 99.1 per cent. (See Table 19.)

TABLE 19

Voting Cohesion by Parliamentary Groups, 1968

	Vote Opportunities	Disciplined Votes	Cohesion Index
UDR	1740	1665	95.7
Ind. Rep.	372	314	84.4
FGDS	342	339	99.1
PDM	198	186	93.9
Communist	198	197	99.4
TOTAL	2850	2701	94.8

Source: Roll call votes reported in detail by *Le Monde*.

The summer's events, then, do not seem to have affected adversely the trend toward greater cohesion in the Assembly. On the other hand, as we shall now see, they had a devastating effect on the same trend in the party organizations.

Regroupment of the Left

Three major events of the summer of 1968 combined to destroy the FGDS—at least temporarily. The riots and strikes raised doubts in the minds of many Frenchmen of the center-left about the prudence of trying to work with parties, such as the PCF and SFIO, which professed to be revolutionary, even though their behavior during the May–June events was quite inocuous. Second, the election setback of the PCF-PSU-FGDS coalition in the June poll led many center-left politicians (especially Radicals) to wonder if the alliance might not be a liability more than an asset. Only 40.7 per cent of the coalition's single candidates on the second ballot drew more votes than the total vote of its candidates on the first ballot. The corresponding figure for 1967 had been 63.0 per cent.[92] However, if the rival parties of the Left had retained all their first-round candidates on the second round, the FGDS would have won 48 fewer seats and the PCF would have won 21 fewer than they did. Nevertheless, many Radical leaders felt that the decline of the FGDS vote was a result of its association with the PCF and of backlash against the latter party because of the May–June disorders.

The third event was the Soviet invasion of Czechoslovakia and the adverse reaction it evoked in France. Despite its immediate and emphatic denunciation of the Soviet action, the PCF fell into further disrepute as a political ally.

Those developments made the Radicals deathly afraid of anything that smacked of sellout to the Reds, including, especially, acceptance of socialist ideology. Yet, the SFIO was so shackled by its rhetoric of six decades that it could not agree to merge in a new party that failed to adopt "socialism" explicitly. As the marriage of the Radicals to the SFIO had been the major purpose of the FGDS, the newly-bared incompatibility brought the courtship to an end. The defection of the Radicals, however, left the SFIO and the FGDS clubs free to consummate a union without making distasteful concessions to the "bourgeoisie."

The agony of the FGDS was brought to a head in September after the convulsive summer of 1968. The federation's committee on structure urged conversion of the FGDS into a "socialist democratic party."

The CIR was the first formation to respond to those recommendations. Its convention in October voted unanimously to join the proposed new party provided it was committed to such traditional marxist principles as "the socialization of the essential means of investment, production, and exchange" and provided it was formed from the base upward by the dissolution of the merging parties.[93] At the same convention, Mitterrand announced his resignation from the leadership of both the CIR and the FGDS. In effect, this act acknowledged the failure of his attempt to unite Socialists and Radicals.

The SFIO National Council, meeting in November, adopted with near-unanimity a resolution that paralleled the CIR motion at all essential points. For all its allegiance to the musty rhetoric of marxism, however, it showed more imagination than the CIR in expressing its view of socialism. Rather than lying down with the marxist corpse on the procrustean bed of "ownership of the means of production . . .", as had the CIR, it advocated "social property which may take diverse forms." On organizational questions, the SFIO was more explicit than the CIR on the manner of forming the new party but said nothing incompatible with the CIR desires.[94] Two smaller groups of political clubs that had belonged to the FGDS— the UGCS and the UCRG—had also indicated by early November their intention to join the new party.[95]

The Radical-Socialist convention in late November, however, confirmed what everyone had expected: the Radicals would not join the new party because it would have "a strictly socialist doctrinal base." Instead, it proposed "a confederal type association" with the SFIO and the FGDS clubs to draft a program for the term of the parliament just elected and to choose an opposition candidate for the 1972 presidential elections as soon as possible. Almost no Radical—not even Billères, who had been a leader in forming the FGDS —urged the party to join the new party.[96]

Negotiations among the remaining partners continued until the SFIO national convention in late December at which time the SFIO majority called for the merger of the local units of the constituent formations early in 1969 and the meeting of the founding convention of the new party by May 1.[97] This process proceeded through the early months of 1969, though not without difficulties. The main problem arose from the desire of the SFIO to institute integral democracy at all levels of the new party while the much-smaller clubs wanted guarantees for minority representation. The founding convention was scheduled for April 25–27.[98] Before it could meet, however, the tension between the CIR and the SFIO became so great that the CIR left the SFIO at the church door. The SFIO went through the ceremony anyway, changing its name to the Socialist Party and absorbing two small clubs. That futile gesture ended effectively the 3½-year effort to unify the French Left through the FGDS.

Given the tremendous expenditure of time and effort since Defferre launched his campaign in September 1963, the French Left has achieved little organizational amalgamation. The clubs have been absorbed, in effect, into a slightly-revarnished SFIO. As the size and political importance of the clubs has always been slight, and they have always fluttered in the shadow of the SFIO, this represents no very substantial change in the picture. Even though the Radical-Socialists have lost much of their past standing, they remain a giant compared to the clubs. Their presence in the union would have signified a real achievement. The new party professes to leave the door open for the Radicals if they have a change of heart. Perhaps the day will come when the principal dividing points—socialist rhetoric on the one side and "redphobia" on the other—will be laid to rest and a true organizational union of the democratic Left can be carried out. Until then, the prospects for joint action seem best in the Assembly—where the FGDS has survived—and in future election campaigns, where the penalties of division are so obvious and painful.

These are meager accomplishments and dim hopes. The fact is inescapable that, despite strong political and constitutional pressures from without, the divisions in the French Left are so deep and wide as to make an early, enduring, and meaningful unification unlikely. The 1968 explosion simply highlighted those divisions.

Conclusions

The net impact of the events of Summer 1968 on the trend toward presidentialism and bipartism in France appears to have been negative. In some respects, such as voting patterns, the trend continued, though at a slower rate. In others, such as the regroupment of the parties, the movement clearly was reversed. Whether the effect will be permanent or merely a temporary deviation remains to be seen.

NOTES

1. By way of comparison, de Gaulle's percentage in the runoff election was less than that of the winners in nine of the thirteen U.S. Presidential elections from 1920 through 1968. U.S. winners' percentage of the vote received by the two major candidates: 1920, 64.0; 1924, 65.1; 1928, 58.8; 1932, 59.1; 1936, 62.5; 1940, 55.0; 1944, 53.8; 1948, 52.4; 1952, 55.4; 1956, 57.9; 1960, 50.1; 1964, 61.4; 1968, 50.4.

2. Jacques Derogy and Jean-François Kahn, *Les secrets du ballotage,* Fayard, Paris, 1966, p. 182, and various issues of *Le Monde* in November 1965.

3. This account of the campaign is drawn largely from field study by the author.

4. *Le Monde (LM)*, November 13, 1965.

5. *LM,* November 11, 1965.

6. Surveys of Institut français d'opinion publique (IFOP), *France-Soir* November 30, 1965; *Le Monde,* November 30 and December 1, 1965. De Gaulle's percentage in the "last wave" of interviews before November 27 was "below 50." See also, Tibor Farkas, *The French Presidential Elections of 1965* (unpublished doctoral dissertation), pp. 160–167.

7. *LM,* November 26, 1965.

8. Derogy and Kahn, *op. cit.,* p. 185.

9. IFOP in *LM,* December 7, 1965.

10. Derogy and Kahn, *op. cit.,* p. 234. Pierre Sainderichin and Joseph Poli, *Histoire secrète d'une élection,* Plon, Paris, 1966, 252 pp., at p. 12, reports his admission as, "We were wrong."

11. For the constitutional and legal framework within which the election was conducted, see pp. 98–104 of William G. Andrews and Stanley Hoffmann, "France: the Search for Presidentialism," pp. 77–138 in William G. Andrews, editor, *European Politics I: The Restless Search,* Van Nostrand, Princeton, 1966, 245 pp.

12. The registered votes numbered 28,239,732 and 661,791 blank or void ballots were cast. Returns from the overseas "rotten boroughs" have been omitted. *L'Année politique 1965,* p. 114.

13. IFOP in *Le Nouvel Observateur,* December 22, 1965, p. 10.

14. For a fuller explanation of this paradox, see Andrews and Hoffmann, *loc. cit.*, pp. 103–104.

15. By way of comparison, the same electoral system was used in 1928, 1932, and 1936 for which elections the numbers of candidates per seat were 6.1, 6.1, and 7.8. Peter Campbell, *French Electoral Systems and Elections since 1789*, Faber, London, 1958, pp. 98–101.

16. A canton is a territorial unit comparable to a New England town in size but having very few governmental functions. Each canton elects one member of the departmental (or general) councils, the principal elective local governmental bodies.

17. *L'Année politique 1961*, p. 692. Overseas territories have been omitted. See also, François Goguel, "Les élections cantonales des 4 et 11 juin 1961," *Revue française de science politique*, June 1963, pp. 289–314. For a study of the intervening, 1964, elections in the other half of the cantons, see François Goguel "Les élections cantonales des 8 et 15 mars 1964," *Revue française de science politique*, June 1964, pp. 556–562.

18. *LM*, September 19, 1967.

19. *LM*, June 13, 1961.

20. *LM*, September 26, 1967.

21. Except that in the 1961 canton elections the Territory of Belfort used a multi-member constituency, majority-ballot system.

22. See Duncan MacRae, Jr., *Parliament, Parties, and Society in France, 1946–1958*, St. Martin's, New York, 1967, 375 pp.

23. The sample was composed of all twelve roll call votes reported in detail by *Le Monde* for the 1963 sessions and all eighteen so reported for 1967, the initial years of the two legislatures.

24. Of the 121 FGDS and affiliated deputies, 68 had served in the 1962 legislature of whom 45 had belonged to the Socialist group and 23 to the Democratic Rally.

25. The CIR is a federation of political clubs.

The fourth "family," Communism, was basically united, of course, at the beginning of the period although a pro-Chinese faction caused the PCF some irritation. The PCF's internal party reforms or "democratization" that were introduced during this period are relevant to our underlying question in that they have eased the problem of cooperation between the PCF and FGDS, but lie beyond the border of our main interest.

26. P. E. Converse and G. Dupeux, "Politicization of the Electorate in France and the United States," *Public Opinion Quarterly*, 1962, p. 10.

27. Andrews and Hoffmann, *loc. cit.*, pp. 104–106.

28. *Ibid.*, pp. 106–128.

29. *LM*, September 11, 1965.

30. *LM*, September 10 and 12–13, 1965; *L'Année politique 1965*, pp. 56–57.

31. The original charter was published in *Bulletin d'information*

radical socialiste, No. 54, September 1965, supplied to me by Professor Tibor Farkas.

32. *LM,* October 6, 1965, and January 13, 1966.

33. *LM,* December 11, 1965.

34. For a remarkable reconstruction of the conference, see Claude Krief, "Le combat des dix sept," *Le Nouvel Observateur,* June 24, 1965, pp. 6–8, supplied to me by Mrs. Nancy Lieber. See, also, Pierre Sainderichin and Joseph Poli, *op. cit.,* pp. 92–104; and Jacques Derogy and Jean-François Kahn, *op. cit.,* pp. 33–42.

35. *L'Année politique 1965,* pp. 542–544.

36. *LM,* September 12–13, 1965.

37. *LM,* January 13, 1966.

38. *LM,* January 13, 1966.

39. *LM,* February 24 and September 24, 1966.

40. *LM,* May 2, 1966.

41. *LM,* March 26 and May 2, 7, and 14, 1966.

42. *LM,* October 20, 1966; *L'Année politique 1966,* pp. 22–3.

43. *Bulletin d'information radical-socialiste,* No. 54, September 1965, p. 34.

44. *L'Année politique 1966,* pp. 22–23 and 68; *LM,* March 15 and July 17–18, 1966.

45. See pp. 40–41 below.

46. *LM,* January 29–30, 1967.

47. *LM,* December 24, 1966; January 21, 22–23, 24, 31; February 10, 16, March 5–6, 1967.

48. *LM,* September 24, October 20, November 1, 8, and 20, 1966.

49. *LM,* December 22, 1966. On the agreement and the events leading up to it, see also Raymond Barrillon, *La Gauche française en mouvement,* Plon, Paris, 1967, 231 pp., at pp. 35–65.

50. *LM,* January 8–9, 10, 22–3, 1967.

51. Barrillon, *op. cit.,* p. 69 *passim.* Barrillon applies the phrase only to March 12.

52. In Creuse 1, Dordogne 3, Drôme 1, Gers 1, Haute-Garonne 6, Jura 2, Lot 1 and 2, Oise 3, and Nord 13 and 19.

53. All but Jura 2, Oise 3, and Nord 13 and 19.

54. Drôme 1, Lot 2, Nord 13 and 19.

55. This account is drawn from *LM,* March 9, 1967.

56. This election law provision excludes from the runoff ballot all candidates whose ballot poll failed to equal at least ten per cent of the registered votes.

57. Barrillon, *op. cit.,* p. 73.

58. Barrillon, *op. cit.,* p. 73. By comparison, in the Popular Front elections of 1936, fifty nine candidates breached discipline. *Ibid.*

59. *LM,* September 2, 1967.

60. Barrillon, *op. cit.,* p. 107.

61. *LM,* March 15, 1967.

62. *LM,* March 18, 1967.

63. *LM,* February 17, 1968.

64. Barrillon, *op. cit.,* p. 149.

65. *LM,* April 14, 1967.

66. *LM,* April 29 and May 11, 1967; Barrillon, *op. cit.,* p. 160.

67. *LM,* November 11 and 17, December 9 and 19, 1967, January 30, February 6 and 23, 1968.

68. *LM,* February 23, 1968.

69. *LM,* October 30, 1967, January 19, 1968.

70. *LM,* October 8–9, 21, 26, 1967, January 11, February 13, March 22, 1968.

71. *LM,* November 7, 1967, January 10, 20, March 18, 1968.

72. *LM,* June 13, 1967.

73. *LM,* September 26, October 3, 1967.

74. These data were calculated from *Le Monde,* omitting for 1967 the constituencies that had been carved from the Seine department in 1966 and which had not voted in 1961.

75. *LM,* March 18, 19–20, 21, 30, April 5, 1967.

76. *LM,* May 13, 1967, January 11, 1968.

77. *LM,* March 31, 1967.

78. *LM,* April 14, 15, 1967.

79. On the negotiations and the agreement, see *LM,* June 17, July 12, August 5, September 7, October 14, 28, 1967, January 20, February 1, 25–26, 1968.

80. *LM,* July 9–10, 1967.

81. *LM,* September 9, 1967.

82. *LM,* February 4, 1966.

83. *LM,* September 15, 1967.

84. *LM,* April 26, 1966, November 21, 1967.

85. *LM,* July 18, October 30, November 10, 17, 1967.

86. *LM,* October 12, 17, 1967.

87. *LM,* March 7, 1967.

88. Much of the research on which this epilogue is based was conducted in France during the 1968 election campaign on a field trip financed by the State University College at Brockport. For a fuller account of the May–June crisis see the author's article, "France 1968: Crisis Election and Long-Term Trends," *South Atlantic Quarterly,* Winter 1969, pp. 1–15.

89. *LM,* June 25, 1968.

90. Compare with Table 11 above.

91. The following day, however, a URD "associate" defected into the ranks of the unaffiliated. *LM,* July 14–15, 1968.

92. *LM,* July 6, 1968.

93. *LM,* October 8, 1968.

94. *LM,* November 5, 1968.

95. *LM,* November 8, 1968.

96. *LM,* November 26, 1968.

97. *LM,* November 24, 1968.

98. *LM,* January 26–27, 1968.

THE FALL OF DE GAULLE

As though neither could survive without the other, de Gaulle and the FGDS disappeared from the political scene in the same month. Hardly had the CIR-SFIO combination collapsed than de Gaulle retired.

The aged president insisted on holding the referendum that had been thwarted in June 1968. Although his term had more than three years to run and he had the "unconditional" support of the most stable and compliant parliamentary majority in the history of the French republic, he threatened to resign if the voters rejected his proposal to transform the Senate into an essentially corporatist chamber and resurrect provinces as units of regional government. With an 80.17 per cent turnout of registered voters (22,881,755 valid votes), the proposal was defeated on April 27, 1969, by 11,989,559 votes (52.4%) to 10,892,196 (47.6%). (Complete returns, except for Polynesia.) None of de Gaulle's erstwhile supporters publicly urged him to remain in office. Despite the fact that his resignation threat had not included—as it had in the past—a threat to refuse to return to office, no one called publicly for his candidacy in the election to choose his successor. De Gaulle resigned when the referendum results were known and made no move to enter the election.

Under the provisions of the constitution, de Gaulle was succeeded in the Presidency by Senate President, Alain Poher, a Christian democratic advocate of European integration. De Gaulle's government remained in office (except that Minister of Justice René Capitant resigned.)

Presidential elections were called for June 1, within the 20- to 35-day period prescribed by the constitution. The runoff election, if needed, was scheduled for June 15. Seven candidates submitted valid nomination papers. Three—a Trotskyite, a left wing socialist, and a "free enterprise" advocate—were "nuisance" candidates. Pompidou, the Gaullist candidate, was endorsed by the UDR and the Republican Independents. The Communists nominated longtime party leader Jacques Duclos. The Socialists nominated Defferre who also sought the endorsement of the Radicals. However, the Radicals, demonstrating again their astonishing political agility and powers of survival, nominated Poher, who also won wide support from Christian democratic and traditional conservative political leaders and even from Gaullists who disliked Pompidou.

Pompidou's election campaign sought to retain de Gaulle's personal supporters while dissociating him from de Gaulle's unpopular policies. Defferre had no chance of success unless he could draw substantial support from non-Socialists. Therefore, he announced that his premier would be former prime minister Pierre Mendès-France, one of the most popular Fourth Republic premiers, who still had a wide following among Radical-Socialists and left wing socialists. Poher's campaign exploited his personal image of calm but unspectacular reasonableness and benefited from the fact that he was too little known to have made many enemies. He sought to draw support from the broad category of Frenchmen who were not Marxists, whether they had been Gaullists or anti-Gaullists during the previous eleven years. Duclos hoped to use traditional Communist discipline to draw about 25 per cent of the vote on the first round and then support Defferre on the second round if the Socialists would cooperate more closely with the PCF. Neither de Gaulle nor the FGDS played any role in the campaign.

The election results gave Gaullism after de Gaulle a big lease on life. Pompidou won a slightly stronger endorsement than de Gaulle himself had received in 1965, with 44.0 per cent of the first-round vote, against 43.7 per cent for de Gaulle in 1965. The Centrists gained even more ground. Poher bettered his 1965 performance, 23.4 per cent to 15.9 per cent. The Left vote, even though divided among four candidates, totaled only 0.6 percentage points less than in 1965, when it was united behind Mitterrand. The radical right, which had supported Tixier-Vignancourt with 5.3 per cent of the vote in 1965 had presented no candidate this time. The complete first-round results:

Registered voters	28,775,876
Participating voters	22,500,644
Abstentions	6,275,232 (21.8%)
Blank and void ballots	289,922 (1.0%)

Valid ballots cast	22,210,722 (77.2%)
Pompidou	9,763,428 (44.0%)
Poher	5,202,271 (23.4%)
Duclos	4,781,838 (21.5%)
Defferre	1,128,049 (5.1%)
Rocard	814,053 (3.7%)
Ducatel	284,820 (1.3%)
Krivine	236,263 (1.1%)

Pompidou's big margin and the Communist decision to abstain rather than to help Poher made him the heavy favorite to defeat Poher in the runoff election on June 15.

The second round balloting gave Pompidou a landslide victory. Complete unofficial returns indicated the following results (omitting overseas possessions):

Registered voters	28,971,637
Pompidou	10,801,932
Poher	7,895,821

With 69.0 per cent of the registered voters participating, Pompidou won 57.8 per cent of the valid votes cast, and Poher won 42.2 per cent. Thus, Pompidou's share of the vote was significantly higher than the 54.5 per cent polled by de Gaulle in the 1965 second ballot. Gaullism seemed to have survived de Gaulle's departure very well—at least initially.

Change in West German Politics
after Erhard's Fall

by George K. Romoser

THE PERIOD UNDER REVIEW WAS NOTABLY RICH IN IMPORTANT developments in West German politics, and even in symbolic events. The most noteworthy of the latter was the death, on April 19, 1967, of Konrad Adenauer. The long-prophesied end of the "Adenauer Era," symbolized by *Der Alte's* passing, was, in fact, taking place in 1966 and 1967.

The political scenery of 1967 was substantially different than that of late 1965. A new Chancellor was in office, the major opposition party of the last decade and one-half now shared governmental responsibility, and an extremist right-wing party, having gained some successes in state elections, may be represented in the Bundestag to be elected in 1969. These changes took place against the background of economic recession—the first substantial economic letdown since the currency reform of 1948—and a search for new foreign policy positions.

Thus, the student of West German politics is confronted by an embarrassment of riches in the attempt to summarize and interpret the events since 1965. Should one begin with the "new nationalism"? With the electoral successes of the NPD (*Nationaldemokratische Partei Deutschlands*)? With the fall of Erhard and the emergence of Kiesinger as Chancellor? With the "Grand Coalition"? [1] With the new initiatives in *Ostpolitik*? With the political aspects of the effort at budgetary reform and economic planning? No matter what the starting-point, it appears that the Germans have retained some of their capacity for surprising the rest of the world in their politics. Yet, the task of the observer

177

of West German politics is to seek to understand the extent to which recent events are, in fact, related to longer-range characteristics of West German political culture and political processes.

Few observers in 1965 saw clearly the approaching changes in the West German political scene. The general election of September 19, 1965, following a campaign noteworthy for its "low temperature" and non-ideological cast, resulted in victory for Chancellor Erhard's CDU. Yet Erhard's position was precarious, a fact which rapidly became apparent during the subsequent negotiations to form a new Cabinet. Because of differences between the CDU and FDP, the CDU and its Bavarian wing the CSU, and within the CDU, Erhard's new Cabinet was destined to be weak and indecisive. Because *Koalitionsverhandlungen*—the process of bargaining among the parties and among factions within the parties—constitute in West German politics a more important level of decision-making than elections, Erhard's difficulties in forming a government were premonitory of further difficulties to come.

Erhard's electoral victory in 1965 also temporarily concealed even more important dimensions of instability in West German politics. One may say that the stability of "normal politics" in West Germany since 1949 has been somewhat deceptive. The events of the last few years have given concrete evidence of the potential for change in processes and policies. The calm of postwar West German politics has been paid for by a certain amount of irrelevancy: these politics were disjointed from the potentially "great issues" of the society. In the review to follow, it will be seen that one of the arguments of the proponents of a "Grand Coalition"—the need to grapple with great issues from the base of broad popular support—was a reaction to this disjunction.

Yet, just as it would have been an error to have been deceived by the superficial calm and continuity shown in the election of 1965, so would it be an error to exaggerate the novelty of the events of 1965–1967. The seeds of these events matured over a considerable period. In one way or another, they all relate to the fact that West Germany is a provisional state, still profoundly overshadowed by the past and deeply uncertain of its future. The events of these two years have shown that this provisional status can have important concrete implications for West Germany's political life. The emergence of these consequences coincided with changes in West Germany's international position, with economic difficulties, and with evidences of instability in the party system.

The underlying nexus of all study of West German politics is, necessarily, this question: how stable are the democratic forms? This question constantly recurs to the observer, not because of abstract speculations about the capacity of the Germans for democracy, but because of the unsettled condition of a large number of vital national concerns. Though the question cannot be given a direct and clear answer, recent events enable the observer to understand some of the conditions which influence the stability of the democratic forms.

West Germany's Grand Coalition represents a substantial departure from the pattern of politics since 1949. It has inspired at least one astute observer to raise the question whether "Bonn is, after all, becoming Weimar?" [2] The emergence of the Grand Coalition is not one theme among many of equal stature in the period under review, but the central event to which other events can be related. It illuminates central characteristics of contemporary West German politics because it is intimately related to the pattern of decision-making in the Bonn Republic as well as to the potential for the emergence of new patterns of decision-making. Viewed from one aspect, the Grand Coalition was an outcome of a particular constellation of political circumstances— dissension within the CDU/CSU, the weakness of Erhard as a political leader, the erratic policies of the FDP, the anxieties and hopes of the SPD. Viewed from another aspect, the Grand Coalition reflects both the structural and policy dilemmas embedded in the West German polity. The fall of Erhard and the formation of the Grand Coalition involved more than just a change of government; they showed the difficulty of changing governments in West Germany, and in this way revealed weaknesses in the party system and constitutional structure. Moreover, the mere existence of the Grand Coalition transforms the categories of political action.

For all these reasons, this essay will focus upon the fall of

Erhard's government and the emergence of the Grand Coalition. From this perspective, both processes and policy issues receive illumination.

I. THE FALL OF ERHARD'S GOVERNMENT

Ludwig Erhard's governing CDU/CSU-FDP coalition tottered toward oblivion throughout 1966. Harried by enemies inside and outside his own party, Erhard proved incapable of balancing the constellation of forces. He himself was the victim of his earlier proclamation that the postwar era of West German politics was drawing to a close.[3] The withdrawal of the FDP from the coalition on October 27, 1966, sealed the Chancellor's fate, though he continued as head of a minority government for a few weeks more. However, the FDP was not crucial in the events of the autumn of 1966. More significant was internal dissension within the CDU/CSU. Nor was Erhard's ineptness as political leader and Chancellor the primary cause of the crisis. Erhard's unhappy three-year Chancellorship permitted emerging problems of the party and constitutional systems to reach exaggerated proportions, and to reach them sooner than might otherwise have been the case. Whether the ensuing Grand Coalition has—or can—solve these underlying problems is, indeed, the central question which binds together the Adenauer, Erhard, and Kiesinger eras. The first of these problems concerns the relationships between the parties and the governing function. In particular, it concerns the CDU/CSU—the party which has, thus far, dominated every postwar West German government.

Bases of Christian Democracy

Since its inception after the war, the CDU/CSU has been based upon a loose alliance of political leaders and interest groups, cemented together by electoral success, strong leadership, and programs and interest in tune with social developments. Measured in terms of electoral success and share in governmental power, the party has been the most successful of the postwar Christian Democratic movements in Europe. It has performed an integrating function by securing support across class and confessional lines. As a broadly-based, relatively non-doctrinaire political grouping, it has been a type of party new to German experience, its formation and success promising to overcome rigid ideological, class, and interest antagonisms. The events of the autumn of 1966 were frequently called a "state crisis," rather than merely a "governmental crisis," because they revealed a deterioration of the political grouping that had both shaped and symbolized the character of West German political life.

The postwar successes of the CDU/CSU have rested upon a peculiar combination of circumstances. Intellectually and programmatically, the party is a product of Germany's traumatic political experiences in this century—the fall of both Empire and Weimar Republic, the period of Nazi rule, the changes in social structure. Its founders and chief leaders have meant it to be an integrating party with sufficient ties to a conservative past to enable it to succeed. In the years after the war, it offered the right combination of ideas at the right time—an emphasis upon economic reconstruction and individual economic initiative, and an absence of governmental experimentation. The latter sentiment found a particularly powerful resonance among those tired of Nazi strenuousness. In one sense, the party appealed to a deep underlying theme of German political psychology—the desire for "community" and "cooperation" rather than pluralism and "interests." The CDU/CSU has been well-attuned to the importance of postwar German striving for security. Adenauer's politics of alliance with the West and hard-line "anti-Communism" rested on this basis. The party established itself as a bourgeois party *par excellence* in a country where the number of bourgeois was rising rapidly. Moreover, its leaders, particularly Adenauer, showed a canny ability to reduce complicated issues to simple terms for increasingly apolitical burghers.

The party also showed considerable tactical sense, and a hardheaded understanding of the loci of social and economic power. It has been closely allied with substantial economic interests, and, despite its conscious, and no doubt genuine, effort to overcome the confessional issue in politics, it could never renounce that part of its heritage from the prewar Catholic Center party. Above all, the CDU/CSU became an engine of electoral success. Its dominant position in federal politics inevitably spawned a host of close connections with interest groups, which it cemented through liberal subventions and subsidies. Adenauer's customary answer to looming difficulties in internal politics was to oil liberally the cranky members in the constellation of interests over which he and his party presided: "To them we'll give some money."

Because the history of the CDU/CSU has been so closely tied to the history of the Bonn Republic, there are many possible starting-points for an understanding of the difficulties which the party encountered in 1966. Since its founding, the party has cultivated the image of being more than merely "one party among many." The word "party" does not appear in the name of either of its components, and this is symptomatic of the claim to be a political force "above parties." The ideology of *Überparteilichkeit* is a key to both the strengths and weaknesses of the CDU/CSU.

Rooted in the German conservative tradition, this ideology assumed its present form during the latter years of Nazi rule and the first postwar years. It was, by and large, the ideology of German conservatives opposed to Hitler's system. The assumption was that of the "coming together" of men devoted to the common weal, not to the interests of class or group. This ideology of consensus, which found resonance after the war in the German middle classes, for years effectively overshadowed the Social Democratic Party, with its continuing aura of class representation. A tested CDU/CSU political tactic has been to cast suspicion upon the willingness of Social Democrats to rule in the "common interest" rather than on behalf of class interests. In effect, the CDU/CSU posture has been a re-formulation, with the necessary adaptation to new political forms, of the prevailing "establishment ideology" of the Second Empire. Thus, it is not completely implausible to compare the mood of the Bonn Republic with the mood of Wilhelminian Germany, despite changes in political forms and social structure, or to speak of "restoration." [4]

Conservative politics had been notably unsuccessful during the Weimar period. Conservatives were pulled toward the poles of extremist nationalism or apolitical resignation. Thus, the genuine new departure by the postwar CDU/CSU represents a significant accomplishment of which practical political success has been but one aspect. Even more important has been its acceptance of the norms of democratic politics, and the elements of idealism and reconciliation contained in the movement.

However, the rhetoric of CDU/CSU politics has tended to

obscure the real underpinnings of success and to cast an ideological veil over the internal contradictions and struggles for influence within the party. The CDU/CSU did not become a successful political operation on the basis of its Christianity or will to reconcile class and interest antagonisms. The events of recent years, and particularly those of 1966, by bringing into the open the antagonisms within the party, necessarily produced a considerable psychological shock to those who had taken the rhetoric of consensus too seriously. These tensions within the party came into the open because the earlier formulas for success had been increasingly undermined. For example, the ruthless struggles for power within the party by a number of leading personalities would be less shocking psychologically if the party had not sought consistently to give the impression that its *modus operandi* was "above" such "political" phenomena. Confronted by a gap between the image the party had cultivated and the realities of its politics, certain CDU/CSU leaders sought in 1966 to evade reality by discovering scapegoats or by intoning repeatedly some "unifying" ideal. Ludwig Erhard was the most prominent scapegoat. As to the second phenomenon, it is no accident that one of the most ardent defenders of the virtues of "national feeling" was also one of the most ambitious Christian Democratic politicians—Eugen Gerstenmaier, President of the *Bundestag* and a prime mover in Erhard's fall.[5]

The CDU/CSU has remained close to its original character as a loose alliance. This has militated against the welding of the party into a reasonably unified whole. It has also militated against planning for future social and political changes. The CDU/CSU shaped the pattern of "Chancellor Democracy" so characteristic of the Bonn Republic, but it did so at the expense of reconciling the diversities in its own ranks, and it mortgaged itself to the continued electoral success of its Chancellors. When this was threatened— whether in reality, or in the minds of prominent party figures— the latent disorganization of the party erupted into a party crisis which was at the same time a governmental crisis. Because the party has emphasized the position of the leader—a tendency reinforced by the constitutional structure of the Bonn Republic—it is especially vulnerable when the leader loses authority and prestige. Moreover, the long years of Adenauer's rule produced a backlog of political ambitions which began to erupt during his last years in office and were fully unleashed under Erhard. One observer summed up the situation succinctly in October 1966:

Erhard is still the rubber lion [*Gummilöwe*], except that he has become porous. Around him stand his friends, with fingers in the openings, preventing the air from escaping. Meanwhile, they consult with one another about the proper moment to take their fingers away.[6]

Leadership Succession in the CDU/CSU

West Germany has not yet experienced a change of government involving the succession to full power by an opposition party. Even in the Grand Coalition, the SPD is the junior partner. The lack of a settled pattern for alternation of governments points to a significant characteristic of the West German political system, involving both party and constitutional issues.[7] The difficulties experienced in changing leaders *within* the largest party indicate, moreover, that one cannot confidently predict the probable pattern of future leadership changes in the West German polity. The problem of succession has profoundly affected West German politics.

The origins of the events of 1966 date from at least 1959. In that year Adenauer reversed his agreement to seek the Presidential office. The problem of succession in both party and government was thereby postponed, but not without revealing its dire potentialities. Two years later, Adenauer again led the CDU/CSU to victory in the Bundestag election, though by a reduced margin. Thus, by the fall of 1961, when Adenauer was obliged to promise his resignation in two years during the difficult negotiations leading to the formation of the post-election CDU/CSU-FDP government, the patriarchal leader had suffered serious losses in prestige.

These developments were intimately connected with internal characteristics of the CDU/CSU, as well as with the changing nature of the issues in West Germany's foreign and domestic politics. In the spring of 1959, voices began to be heard within the governing party, particularly among its MPs, calling for Adenauer's replacement by Ludwig Erhard, reputed manager of the "economic miracle." They reasoned that a period of time would be necessary to transform the Minister of Economics into the new "election locomotive" of the party. This was the origin of Erhard's unhappy career as Chancellor. The primary concern of Adenauer's opponents was that the party acquire an effective political star for the future. Erhard's policies or leadership capabilities took second place to the dominant concern: to keep the party in power. This judgment implied that the unity and discipline in the party rested upon unbroken electoral success.

By 1961, policy issues began to play a more important role in intra-party maneuvers. Other developments contributed to differences within the party. Most noteworthy was the increasing weight of the CSU; in March 1961, the ambitious Franz Josef Strauss became its Chairman. By the fall of 1961, Strauss was urging the immediate replacement of Adenauer by Erhard, and openly designating the CSU a "fourth party" alongside the CDU, SPD, and FDP. At this point, Strauss probably hoped to become foreign minister in an Erhard government. While Erhard refused to compete against Adenauer, it was with strong CDU/CSU support that the FDP secured Adenauer's promise to resign by 1963.

The "*Spiegel* Affair" of late 1962 further weakened Adenauer's prestige and that of his party. While it also led to the departure of Strauss from the Cabinet, the appearance of his eclipse was deceptive. Strauss became Chairman of the CSU parliamentary fraction in Bonn and, from this position, worked diligently to rehabilitate himself and weld a personal following in the Bundestag.

Throughout the period since 1959, important changes were developing in the issue horizons of West German politics. Lack of progress on reunification, changing relationships between the United States and West Germany, and de Gaulle's policies began to cast doubt on the ability of the old CDU/CSU foreign policies to retain their appeal to West German elites and masses. Purported controversies between "Atlanticists" and "Gaullists" often rested on a fundament of intra-party struggles for personal power rather than upon principled issue disagreement, but new aspects of West Germany's international position also signaled the coming of a period of foreign policy re-examination. New issue patterns were also emerging in domestic policy. The period of rapid economic expansion was being succeeded by a period in which problems of economic distribution loomed larger and were reflected in tensions among the many groups allied in the CDU/CSU.

Finally, the behavior of the Social Democratic opposition began to change, signaled by the adoption of the "Godesberg Program" in 1960. In response to the success of the CDU/CSU and as a result of the ascendancy of Herbert Wehner in the party, the SPD altered its image and behavior to compete with the Christian Democrats for middle class votes. In short, the differences between the two major parties were rapidly being reduced, and this change raised for the CDU/CSU the specter of possible loss of power. These anxieties increased the pressure on the party to guarantee continued electoral success, but inevitably also increased the differences about how to do so.

In fact, the party never undertook a systematic review of its structure, policies and future. True to its original impulses and its heterogeneous composition, it drifted in the direction of the lowest common denominator: reliance upon Ludwig Erhard as the "election locomotive" to maintain it in power. The dangers of this drift were accentuated by the inattention to thorough party organization at the local level. At the same time that increasing numbers in the party waited impatiently for Adenauer to be succeeded by the new popular hero, Erhard, the party, in fact, hoped to be able to continue to profit from the methods and policies of the Adenauer years. Differences of opinion within the party tended to assume the form of personality clashes, and there was an inability to thresh them out on their merits.

Erhard assumed office in October 1963 and successfully played the role of popular leader in the election of 1965. Yet, even before the election it was apparent that he had formidable enemies inside the party. Adenauer directed a running fire at him, though he had not supported an alternative candidate at the time Erhard was selected. Moreover, would-be displacers of the "rubber lion" were increasingly restive. These included Gerstenmaier and Rainer Barzel, who in 1964 became Chairman of the CDU/CSU fraction in the Bundestag. The diversities in the motivations of Erhard's opponents could not obscure two points of agreement: Erhard must lead the party in the 1965 election, and Erhard must be deposed sometime before the next Bundestag election in 1969. Indeed, the campaign of 1965 was marked by increasing rumors about the possibilities of a Grand Coalition between CDU/CSU and SPD. Erhard set himself rigidly against the voices inside and outside his party—including Heinrich Lübke, the Federal President—who were known advocates of the Grand Coalition.

Erhard's Isolation

Erhard's isolation was gradual and his fall was marked by no dramatic debates or confrontations in the Bundestag. Instead, Erhard and his opponents maneuvered intensely behind the scenes and issued a long series of statements and interviews.

These methods cast light upon important features of the West German political system. Parliament plays a subsidiary role in this Chancellor or Cabinet-oriented system, and politicians tend to appeal beyond it directly to "public opinion." Moreover, in the intra-party intrigues leading to Erhard's fall, the MPs were largely by-passed; the struggle was one among leading personalities in the party, and this is the way it appeared to the public.

Erhard sought to surmount his difficulties within the Cabinet and party by appealing directly to the public. However, these appeals were notably abstract and unrelated to concrete policy programs. In the main, they consisted of vague assertions of his willingness to lead and of his ability to deal with national problems. Erhard's vacant phraseology was ultimately unconvincing, both because of his own inability to control the direction of events and because of the obviousness of the campaigns proceeding against him. His oft-repeated concept of the *"formierte Gesellschaft"* lacked specific policy content. In effect, it was merely a phrase which promised consensus and accomplishment without showing the path to them. In this sense, Erhard merely expressed the dilemma of his party, whose phraseology, in contrast to the forties and fifties, had become increasingly irrelevant to emerging issues.

Too great an emphasis upon the role of personalities distracts attention from underlying characteristics of West Germany's political system. Nevertheless, Erhard's isolation was to some extent the result of his own unrealistic approach to the problems confronting him. He had no talent for in-fighting in coalition and party, and his appeals to the public gradually lost their effectiveness. Polls showed that more than half the voters approved his conduct of the Chancellor's office in the fall of 1965, but only one-third did so a year later. Moreover, Erhard did not assume the Chairmanship of the CDU until March 1966, and then only after long hesitation which further undermined his prestige. In the meantime, Ade-

nauer remained party chairman, and used this position to keep up a
drumfire of criticism against the Chancellor. In November 1965,
the Strauss-dominated *Bayernkurier* launched an open attack upon
Erhard, but even the more objective press was increasingly hostile.
Erhard's *Volkstümlichkeit,* sufficient to win the election of 1965,
had little influence thereafter in face of his own inability to consolidate his leadership, the attacks upon him, and the policy issues
which emerged fully into the open during the period under review.
At the same time that Erhard was demonstrating his own ineffectiveness, his opponents were using the mood of crisis engendered
by economic and foreign policy issues to heighten the antagonism
toward him.

Economic Issues

Erhard's Chancellorship stood under unfavorable economic signs
almost from the beginning. During 1965, federal spending exceeded budgetary estimates by almost two billion marks. During
this election year, the parties liberally used the old tactic of
subsidies to increase electoral support. Federal expenditures increased approximately eight and one-half per cent the following
year, state expenditures increased eleven per cent, and local government spending rose thirteen per cent. Several billion marks of
federal expenditures during 1965 represented *additions* to existing
subventions or subsidies of one sort or another, presented as "electoral presents." Between 1962 and 1965, *direct* subsidies increased
approximately one-third overall, as shown by the following table:

Recipient	Total, 1965, in millions of marks	% Increase, 1965 over 1962
Agriculture	3,956	35.3
Business	565	47.5
Transportation	489	21.1
Housing	530	19.4
Other	1,246	53.0
Social Security and Welfare subsidies	8,441	29.7
Totals	15,227	32.5

Indirect subsidies in the form of tax write-offs, interest-free loans
and so on, amounted to an additional fourteen and one-half bil-

lion marks in 1965, representing an increase of more than fifty
per cent over 1962.[8]

Largesse by the federal government was, however, only one aspect of West Germany's recent economic difficulties. By the end
of 1965, indices of an economic recession were everywhere. Prices
had been rising steadily, and the Federal Republic's favorable
trade balance falling. The economy had obvious soft spots, the
most noteworthy being the coal industry of the Ruhr. At the same
time, the pressure for increased federal, state and local expenditures for purposes other than subsidies was persistently on the upsurge. Problems in scientific development, education, and urban
and rural planning were becoming more evident, demanding greater
outlay of resources. Large expenditures were devoted to West
Germany's complex social security and welfare systems. Expenditures connected with Bonn's foreign policy have been substantial and, as will be seen, of great political sensitivity. Finally,
federal and state authorities had been competing increasingly
for tax revenues. State expenditures have been rising proportionately faster than federal expenditures, and Bonn's share of total
tax revenues has fallen.

For many years it has been a commonplace to say that the
stability of West Germany's democracy requires testing in the
cauldrons of economic crisis. It would be absurd to say that West
Germany entered upon a period of disastrous economic depression
in 1965 and 1966, but the recession had enormous implications
because of its psychological impact, because the large governmental
expenditures had substantial political content, and because of inattention to economic planning or inability to put such planning
into effect.

West Germany's postwar economic boom was an integral ingredient in the success of the CDU/CSU. Moreover, relationships
between interest groups and government developed in such a way
that the former gained direct access to highest levels of decision-
making. For example, business interest groups established direct
connections with the Chancellor's Office. Members of the Cabinet
tended to be spokesmen for the interest groups related to the
subject matter of their offices. The substantial business and agricultural interests supporting the CDU/CSU were initially suspicious of Erhard because of his reputation as an advocate of

competition and laissez faire. They feared limitations upon the paternal beneficence which had characterized Adenauer's governments. To solidify support, the Erhard governments could not very well undertake thorough revision of the pattern of subsidies. Erhard spoke frequently of the economic wisdom of his governments, but his policy speech of November 1965, following the investiture of his new Cabinet, was even vaguer and more lacking in concrete proposals than had been earlier statements. Moreover, Erhard's relationship to the prominent state politicians of his party was far weaker than had been Adenauer's. The growing appetite of the states for revenues further diminished the possibility for Bonn to undertake rational economic and financial planning, which would have involved hard choices affecting the interests of many of the groups making up the CDU/CSU's loose alliance.

In short, as West Germany's economic boom leveled off and the economy showed signs of recession, hard issues about the distribution of resources pressed for decision. No longer could the economic boom sustain political equilibrium. The latent competition for benefits within the country, and especially within the CDU/CSU, became politically important. Erhard's indecisiveness in planning the future distribution of resources was intimately related, not only to his own personality, but most of all to the constellation of economic and political interests confronting him.

At the turn of the years 1965–66, surveys showed that the West German public, for the first time in years, was evaluating the economic future darkly. This mood, far more than the objective economic situation, contributed to Erhard's fall. The crisis of confidence fed upon itself. Moreover, the psychology of crisis was deliberately used by Erhard's opponents against him; the Cassandra-like intonations of Strauss, Gerstenmaier and others intensified the mood of crisis. In all this, there was no assurance that the opponents would be more effective in meeting the genuine changes in West Germany's situation: the fall of Erhard was not the result of a rational confrontation of an alternative policy to his policies, but of a complex web of objective difficulties and subjective ambitions which increasingly led Erhard's government into complete immobilism. This development showed that the pattern of active "Chancellor Democracy" could easily be succeeded by inactivism, immobilism, and confusion, once the economic and political fundaments of activism dissolved.[9] Erhard remained Chancellor for a long period after the attacks on him began and after he lost the confidence of the CDU/CSU as an electoral star. He was incapacitated for action, but there was no decisive and clear way to change the government.

A major objective problem confronting West Germany in recent years has been the pace of technological progress, which is intimately associated with sustained economic growth. This problem has a large foreign policy content, for it is related to levels of expenditures for military purposes, to allocation of expenditures within the military sector, and to atomic technology. Thus, events such as the "Starfighter" episode and the "offset payments" controversy of 1966 and 1967 involved issues of both domestic economic policy and foreign policy. In the developments leading to Erhard's fall, it was difficult to differentiate these two fields. Both are related to forebodings about the ability of the nation to sustain security effectively and to obtain reunification. Moreover, both domestic economic policy and foreign policy are, in an interrelated way, matters of great interest to business groups in the Federal Republic.

Isolated Germany?

The foreign policy content of the clashes about Erhard's leadership was apparently very substantial. Commentators inside and outside West Germany have seen in the controversies concerning the direction of Bonn's foreign policy one of the major sources of the Chancellor's weakness.[10] There has been much discussion of the conflict between "Gaullists" and "Atlanticists" in the CDU/CSU, and considerable emphasis upon West Germany's changed relationships with the United States as a source of resentment against the "Atlanticist" Erhard and his foreign and defense ministers, Gerhard Schroeder and Kai-Uwe von Hassel.

These issues were undoubtedly important in West German domestic developments in 1966 and 1967, but their precise relationship to the complex story of Erhard's fall has often been unclear. As in the case of economic issues, several phenomena were involved: substantive disagreements about the direction of West German foreign policy; the use of foreign policy arguments by Erhard's opponents as weapons against him; a mood of confusion and crisis which had little to do with specific foreign policy alternatives, but which undermined Erhard's authority and prestige. Erhard did not fall from power as a result of any specific set of foreign policy alternatives, but partly as a result of disagreements about the future of West German foreign policy. All these disagreements, in turn, were related to frustrations over West Germany's influence in international events. These frustrations created the setting in which the other elements weakening the Chancellor could be accentuated.

Adenauer's foreign policy had been based upon three fundaments: rigorous opposition to the Communist world, with the postulate of reunification through strength; close alliance with the United States, involving German rearmament; and, cooperation with other Western European countries in a movement toward supranational integration. These lines of policy were set early in the Bonn Republic; indeed, they were conditions for the establishment of a separate West German state. For at least ten years thereafter, other foreign policy alternatives stood little chance because the set policies were part of the "package" of German security, which was guaranteed by the United States, and which materially and psychologically permitted primary attention to internal economic development. In effect, dissent about foreign policy and national goals fell on sterile ground for more than a decade. Since 1959, and particularly in the past few years, there has emerged the type of debate and confusion which might have been expected earlier, had not the West German state, under the pressure of the Cold War, been rapidly established.

The difference in recent debates is that now, clearly, "time has not worked on the side of the tactics of postponement, of simple stand-pat positions, or of an automatic connection between a Western-oriented policy, a continuing economic miracle, and reunification."[11] Frustrations have been engendered by dawning awareness of the unsolved dilemmas of West Germany's position, and political ambitions feed upon these frustrations.

West German reactions to changing international politics, particularly since the building of the Berlin Wall in August 1961, may have been exaggerated beyond the objective significance of these changes. Moreover, both the attitudes inside West Germany and the relationships between Bonn and other states are very diverse and complex. The fact remains that a fear of becoming isolated, and a desire for more influence in international politics, took hold in Bonn during this period, and that the concomitant effect of this mood has been, in the words of one perceptive commentator, to make "the Germans feel like Germans again." [12] The origins of these new tendencies lie in several developments: doubts about the reality and effectiveness of American support of West German interests, particularly defense and reunification; the American policy of relaxing tensions with the Soviet Union, leading to the specter of East-West agreement to maintain the status quo of a divided Germany; the disintegration of NATO; the unrealized hopes for West European integration. The essential preoccupations are security and reunification, the essential effect of the changes, a search for independent West German policies. Clearly, this review can do nothing more than depict the form which foreign policy issues assumed during the process leading to Erhard's fall.

Foreign policy issues played practically no role in the campaign of 1965. When Adenauer sought to raise foreign policy issues during this campaign by denouncing American efforts to reach agreement with the Soviet Union on the prevention of nuclear proliferation, the Christian Democrats hastily tried to patch over the disagreements within the party by issuing ambiguous statements. Parties were unwilling to open the Pandora's box of controversy about foreign policy, for the simple reason that they disagreed within themselves, and were uncertain about the electoral effects of such controversy. Thus, the campaign was conducted about marginal issues, not about central questions.[13]

This situation illustrated a major characteristic of West German politics: the inadequate articulation of issues before the public. This characteristic is related to the gap between party leaders and voters: the "big issues" are fought out behind the scenes. None of the parties, especially not the CDU/CSU, elicits strong participation at the local level. This alienation between parties and voters creates a potential source of appeal for new groups which promise closer ties with the public and criticize the "bosses" of the established parties.

The reputed conflict between "Atlanticists" and "Gaullists," one of the first manifestations in West Germany of changes in the international situation, continued to be of some importance during the period under review. However, the designating terms were even more misleading than they had been earlier. Behind these terms lay, in fact, the political ambitions of "Gaullists" Gerstenmaier and Strauss, a mood of resentment against the United States, a concern that the CDU/CSU was losing or would lose electoral support as the unsolved issues of Germany's reunification and influence in world affairs became matters of public concern, and a considerable degree of national feeling. Long before 1966 it had become apparent that de Gaulle was by no means a defender of peculiar German interests such as reunification and eventual re-acquisition of the "lost territories" in the East. The "Gaullists" presented no consistent program other than the program of working against "Atlanticists" Erhard and Schroeder. Rudolf Augstein, publisher of the muckraking news magazine, *Der Spiegel,* explained this situation in his usual polemical form, in writing of the "destruction process" against Erhard and the alliance of Strauss, Gerstenmaier and Adenauer:

Here there is crystallized a collection of all conceivable disappointments: about the Americans, about DeGaulle, about lost offices, about unobtained offices, one could even say about the world and life altogether. The trick is simple. One grumbles that the Americans don't do anything for us, that they have deceived us, that they steal money out of our pockets, that they drown us with their investments, invest in the wrong things, etc. Conclusion: we have to seek refuge with DeGaulle.

But now DeGaulle has disappointed the disappointed, even more. He recognized the Oder-Neisse line, quarantined the Germans from nuclear weapons, shattered NATO, which had been the hopeful dream of all the disappointed, and, in brief, undermined Bonn's policies, which were deficient anyway.[14]

The inconsistencies of the Strauss-Gerstenmaier-Adenauer line as a *program* were also shown by developments in West Germany's policies toward the countries of Eastern Europe, including East Germany. While Foreign Minister Schroeder and Erich Mende, leader of the FDP, and Minister of All-German Affairs in Erhard's government, moved in the direction of at least talking about improving relations with these countries, their opponents inside the CDU/CSU continued to speak the "hard line," until the time that the emergence of a new government made it possible for them to identify themselves with policies of relaxation. The Strauss-Gerstenmaier-Adenauer line was consistent, however, as an attack against Erhard and Schroeder. The latter, with strong backing in certain sections of the party, and with a considerable capacity for survival in political in-fighting, was considered one of the main obstacles to increased prominence for Strauss and Gerstenmaier.

The path toward relations with Rumania, for example, concluded under the Grand Coalition, had been begun under Schroeder. However, Erhard and Schroeder had too many enemies within the party to be able to carry through new policies vigorously. In fact, West Germany's *Ostpolitik* was in an ambivalent state throughout Erhard's Chancellorship. The first steps toward changes in the "hard line" were tentative, and carried out only within narrow limits. Since the West German position was complicated by the reunification problem, and by the issue of the "lost territories" in the East, new initiatives were constrained and rather feeble. Though there was increasing discussion of *Ostpolitik* during the last years of Adenauer's Chancellorship, there were few concrete results. Under Erhard, Schroeder, who had become Foreign Minister in 1961, had greater room for initiative, but he was restrained by the considerable influence of refugee groups in the party, and by the heritage of "hard-line" anti-Communism which had been stressed during the Cold War, and which was a pervasive mood in the Christian Democratic electorate. On the other hand, some business interests behind the CDU/CSU undoubtedly supported the development of economic ties with Eastern Europe.

However, the desire for relaxation was even stronger in the FDP and SPD, and during the last two years of Erhard's government, these parties spoke more and more of contacts with East Germany as well as with other countries in Eastern Europe. The Middle East imbroglio of early 1965 enormously compromised the principle that West Germany would regard as an unfriendly act the recognition, by a third party, of East Germany as a sovereign state (the "Hallstein Doctrine") and exposed to the world the disagreements about *Ostpolitik* within the Federal Republic. Erhard's government seemed incapable of developing and sustaining a coherent *Ostpolitik* against opponents within the

CDU/CSU. Erhard and Schroeder were plagued with too many weaknesses and liabilities to enable them to make new directions in *Ostpolitik* a source of political strength for themselves.

While problems of *Ostpolitik* were increasingly important during Erhard's last two years in office, they were still overshadowed by problems arising from Bonn's long-standing security and economic ties to the United States. Here, the attacks of Erhard's opponents could find fertile ground for political advantage, and these possibilities were fully exploited. When Strauss stated, after the Hessian and Bavarian state elections in November 1966, that the successes of the NPD could be attributed to resentment at the dependence of West Germany upon the United States, this was but a particularly crass way of expressing the desire for "independence" in West German foreign policy and of stimulating and playing upon that desire for political advantage.

It must be emphasized again that talk of "independence" signified less a specific program of alternatives than a diffuse array of uncertainties and dissatisfactions among political and other elites. Concern about policies toward West and East was a symptom in its own way of the changing climate in world affairs and the engagement of the United States in Southeast Asia. A set of established and predictable relationships—NATO, the Hallstein Doctrine, the isolation of East Germany—was breaking down, opening up a wide vista of diplomatic possibilities. However, the more uncertainty there was about concrete policies in this new situation, and the less clarity about what "independence" would actually mean, the more pervasive became the mood of crisis, the more Erhard's position was undermined, and the more his enemies multiplied and clamored for change. Just as the change from a CDU/CSU-FDP government under Erhard to a CDU/CSU-SPD Grand Coalition did not represent a tidy succession, carried out after a grand confrontation of leaders and policies before the Parliament, but a gradual change effected through negotiations among the parties, so the confrontations on foreign policy issues were not clear-cut. In part, they were no genuine confrontations at all. For, when all was said and done, West Germany's mobility in foreign policy is, at least for the immediate future, relatively narrow.

Thus, if one seeks to disentangle the specific content of pressures for change in American-West German relations from the rhetorical surroundings, considerable attention must be given to the economic component of West German dissatisfaction. Some of these economic issues became clear to foreign observers only after the advent of the Grand Coalition, most notably in connection with the proposed treaty on nuclear non-proliferation. Before this, however, the *costs* of American involvement in West Germany were of concern to business groups in that country. Such costs included those for the stationing of American troops, partly financed by West Germany through "offset agreements" for the purchase of arms from American suppliers. "Indirect costs" related to West Germany's dependence on American nuclear technology, given Bonn's non-participation in nuclear development, which has purported "spin-off" values. This issue has been closely associated with schemes for some type of multilateral nuclear sharing which, in the form of the Multilateral Force (MLF), was already on its deathbed in the Kennedy administration and was finally laid to rest under Johnson. Strauss, in particular, has agitated for years about the nuclear issue. His attacks have had a dual thrust: (1) West Germany should have some share in decision-making about the use of nuclear weapons in Europe and, failing to obtain this, should look to a European nuclear force for protection rather than to the United States;[15] and (2) West Germany is at an economic disadvantage by being excluded from a wide range of nuclear development. Many thought that Strauss wished, in the long run, for West German (not for a share in *European*) nuclear arms. However that may be, these arguments were sufficient to promise political dividends, at least among elite groups.

The issue of nuclear technology is associated with the progress of West German scientific research and with the maintenance of the competitive ability of West German firms in domestic and overseas markets. Concern about the "spin-off" value of nuclear arms production forms part, though not the whole, of West German concern about efficient cost control, and research and production sophistication. Doubts about the ability of West German industry to compete effectively, particularly with advanced American technology, had already been stressed by the SPD in the 1965 campaign. Increasing American investments in German firms, establishment of affiliates of American companies in West Germany, and dependence on American patents and licenses, have added to these concerns, as they have in other Western European countries.

Here one notes a major underlying motivation of the Grand Coalition. At the very least, voices in the CDU/CSU began to be raised about the possible political capital which opposing parties could reap by stressing economic development issues. The criticism of Erhard's government as bumbling, inefficient, and inattentive to West German interests could find support here across party lines.

Two major concrete incidents became focal points for West German unease about military and economic relationships with the United States during this period: the offset payments question and the Starfighter controversy. Because both erupted after the election of 1965, they were central problems for Erhard's government at a time when it was under constant attack.

Given developing economic difficulties and changes in international politics, the military budget in West Germany was likely to be a sensitive subject. This sensitivity was compounded by the fact that the Defense Minister, Kai-Uwe von Hassel, had succeeded Strauss when he was removed from the Cabinet at the time of the Spiegel Affair in late 1962. Moreover, Hassel was reputed to be an "Atlanticist," and his administrative competence and judgment were questioned widely. Finally, foreign policy issues were tied, in one way or another, with issues of the role of West German armed forces and the armed forces of its Western Allies stationed on its territory.

Under its own economic compulsions, particularly since the massive increase of American participation in the Vietnam war, the United States, with Secretary Robert McNamara playing the leading role, has been insistent on West German purchases of arms and weapons systems from American suppliers to offset balance-of-payments losses to the United States from expenditures in Germany by American troops. In November 1964, the latest of these agreements, signed by von Hassel in Washington, provided for purchases in the amount of approximately one and one-third billion dollars prior to June 30, 1967. This windfall for American arms and aerospace manufacturers[16] irritated West Germany both for budgetary reasons and because of its connection with more general policy questions. This was succinctly pointed

out by Lt. General James M. Gavin, Ret. during testimony before
the Senate Foreign Relations Committee:

. . . Western Germany . . . would be buying weapons systems from
the United States that it would much prefer to buy from, or develop
with, its European allies. Weapons systems jointly developed by western
European nations for the defense of Europe would add to the over-all
military strength of Europe.
  Their own industries would be developed, they would share to an
increasing extent in the development and use of weapons systems of
common characteristics and, all in all, the result of the integration would
be to enhance their military prospects in defense.[17]

In a post-election visit to the United States in December 1965,
Erhard found the Americans commencing to tie the offset payments question to the level of American troop commitments in
been better designed to make Erhard subject to charges of weak-
West Germany under the NATO agreements. Nothing could have
ness, ineffectiveness, and inflexible adherence to "pro-American"
policies than this development, which was, indeed, frequently used
against the Chancellor. In any case, he secured no concessions on
offset payments, and by the time of the government crisis in September 1966, Germany still owed more than $1.2 billion by the
terms of the 1964 agreement. In a meeting of the CDU/CSU
parliamentary fraction, Strauss suggested that West Germany,
after purchasing the unneeded arms, dump them in the North Sea:
"That way, we would satisfy our American friends and at the
same time demonstrate our peaceful intentions to the world."
  Beginning in the mid-fifties, the West German Defense Ministry,
under Strauss' leadership, moved toward the procurement of
nuclear delivery weapons systems. Warheads for such systems
were to remain under American control. In 1958, Bonn made
an agreement with Lockheed Aircraft Corporation to obtain 700
F-104 Starfighter planes, which had been put into service by the
United States Air Force in 1954. Ninety-six of these were to be
built by Lockheed in the United States, the remainder in West
Germany under Lockheed licenses, with substantial procurement
of parts from the United States, the purchases forming part of
offset agreements. Since West Germany wanted an "all-round
plane," the Starfighter required extra equipment, and it also re-

quired special equipment to cope with West Germany's poor flying weather.

The Starfighter proved to be a "problem plane" in West Germany. It has been involved in a very large number of crashes. These led to the crisis which erupted in the summer of 1966. The decision to obtain the Starfighter had, under West Germany's system of civilian control of the armed forces, been made by civilians. In August 1966, three top-ranking Bundeswehr officers, including the commanding general of the Luftwaffe and the highest-ranking officer in the Bundeswehr, resigned under pressure. They charged that the whole administrative system of the Defense Ministry exercised too much control over plans for Starfighter development and use, and that this reflected general conditions in the relationships between civilians and military in the defense establishment.

The controversy had overtones of the old issue of military-civilian relationships in politics in Germany. More important, in reality, was the fact that the CSU took the side of the departing generals, and that the issue contributed to the impression of confusion in the government.

Erhard's Last Months

The "interview war" assumed an intensified form in the late autumn and early winter of 1965–1966. Following his return from Washington in late December, Erhard was confronted by the need to rally support against advocates of a Grand Coalition between CDU/CSU and SPD. The most recent discussion of this idea in party circles and in the press had been launched by President Lübke, and by Minister of the Interior Paul Lücke, one of its major supporters in the CDU. Erhard withstood these attacks temporarily, and in mid-January the immediate crisis subsided with an explicit declaration by the parliamentary party that it rejected the suggestion of a Grand Coalition and supported the existing coalition. Rainer Barzel, who at this time enjoyed a reputation as the coming man in the party and a likely successor of Erhard, played a major role in enabling Erhard to surmount this looming crisis.

The election of the party chairman took place in March, but it was certainly not to support Erhard for that office that Barzel had calmed stormy waters in January. In fact, he sought to succeed Adenauer as chairman and was checkmated only because Erhard brought himself to take this post. In reality, this was far from a victory for the Chancellor; what earlier would have been seen as a logical step for the Chancellor was now interpreted as a sign of desperation. In any case, Erhard had few ties with party notables, either in Bonn or the provinces. Barzel became Erhard's first deputy as party leader. His position as Chairman of the parliamentary fraction assured him, in any event, of a key position.

The succeeding months were marked by continual maneuvering among Erhard's potential successors. In a New York speech in June, Barzel made a further bid for prominence by criticizing openly the inflexibility of his government's *Ostpolitik*. In August, the Starfighter Affair erupted. In the same month, Gerstenmaier launched an attack on Erhard. However, the state election in North Rhine-Westphalia on July 10 was the hardest blow for Erhard. The CDU suffered a serious defeat, losing ten of its seats in the state parliament. Its vote fell from 46.4 to 42.7 per cent. The SPD rose from 43.3 to 49.5 per cent and the FDP rose from 6.9 to 7.4 per cent. The real significance of the result lay in the fact that Erhard had continually proclaimed the election as a mandate. The CDU's poor showing undermined his reputation as an electoral star, destroying his last source of strength in the party. Moreover, the CDU and FDP re-formed the government, despite the clear victory of the SPD. This coalition also collapsed in November.

In mid-September, Erhard undertook his annual visit to Washington, where he unsuccessfully sought to secure concessions on offset payments. Upon his return, he was faced with a crisis which lasted until the installation of the Grand Coalition.

Most commentators had expected some sort of Cabinet reshuffle in the autumn. On September 15, Lüdiger Westrick, Erhard's state secretary in the Chancellor's Office, who was unpopular with many in the party, resigned.

While Erhard was in Washington, Gerstenmaier gave an interview to the *Rheinische Merkur,* a pro-CDU journal. He affirmed his "loyalty" to Erhard, but also spoke of the possibility that at some juncture "loyalty to the country" might have to take precedence over loyalty to party or person. He declared his availability for the Chancellorship under such conditions. Gerstenmaier then invited Josef-Hermann Dufhues, leader of the Westphalian CDU and a prominent CDU party manager; Bruno Heck, federal Family Minister and chairman of the CDU presidium; Helmut Kohl, leader of the CDU in Rheinland-Pfalz; and Kurt-Georg Kiesinger, CDU Minister-President of Baden-Württemberg for "conversations" to his country home near Bonn. Such conversations between the Bundestag President and other CDU leaders were yearly events, but on this occasion the meeting was in the service of Gerstenmaier's ambitions. Kiesinger was the only invitee who did not attend. His lack of involvement in the Bonn maneuverings stood him in good stead later as a symbol for party unity.

On September 28, the state chairmen of the CDU strongly advised Erhard to make personnel and policy changes prior to the elections in Hesse and Bavaria. However, the crisis had already moved rapidly away from a mere re-shuffle of ministries to an elimination of Erhard himself.

The public debate about Erhard lasted until the following Wednesday, October 5. In the meantime, in interviews and statements, Adenauer, Strauss and others flayed Erhard for his lack of success in Washington and his inattention to relations with France. Finally, on October 4th a long, stormy meeting of the CDU/CSU parliamentary party sought to pacify what one radio journalist termed the "neurotic campaign of tearing Erhard down." The group issued a statement that "Ludwig Erhard is and remains Chancellor," and Barzel assured the press that "with this, the public debate is closed." Gerstenmaier asserted his loyalty to the Chancellor, and expressed his satisfaction that the fraction had discussed the policy issues which, he claimed, his *Rheinische Merkur* interview had been intended to help clarify.

The ensuing calm was brief and hardly convincing. A young CDU deputy during the October 4 meeting spoke more to the point: Erhard, Strauss, Barzel, Gerstenmaier and Schroeder should, as in the case of elections to the papacy, be locked in a room until they reached agreement. Both Barzel and Gerstenmaier had, clearly, moved too soon, though the latter was now in a poorer position than Barzel, who was attempting to appear as a unifier of the party. Kiesinger began his move on October 5 with a comment that the crisis in Bonn was not only "the Erhard case," but a crisis in the CDU. Kiesinger declared that the latest opinion polls showed that only 25 per cent of the electorate supported the party. The same day, Kiesinger, as spokesman for the state Minister-Presidents, reported to Erhard that the states would not permit the federal government to obtain 39 per cent of income and corporation taxes in 1967, but would demand a return to the earlier level of 35 per cent.

Erhard's coalition collapsed over the next three weeks, the immediate cause being disagreement between the coalition partners on the balancing of the Federal budget. The FDP favored a cut in expenditures, while Erhard pushed for higher taxes. Some expenditures had been cut, and some taxes raised a year earlier, but the new budget crisis was not only far more serious, but took place in the context of Erhard's demise. The FDP, which withdrew its four ministers from the Cabinet on October 27, was formally responsible for the establishment of a minority government (Erhard filled the four Cabinet seats with CDU ministers), but it was encouraged by Erhard's opponents in the CDU and by the CSU, which at this time, under Strauss' leadership, was functioning clearly as a fully separate party. In discussions with the FDP leadership, Barzel made the finance question—which, in the past, had frequently arisen among the coalition partners—an absolute test of the coalition. For several reasons of its own, the FDP was no longer reluctant to leave the government. Erhard's opponents in his own party, meanwhile, sought to depose Erhard without overturning him in Parliament. Under the "constructive lack of confidence" provision of the Basic Law, this required prior majority agreement in the Bundestag on Erhard's successor. Such agreement was lacking because no master hand guided the course of the crisis. The crisis proceeded in three stages: collapse of Erhard's government; designation of Kiesinger as CDU/CSU candidate to succeed Erhard; formation of the Grand Coalition, rather than either a small coalition of CDU/CSU-FDP or SPD-FDP.

The FDP

The coalition between CDU/CSU and FDP began in 1949 as a coalition based ideologically on a measure of agreement on economic policy. In foreign policy, particularly concerning relationships with East Germany and other countries of Eastern Europe, most of the leaders of the FDP had for years been critical of CDU/CSU caution. Thus, when a serious dispute on the budget broke out under the economic conditions of 1966, one of the most important bulwarks of the coalition was removed, especially since the SPD had moved much closer to the CDU/CSU on economic policy after 1959.

However, this dispute in itself probably would not have been sufficient to induce FDP withdrawal. The special circumstances of the political situation were more important. The major preoccupation of the FDP leadership is survival as a political party; the major preoccupation of the business interest groups which compose a substantial part of its constituency is economic policy. Much of the latter support has been conditional upon the party's success in participating in government. By the fall of 1966, the leaders of the FDP, and especially some of its younger leaders, began to see cooperation with the quarreling CDU/CSU as a liability rather than a benefit. Had the CDU/CSU been unified, it probably could have split opinion in the fragmented and extremely eclectic FDP, as it had done several times earlier. However, the disunity of the Christian Democrats was precisely the source of the FDP's hesitation at remaining bound to a party that was losing popular support rapidly. Several times in the past, the leaders of the FDP had "flipped" back to cooperation with the CDU/CSU despite earlier threats of withdrawal. This behavior—induced by the business interests behind the party who wished to have a share in governing—damaged its image.

Related considerations played a role in the FDP decision. Some party leaders feared losses to the emerging NPD in the forthcoming state elections if the FDP did not make clear its distance from the "establishment" in Bonn. Moreover, at various times, the more leftward-tending wing of the party had sought to cooperate with the SPD. Since all appeared in flux, a coalition of SPD and FDP might conceivably emerge from the crisis. Thus, all factions of the party, for their own reasons, saw advantages in disassociating themselves from the Christian Democrats and this mood was encouraged by Erhard's opponents inside the CDU/CSU.

The Constitutional Situation

Characteristic of the crisis of September to December was its prolongation without a formal vote on the status of Erhard's government in Parliament. Under the Weimar Constitution (1919–33), the SPD and FDP together could have deposed Erhard's government and precipitated negotiations for a new government that would have the support of a parliamentary majority. The "constructive vote of no confidence" whereby Parliament cannot vote lack of confidence without simultaneously proposing a successor as Chancellor, was supposed to prevent prolonged negotiations about new governments, and guard against immobility in the executive. In fact, as Karl Dietrich Bracher has pointed out, this provision of the Bonn Basic Law has been "much overrated" in its effects.[18] Erhard remained head of a caretaker minority government for more than a month following the withdrawal of the FDP. On November 8, the Bundestag passed an SPD-FDP resolution asking Erhard to place before the house a confidence motion, but the resolution had no effect and no other constitutional measures were taken.

Erhard reigned—but did not rule—for even longer than the month, as a consequence of the immobility created by the party crisis. The creation of an effective government awaited the resolution of this crisis and the outcome of the state elections, to which all three parties were looking before making decisions on the future government. Because of the fears of the CDU/CSU and FDP and the cumbersome and limited powers of dissolution under the Basic Law, a dissolution of the Bundestag and calling of new elections was never a real possibility. Even the SPD never pressed this issue. A dissolution would have been possible only if all the following conditions had been met: (1) if Erhard had proposed a vote of confidence and lost; (2) if the Bundestag had been unable to elect his successor by absolute majority; (3) if Erhard had requested the President to dissolve the Bundestag; and (4) if the President had done so. Thus, it seems clear that the constitutional structure is not in itself capable of preventing long periods of governmental immobility in the absence of either a two-party system with unity in both parties or a multi-party representation in the legislature with unity among the coalition partners or within the governing party.[19]

In fact, Erhard did not even propose that the parliamentary fraction of the CDU/CSU vote on his leadership. His departure followed the informal pattern characteristic of the whole crisis. Proclaiming his intention to remain in office, he plunged into the Hessian election campaign on the last weekend in October, telling voters: "I will stay in office. . . . I have become immune to all the things that are being said about me in Bonn." The following week, the CSU ministers in the Cabinet, under pressure from Strauss, threatened to resign. By Wednesday, November 2, Erhard was persuaded to agree to stand aside if he could not find a new majority. This temporary formula meant, in effect, his resignation. The CDU/CSU now set about to complete the negotiations for the succession, to repair its image, and to heal the party crisis which had become a governmental crisis.

The NPD

The following Sunday brought election results which heightened the impression that the governmental crisis had become a crisis of the Bonn state. The right-wing National Democratic Party, which had not existed at the time of the previous Hessian election in 1962, won 7.9 per cent of the vote and 8 seats in the Hessian legislature. The SPD, long a power in the state, very slightly increased its absolute majority, while both CDU and FDP declined slightly. Two weeks later, the NPD, again contending for the first time, won 7.4 per cent of the votes and 15 seats in Bavaria. Both major parties—SPD and CSU—gained slightly, while the FDP and Bavarian Party declined. These elections focused the attention of the world on developments in West Germany.

The NPD won only 8 of 200 seats in Hesse, and 15 of 204 seats in Bavaria, but it was, relatively, more successful in making inroads on the major parties in Hesse, a circumstance related to the conservative and well-organized character of the CSU in Bavaria, which enabled it to hold its own and even increase its share of the vote by 0.6 per cent (a larger gain than the SPD). Moreover, in Hesse the conservative All-German Party (GDP) had gained 6.3 per cent of the votes in 1962; this fell only to 4.3 per cent in 1966. In Bavaria, GDP votes fell from 5.1 per cent to 0.2 per cent and votes for the Bavarian Party from 4.8 to 3.4 per cent. Some of the NPD votes undoubtedly came from former GDP and Bavarian Party voters. Nevertheless, numerous studies by political scientists and sociologists after the elections have shown that not all former GDP and BP voters went to the NPD, and that the success of the latter party cannot be explained adequately this way. The upsurge of the NPD evidenced a new development.

The NPD had been founded from the remnants of extreme right-wing groups in November 1964. Careful studies have shown that the strength of the party in the 1966 elections resulted from the existence of a right-wing "reservoir" with a potential strength of 8–18 per cent in the West German electorate, 8 per cent representing a relatively "hard core," and 10 per cent a potential bloc, willing to support the NPD or similar groups under particular circumstances.[20] In the 1966 elections, the reservoir, rather than being split among several groups, went in considerable degree to the NPD because this party was well-organized.

Thus, the NPD successes were related to the condition of West German politics in 1966, but this relationship must be specified more precisely in terms of the functional disarray in West German politics.

The NPD vote has been analyzed as an "oppositional" vote. Neither the SPD nor the FDP have been able to monopolize or even derive great benefit from opposition to the CDU/CSU. To express the matter another way: the crises within the CDU/CSU, which weakened it electorally, probably did not benefit the SPD or FDP substantially. Rather, they benefited the splinter parties, old or new. This tendency is strengthened by the limited proportional representation system in West German elections, which encourages the formation of parties. Also, it is favored by the gap between party leaders and voters among the established parties—the inadequate communication between parties (particularly the CDU/CSU) and public. This alienation effect is likely, of course, to increase in times of stress. In 1966, the crisis in the CDU/CSU coincided with economic downturn—psychologically exaggerated, as has been seen—and with the emergence of a "new nationalism."

The "ideology" or program of the NPD has a content based largely upon the alienation effect and—as was typical of the National Socialist Party—resentments. Its thrust is "anti-establishment." Moreover, many of the criticisms of West Germany's weakness in international politics, its subservience to the United States militarily and economically, and its inadequate attention to reunification only repeated in more extravagant form criticisms being voiced within the "establishment" itself. The "new nationalism" of 1966 was here mirrored in an extremist form. Finally, the transformation of the SPD since the Godesberg Program gave opportunities to a new "oppositional" party in West Germany.

The Hessian and Bavarian election results undoubtedly contributed to the establishment of the Grand Coalition. Politicians of the CDU/CSU and SPD were torn in several directions. Opposing extremist nationalism, they were nevertheless cautious about appearing "anti-national." They feared radicalism and the destruction of moderation in the political spectrum. The Grand Coalition appeared to be a way to solve economic difficulties, give attention to "national" problems and, possibly, reconstruct the electoral system so as to minimize the chances that extremist groups could gain further influence.

II. THE GRAND COALITION

The Selection of Kiesinger

On November 10, when Kurt-Georg Kiesinger, Minister-President of Baden-Württemberg, was chosen by the CDU/CSU as its candidate for the Chancellorship, plans for the Grand Coalition were already underway behind the scenes. Yet, Kiesinger did not appear to the public to be the future Chancellor of a Grand Coalition. It was not even certain that he would become Chancellor at all. Other possibilities were still open, though they were being foreclosed rapidly by agreements between leaders of the two major parties. Their main concern was to ensure that the formation of the Grand Coalition would not fragment each party. This was a far more serious matter in the SPD than in the CDU/CSU. Kiesinger was chosen as Chancellor candidate of the Christian Democrats for several reasons, but one of the most important was that he was acceptable to the SPD leadership as the leader (or co-leader) of a Grand Coalition.

Following Erhard's announcement that he was willing to stand aside and the Hessian election, the Christian Democrats moved rapidly to designate Erhard's successor. Being loosely organized and long inclined to present itself to the electorate through the image of its leader, the CDU/CSU inevitably selected its new leader rapidly. Moreover, with the dramatic flair surrounding the selection, the party sought to give the public the impression that it was choosing a new Chancellor, not merely one party's candidate for that post. The party still commanded more Bundestag seats than any other party. An additional impetus to speed was provided by the Bundestag vote of November 8, in which SPD and FDP joined in asking Erhard to place the question of confidence before the chamber. Barzel, who played a central role in urging rapid action, arranged that the party presidium nominate four candidates on November 8. The following day, the parliamentary party decided to vote on November 10.

The four nominees were Barzel, Gerstenmaier, Schroeder and Kiesinger. The party presidium indicated that other candidates might be nominated at the meeting. While some speculation concerned Lücke and Walter Hallstein, no substantial movement developed in either direction. The outcome of the election was determined no later than the previous evening. Gerstenmaier withdrew and threw his support to Kiesinger prior to the meeting. Wednesday evening, the day before the vote, Strauss announced that the CSU would support Kiesinger. The same day, the *Bayernkurier* had indicated this step by arguing that the party's choice should not have been involved in the Erhard crisis. The first ballot gave 97 votes to Kiesinger, 76 to Schroeder, 56 to Barzel, and 14 to Hallstein. By the third ballot, Kiesinger had won the required majority with 137 votes to 81 for Schroeder and 26 for Barzel.

Barzel, Gerstenmaier, and Schroeder had too many opponents within the party to succeed. Barzel's support evaporated with the emergence of Kiesinger and with his own inelegancies in pursuit of the post. He had, for instance, promised positions to supporters before he was assured of success in the vote. Gerstenmaier withdrew as part of the arrangement whereby the CSU played a decisive role in bringing about Kiesinger's selection. Schroeder was both the strongest and the weakest barrier to Kiesinger's selection. Because of his known opposition to a Grand Coalition, his "Atlanticist" views, and his northern Protestant support, he was a major enemy of the CSU. Thus, he could not hope for election as long as the CSU agreed on an alternate candidate acceptable to sufficient CDU members. Yet his bloc of supporters remained loyal to him through the final vote, and this indicated the possibility of continued tensions within the CDU/CSU after the crisis of succession was settled.

The candidates did not present formal statements or programs to the parliamentary party prior to the voting. They did not indicate how they proposed to find a Bundestag majority to support a new government. They did not declare formally what emphasis they would place upon different aspects of foreign policy. The choice of a personality was in the foreground of attention, and the prime requirement was that he be reasonably acceptable to all factions in the party, especially to the CSU. The decisive elements in Kiesinger's selection were Gerstenmaier's withdrawal, the support of the CSU, and his support by powerful provincial leaders of the CDU.

Kiesinger had been removed from the hothouse of Bonn politics since 1958. After having served as a prominent Adenauer lieutenant for years, he had become Minister-President of Baden-Württemberg. He had been Bundestag foreign policy spokesman of the CDU/CSU for eight years and chairman of the Bundestag Foreign Relations Committee for four years. His lack of direct involvement in the intra-party clashes of the previous eight years was one of his strongest advantages. He was reputed to be a mediator and conciliator. He was also thought of, however, as not particularly strong and decisive, somewhat easygoing and laconic in leadership and administration. He was known as an accomplished and persuasive speaker, master of the golden phrase on every occasion, and thus likely to be an accomplished electoral leader for the party. An attentive devotee of opinion polls, Kiesinger was highly attuned to the importance of "images" in politics.

His own image was endangered prior to the vote by his activities during the Nazi regime. He joined the party in 1933 at the age of 29 and was deputy leader of the radio section in the Foreign Office during the war. This position required him to have extensive contact with Goebbels' Propaganda Ministry and it has been charged that he functioned as a liaison man between the Foreign

Office and the Propaganda Ministry. After the war, he was interned by the Allies for 18 months.

Just before the CDU/CSU meeting of November 10, photocopies of a document concerning Kiesinger's activities in the Foreign Office during the war were distributed to the gathering politicians. In the document, two Nazis complained to their superiors that Kiesinger criticized the regime and attempted to protect Jews. The previous day, Kiesinger had explained his activities between 1933 and 1945. He asserted that he had joined the party in order to turn the course of events in the proper direction and, like many others, had been deceived. He claimed to have become disillusioned a year and a half later, at the time of the Röhm putsch, though he remained a party member.

Except that the press—for example, *Die Zeit*—expressed some concern and some student groups protested, Kiesinger's activities during the Nazi period did not cause much controversy within West Germany, certainly not within the leadership of the major parties. Indeed, the Grand Coalition that he formed with Brandt (who had emigrated and served in Norwegian uniform against Hitler) and Wehner (formerly a Communist) was said by many to symbolize reconciliation and unity in Germany. Kiesinger was selected as a result of the current political situation. His selection showed that matters of the past have little importance in determining such decisions.

In fact, few doubted Kiesinger's loyalty to democratic procedures in 1966 or charged that he had participated in any Nazi crimes or been a "typical Nazi." His attitude in 1933 and during the Nazi regime was undoubtedly typical of many German conservatives. Profoundly affected by the cultural pessimism after the First World War and dismayed by the disorderly Weimar years, they looked for a "conservative renewal" and were deceived by the claim of the Nazis before 1933 that they were true conservatives. Hitler came to power as the spokesman of this heralded "conservative renewal," and the practical successes of the Nazi movement in achieving political power had great attraction for conservatives who would have been limited to romantic reveries or literary exercises otherwise. As soon as it became obvious to these conservatives that the Nazis brought—not renewal, order, and culture—but an accentuation of what they termed "mass society," they turned aside.

One of the writers that Kiesinger admired most was Ernst Juenger, a symbol for those with a contempt for "cultural decline" and a vague, ill-defined longing for "true leadership," "unity," and "order." Juenger opposed the Weimar Republic violently, but never supported Hitler, who was also a symptom of decline to him.

Kiesinger may have become involved with the purported "national renewal" of 1933 because his personal decency was neutralized by an amorphous ideology that clouded his judgment and by a certain passive openness in his nature that permitted him to experiment with this new phenomenon. This deception became evident to him rapidly after 1933, as it did to many others who had been caught up in the mood of the times and who lacked coherent intellectual defenses.

At the time he was elected, Kiesinger was reputed to tend more toward the "Gaullist" than the "Atlanticist" side. He had long had contacts with Baron Karl von und zu Guttenberg, a CSU politician with pronounced pro-Gaullist views who had been involved in discussions concerning the possibility of a Grand Coalition as early as 1962. Guttenberg became parliamentary state secretary to Kiesinger when the Grand Coalition was installed. Yet, it was characteristic of the process by which Kiesinger was selected, as well as, perhaps, of Kiesinger's outlook, that knowledge of the new leader's pro-French leanings was notably rudimentary and imprecise. Strauss and his supporters insisted, of course, that he take a harder line than had Erhard on the offset payments question and that he seek a demonstrative reaffirmation of the Franco-German Treaty. Kiesinger did not express policy choices until after he was selected leader, and then only tentatively. In short, he was not put forward to represent a definite position; he was thrown forward by the crisis in the CDU/CSU and by the belief of the CDU/CSU leaders that they would benefit by change.

The Search for a Majority

With the selection of Kiesinger, at least five possibilities for the construction of the government remained open theoretically: an indefinite continuation of the Erhard government, tolerated as a minority by the SPD; a reconstructuring of the CDU/CSU-FDP coalition under Kiesinger's leadership; an SPD-FDP coalition; a coalition of all parties; or a coalition of the CDU/CSU and SPD.

For all these alternatives, the behavior of the SPD leadership was crucial. Even the alternative of a new CSU/CSU-FDP coalition under Kiesinger would have been likely only if the SPD had chosen to distance itself from governmental participation prior to new elections. Such was not, however, the major thrust of the SPD leadership. In fact, it was toward immediate participation in the Cabinet. This fundamental tendency, vigorously pursued by Wehner, supported enthusiastically by Helmut Schmidt, and with somewhat less enthusiasm by Willy Brandt, foreclosed several alternatives and made the Grand Coalition the most likely result of the crisis.

All three parties were active in negotiations between November 11 and November 30, especially after the Bavarian election on November 20. Rumors about the coalition to be formed occupied Bonn's attention for a considerable period. However, much of the activity which came to public attention served only party tactical purposes, being intended to strengthen one or another party in its negotiations with the others. The only two alternatives which were pursued seriously were an SPD-FDP coalition and a Grand Coalition. Tactical maneuvers by the three parties played some role in influencing the final outcome, but were not decisive. The SPD-FDP coalition failed to develop, not primarily because of tactical errors by the FDP—though these existed—but because of the intentions of the SPD leadership.

The SPD leaders did not seriously consider tolerating the Erhard minority government for an indefinite period. Such a policy seemed to them to present the danger that the old coalition partners would agree on a new government eventually. The CDU/CSU played on such fears by sporadically appearing to want to reconstruct the coalition. The SPD also feared the consequences of minority government for the stability of the political system. Finally, they saw a chance to participate in the government immediately and preferred this alternative to the uncertainties of an eventual overthrow of the Erhard government and new elections. They wished to compete in an election under more favorable auspices—after having been in power or after having helped revise the electoral law or both.

In the CDU/CSU, also, reconstruction of the old coalition under Kiesinger met considerable resistance. Although at the time Kiesinger was selected, this solution still appeared possible, it had already been undermined by growing sentiment for a Grand Coalition and by the indicated willingness of the SPD leaders to participate in such a government. Wehner had been pursuing the Grand Coalition for years and as early as the beginning of October Brandt had publicly hinted at its possibility. The two major parties in November were negotiating less the existence of the Grand Coalition than its terms: its program and the distribution of ministries between the parties. Almost immediately after his selection, Kiesinger began to present himself to the public as an advocate of the Grand Coalition, for example, in a speech to the party's youth organization in Würzburg a few days after his selection.

The CDU/CSU saw in a Grand Coalition the chance to remain in power, to involve the SPD in hard decisions about economic policy, and to escape their dependence upon the FDP. Moreover, the FDP still opposed a Cabinet seat for Strauss, who had played a leading role in the deposition of Erhard and the choice of Kiesinger. Even before Kiesinger's selection, the *Bayernkurier,* voice of the CSU, concentrated a constant fire of criticism against the FDP. Undoubtedly, the CDU/CSU leaders believed that if Kiesinger could become Chancellor of the Grand Coalition, the party would profit from his effective campaigning in future elections. Fears about Kiesinger's effective campaign techniques were, in fact, one reason some provincial SPD leaders opposed the policy of their national leaders. A deputy from Baden-Württemberg, familiar with Kiesinger's style, argued that if Kiesinger should lead the CDU/CSU into the next national election as Chancellor, the SPD in that state "might as well give up."

Insofar as there was hesitancy within the CDU/CSU about a Grand Coalition, it pertained to doubts about the SPD's possible flexible policies toward Eastern Europe, including East Germany. Since the FDP was perhaps even more consistent than the SPD in its wish to escape the "hard line" policy championed for years by the CDU/CSU, these doubts did not necessarily make the FDP a more attractive coalition partner. Even in the minds of these "hard liners," the important thing was to insure that the CDU/CSU ministers in the Cabinet restrain the SPD. In short, the CDU/CSU leaders faced far fewer difficulties in winning their party's support for the Grand Coalition than did the SPD leaders. The CDU/CSU remained badly split on many policy issues, but its desire to remain in power, and the ambitions of many of its leaders, at least temporarily overcame these splits. This was indicated by the fact that Strauss, who had the reputation of being a "hard liner" toward the East, was a strong advocate of the Grand Coalition.

In any event, the FDP showed little consistency in pushing for a reconstruction of the coalition. Before the election in Bavaria, the FDP leaders attempted to hold open their dual possibilities of remaining in the government, though they tended toward a coalition with the SPD. After their losses in Bavaria, they became more eager for that solution. In effect, however, they had become irrelevant to the plans of the national leaders of the two major parties. Moreover, the party was not sufficiently united, nor were its leaders sufficiently skilled, to work efficiently for an SPD-FDP government. This solution to the crisis had less chance of realization than appeared at the time, for Wehner used the threat of an SPD coalition with the FDP as a tactical weapon against the CDU/CSU in the negotiations between the major parties.

The SPD leadership explained its unwillingness to enter a coalition with the FDP primarily by reference to the slim six-vote majority which such a government would enjoy in the Bundestag. They feared that this was an unreliable majority for difficult legislative decisions, especially in view of disunity within the FDP. Illness might affect the reliability of majorities, and several FDP deputies were known to be extreme conservatives who might not even vote for the installation of an SPD-FDP government, much less for later policies heavily influenced by the SPD. The majorities in the committees would be particularly precarious. Only voting rights for the twenty-two Berlin deputies, most of whom were SPD, would have given such a government a stronger majority. While this possibility was discussed briefly, it was never a crucial issue because the Allies reaffirmed their position that, in order to maintain the "international" status of Berlin, Bundestag deputies from Berlin should not become voting members rather than observers.

Undoubtedly, the fears of the SPD leaders about the FDP had real substance. Moreover, the behavior of the party in November was not conducive to overcoming these fears, though after the Grand Coalition was formed, the party complained loudly that it had been deceived and that the SPD had not negotiated with it in good faith. For example, the FDP leaders never conducted an actual vote within their parliamentary party to determine how many deputies would vote with the SPD to depose Erhard and form a new government. Moreover, despite their solid support of the SPD motion of November 8 to request Erhard to place the confidence question, the FDP deputies later, in a meeting of the Bundestag Budgetary Committee on November 25, voted against an SPD motion to reject the budget.

Despite the difficulties of collaborating with the FDP, however, the decisive push to the SPD decision to join a Grand Coalition was the desire of the party's leaders to participate in a government where they would run minimum risk of being blamed for failure. The SPD leaders sought to balance the desire for governmental participation with a policy of minimizing risks. In return, they were willing to accept some limitations on their freedom to formulate policies. This attitude, corresponding to the long-standing devaluation of programs in the party, is a key to an understanding, not only of the SPD's behavior, but also of the implications of the Grand Coalition.

The long years of transformation changed the SPD into a "middle-class" party, or, more precisely, into a party which wished to convey the impression that it was not eternally in opposition. This change was shown in the campaign tactics of the party and its votes in the Bundestag. Participation in a Grand Coalition was an extension of this transformation. Curiously, the notion of participating in a Grand Coalition became ascendant among party leaders precisely because the "de-radicalization" of the SPD, while probably gaining it some support, did not achieve *sufficient* electoral gains. The results of both the 1961 and 1965 elections did not live up to SPD expectations. In 1962, Wehner commenced to plan in earnest for SPD participation in a Grand Coalition.

In short, once having started to re-cast its image and, to a certain extent, its policies, the issue of participation in a Grand Coalition had, in effect, already been decided. For, if the policy of adaptation to the non-ideological, non-issue style politics of the CDU/CSU did not bring sufficient electoral dividends, it would be much easier to take the party a further step along this path than to revert to the style and stance of opposition.

Even during the Weimar years, however, the SPD had not been radical in programs and policies. At least by the early years of the Bonn Republic, a more precise term for its behavior would have been "oppositional," indicating not so much adherence to ideology as a certain style of behavior. Thus, under its first postwar leader, Kurt Schumacher, the SPD pursued oppositional politics which, in content, were not alway easy to reconcile with Socialist ideology. As has been indicated, its transformation, particularly after 1959, involved some changes in program, but the main thrust has been in behavior and style. It has sought to escape the image of a party in eternal opposition and present itself as a group of alternative leaders whose election would signify relatively slight policy changes.

The fundamental thesis underlying the party's transformation has been that more votes may be gained by minimizing the distinctions between the two major parties than by maximizing them. However, this thesis is open to some doubt, at least with regard to attracting sufficient votes to become the largest group in the Bundestag. Changes in social structure may bring results only to a certain point. Beyond this point, "floating votes" may go to other groups. Such votes, as in the case of the NPD constituency, are not identifiable with a particular social grouping—e.g., the middle class. Especially under the present electoral law, which encourages minor parties somewhat, the SPD may find it difficult to attract sufficient votes to become the largest party in the Bundestag.

The tendency toward a two-party system in legislative representation has existed throughout the Bonn Republic, but has not produced such a system yet. Indeed, there are indications that under conditions of uncertainty in the society—e.g., in the economic system or in foreign policy—the trend may actually be reversed. In order to win a larger share of the vote, the SPD has had to displace third parties, win recruits among new voters, or change the habits of some CDU/CSU voters. The first two expectations have been fulfilled in part, but further gains are unlikely. Even in the case of new voters, the trend does not promise the certainty of great results for the party. Thus, once started on the path of winning votes by minimizing the differences between the major parties, the SPD is driven, by the logic of the premises of its own national leadership, to further steps in this direction.

The Grand Coalition is the stage in this process when the SPD enters upon the governing function in order to overcome lingering middle-class suspicions of its "respectability"—i.e., its freedom from remnants of radicalism—hoping, thereby, to win votes from the CDU/CSU. Because this may be a miscalculation, it spawns tensions within the party. This helps explain why certain SPD groups opposed formation of the Grand Coalition.

The desire of the SPD leaders to participate in the Cabinet did not arise solely from calculations of *future* electoral advantage. A desire to help shape policy and give the party's major supporters direct access to policy-making probably played an even greater role. The desire to participate rests on the implicit thesis that the governing and administering functions in the modern state are more central to the concerns of a political party than are the functions of formulating programs, discussing them before the voters, and shaping public opinion. In short, it assumes that elections are becoming less important and executive decisions more so in determining "who gets what." The newly-elected parliamentary party leader of the SPD, Helmut Schmidt, a Social Democrat of notably non-ideological and "modern" bent, expressed this view in clouded form during the Bundestag debate immediately after the Grand Coalition was installed. Schmidt stated that it was "not the task of the Social Democrats to worry about being a strong opposition in the Budestag," but, like all other parties, to emphasize how to "realize the aims of the party and its voters in practice."

A corollary to this guiding thesis is that a gap exists between parties and people, the latter being more the object of periodic election campaigns conducted with non-programmatic showmanship, personality contests, and advertising techniques, than an active participant in the formulation of public policy. The people, fragmented into various interests, must find channels of influence other than elections and the legislature. This tendency of the

West German party system has been emphasized by Bracher and other observers and is further manifested by the low level of citizen participation in party affairs at the local level. Bureaucratization of party structures correlates with bureaucratization in the policy-making process.

The thesis also involves a changing meaning of the term "goals," a retreat from programmatic goals to the simple goal of sharing in the administration of government and, thereby, in decisions on the distribution of benefits. "Goals" become immediate, tangible, and pragmatic rather than long-range and coherently bound together by programs and theories. This, to be sure, is only tendency. The SPD leaders continue to insist that their program has changed far less than the method to achieve it. During the negotiations with the CDU/CSU, the party published an eight-point program which, it said later, the Christian Democrats had accepted as a basis for the Grand Coalition. It included four points on foreign policy and four on economic policy. However, they expressed concrete proposals less than general statements of intent, e.g., to establish priorities in distributing revenues to federal, state, and local governments and to normalize relations with Eastern Europe. Clearly, the specific meaning of such phrases would depend upon negotiations among the coalition partners. The SPD would bring to these negotiations less a definite plan than a general approach sympathetic to planning and a new set of ministers and officials, especially as several leading Social Democrats were important provincial officials likely to resist curtailment of state expenses in favor of federal spending.

The parties reached essential agreement on November 24, four days after the Bavarian election, but they did not agree on details until two days later and the final distribution of ministerial posts was not set nor the agreement ratified in its final form by the parliamentary parties until November 30. The Grand Coalition was installed on December 1. The Bundestag vote on Kiesinger's nomination showed 340 in favor, 109 opposed, and 23 abstentions. Sixty deputies from the two major parties—almost all from the SPD—had opposed the new government and 23 had abstained. Formally, the coalition parties controlled 447 of the 496 seats (472 deputies were present and voting).

The voting was a testimony to substantial opposition to the

Grand Coalition inside the SPD. In fact, in the week before the vote Wehner, Brandt and Schmidt had converted a sizeable number of deputies to support of the new coalition, and for weeks afterwards they were occupied in attempting to calm protests from the provinces. SPD leaders in Baden-Württemberg, Bavaria, and Schleswig-Holstein were especially vocal in opposition, demanding an extraordinary national party conference to examine the new agreement. Protest telegrams inundated SPD headquarters and the Bundestag delegation. In several university cities, many students protested, with slogans such as "Black + Red = Democracy Dead" and "Black + Red = Brown" (the Nazi color). Yet the opposition was disorganized and lacked a coherent structure of action. Wehner had, over the years, organized the party centrally and the position of the national leadership was strong. The installation of an SPD-FDP government in North Rhine Westphalia in early December partly reflected the strength of opposition in the SPD. Brandt, in a meeting with the leaders of that state's party, had taken a "hands-off" stance in deference to the unrest in the party. Thus, the SPD-FDP government that the protesters desired came into being, but in Düsseldorf, not Bonn. However, the formation of this coalition was at least equally attributable to the strength of the two parties in the state. It had been delayed only temporarily since the July election.

The Grand Coalition and the Political System

Evidently, the import of the SPD's participation in a Grand Coalition is related to central tendencies of the West German political system, as is the Grand Coalition itself. The implications of the Grand Coalition are less important with regard to policies than with regard to the manner in which the West German polity functions. It emerged less as a result of policy agreements than as a result of the inability of the political system to produce any other stable majority government. Thus, it is at one and the same time an expression of difficulties in the functioning of the political system and a method intended to overcome those difficulties. It represents an unusual method of governing because it departs from the pattern of government and opposition postulated by the theory of the Bonn Basic Law and carried out in practice in West Germany previously. In short, the forming of policy and the function of governing have, with the emergence of the Grand Coalition, been conferred upon a Cabinet, not by an election, following which one of the major parties assumed the main responsibility, but by agreement between the two main contending parties.

The notion of a government by the two major parties, with only weak opposition in the legislature, is not without theoretical support. Theories of popular government stress the achievement of consensus as the outcome of popular sovereignty. Indeed, without assuming that popular sovereignty will lead to beneficent and wise authority, as well as controls on that authority, the theory of popular government would be subject to the ancient criticism that it leads to anarchy through fragmentation. The free exchange and competition of opinions should lead to consensus on policy, not to divisiveness and stalemate.

Moreover, it has been argued that the "waning of opposition" in industrial societies, resulting from the fact that parties no longer represent single social groups, but diverse mixtures of groups, renders the notion of "government" *versus* "opposition" obsolete and justifies a system in which all groups participate in governing, controlling one another in the executive branch.[21]

The latter theory may be criticized from several standpoints. It assumes that the distribution of benefits will not be stalemated by claims and counter-claims of the various groups. It implies that conflicts and opposition are concealed from the public. Because all groups are involved in governing, they all have an interest in concealing antagonisms and conflicts that might lead to rejection of the system. The process of creating policies through negotiations among the groups, away from the public eye, reinforces the gap between the electoral process and decision-making. Extremist movements in the West in the twentieth century have generally attacked democratic procedures at precisely this point: the dominance of "interests" in governmental decision-making rather than the "rule of the people." For example, in its propaganda the Nazi Party effectively played upon popular feelings of alienation from "the government" and "the politicians," and the NPD has tended to operate in the same manner. Populist anti-democratic extremism of the Right does not, in the style of more traditional conservatism or authoritarianism, simply attack the lack of "authority" and the weakness of the governing function in democracies. It charges that the authority or control which exists is not "genuine" because it serves "interests" remote from the populace. It promises genuine popular participation and genuine authority. Such notions have deep roots in Germany, where the concept of unity in the populace, and between populace and leaders, has often been counterpoised to the pluralism of "the West."

In part, the Grand Coalition itself is a concession to the notion of "genuine authority" (the two major parties controlling an overwhelming majority of legislative seats) acting on behalf of the common weal. The rhetoric accompanying its founding was cast in heroic terms. The government was presented, not as the consequence of an inability of the political system to produce any other majority, but as a creation necessary and desirable in itself. Yet, these explanations were curiously ambivalent and ambiguous. The government was presented over and over again as a temporary solution, designed to prepare the way for stable majorities in the future. The avoidance of an all-party government, which was mentioned only hesitantly and sporadically by a few individuals and journals, reinforced this impression of transitoriness. Yet, the concurrent emphasis upon the difficulty of the problems confronting the nation, together with the indicated delay of electoral reform implied relative permanence (at least six years) for the coalition. Aside from mere statements, as of late 1967 the Grand Coalition had not created the new electoral law which would help prepare its demise, and the leaders of the government clearly do not believe that they have accomplished even a substantial part of their work in coping with pressing national issues. Indeed, the definition of these issues has been so vague in part that it might be impossible to determine when they had been accomplished (e.g., more independence in foreign policy).

Not opinions or theories, but the functional place of this unusual government in the West German political system stimulate these observations about the Grand Coalition. The Grand Coalition is supposed to function as an aid to consensus in a system where the preceding consensus was insufficient. The potential instability of the political system which is implied by recent events would become evident were the Grand Coalition unable to deal effectively with real problems and become merely a more or less permanent method of governing, or were it, *together with the democratic forms altogether,* to be attacked as incompetent and fraudulent. The theory of popular sovereignty and consensus to which I have alluded certainly requires that the consensus on policy relate to real problems of the society, and that it lead to solution of these problems. Strong government is not the aim, but strength is defended as an aid to competence.

The Grand Coalition is a substitute for strong and effective majority government through the competition of parties. To prevent such substitutes from becoming a permanent way of governing, the Grand Coalition must make itself obsolete. Yet, it cannot make itself obsolete until it has created the conditions for majority government to emerge through the competition of parties. According to the theory underlying the Grand Coalition, this requires the pacification of issues which cause fragmentation—for example, the establishment of definite patterns in economic and foreign policy and the interment of obsolete controversies—and the creation of an electoral law structure that will encourage the emergence of a two-party system. Once again, however, to speak of a "theory" of the Grand Coalition may distract attention from the fact that this government was in large measure the result of a flight away from stalemate rather than a rational plan, and that the conditions of stalemate may persist within it. For example, the substantive aims of the government, despite the rhetoric about national needs, are not at all clear; they tend to reduce themselves to assertions of the need to act, without indicating what kind of action will win approval of the coalition parties and their fractions. The Grand Coalition is to some extent condemned to be cautious in its policies, while the justification for its existence is that it be bold.

The Grand Coalition must deliver successes to retain its legitimacy. Such successes, however, may not be assured. Failure, which under conditions of party competition, could be placed upon one party or one governing coalition, might be directed against the political system as a whole. West Germany, with its fund of unsolved foreign policy problems and possible cycles of economic recession, has a number of potentially stubborn issues for which no easy solutions are likely. In forming the Grand Coalition, both parties manifested concern that economic difficulties, together with the unsolved problems in foreign policy, might aid extremists of the Right. Yet these very reasons, advanced in justification of the Grand Coalition, tended to conceal the fact its formation might worsen the penalties for failure, leading either to an habituation to government without opposition, *but also without effective decision-making abilities*, or to growing influence of extremists outside the "establishment." The apparent stability purchased through the Grand Coalition might, under these conditions, result in greater instability. If the existing system could not cope with national issues even by unusual means, the way had been prepared for even more unusual means. In short, by emphasizing the existence of unusual circumstances, or a "crisis," it increased the potentialities for crisis.

The parties of the Grand Coalition could not avoid using some of the rhetoric of crisis to legitimize their undertaking. Through doing so, however, they became to some extent prisoners of the mood they had helped create. Yet, they undoubtedly had considerable confidence that the existing problems could be solved and that the crisis was less extensive in fact than in rhetoric. The emphasis on the temporary nature of the new government was meant to convey this opinion. Structural changes and economic and emergency legislation to discourage extremist groups were its primary practical aims. The SPD placed considerable emphasis upon reducing the influence of right-wing groups—for example, hard line refugee groups devoted to retrieving the lost territories and to reaction internally—in government and administration. The departure from the Cabinet of Hans-Christoph Seebohm, representative of Sudeten Germans unreconciled to final loss of the Sudetenland, symbolized this change.

Whether the Grand Coalition will actually lead to the problems mentioned cannot be discovered abstractly, but only by observing its actual effects. The discussion of the Grand Coalition as a symptom of difficulties in the West German political system provides the necessary frame of reference to evaluate the significance of political events under it. The following pages will discuss those events during its first year or so of existence.

The spokesmen of the Grand Coalition were sensitive to criticism during the period under review. Kiesinger noted in his first declaration of policy to the Bundestag in December that the hour did not herald the birth of a new nationalism in West Germany. The shapers of the government depicted it, rather, as the substitution of competence, energy, and imagination for past stagnation, confusion, and entrapment in sterile slogans. They pointed to the unwillingness or inability of previous governments to grapple with fundamental issues of economic policy, education and research, and foreign policy. The Grand Coalition brought to the federal government new men of talent, with declared penchants for hard work and confidence in their ability to undertake rational projects for the welfare and progress of the polity. To many advocates of the Grand Coalition, doubts about the potential stability of the system appeared to be abstract speculations, and reservations about the methods of achieving the purported ends unrealistic.

The student of comparative politics will recognize in the emergence of the Grand Coalition similarities to developments in other countries—for example, France—in the emphasis upon administrative and technical efficiency and upon the definition of national needs. At the same time, he must relate these developments to the way the political system deals with the central issues of politics: the distribution of power and influence, the interaction between leaders and public, the appropriateness of the decision-making process to standards of stability and justice. He cannot focus solely upon policy tendencies, but must seek to disentangle claims from realities. Most of all, he must seek to grasp the significance of political changes for the way in which the political system determines answers to the central issues of politics.

From this standpoint, the major significance of the emergence of the Grand Coalition is that this change took place without a popular electoral mandate. Its existence testifies, not to consensus in the society, but to the absence of consensus or, at the very least, to the failure of the political parties to transmit such consensus. Its proclaimed purpose was to create the conditions for a more adequate marriage of popular participation and effective government in the future.

No doubt, much of the rhetoric at the time the Grand Coalition was formed, with its emphasis upon policy and structural reforms, consciously or unconsciously concealed the root causes of the 1966 political crisis: disagreements about policy choices and conflicting political ambitions, both expressed through stalemate and the inability to form any other government. These root causes, in turn, indicate the possibility of insufficient agreement in the society or insufficient articulation of such agreement by the political system, resulting in stalemate and drift in domestic and foreign policy. Thus, the observer of West German politics under the Grand Coalition must be attentive to several dimensions of political life under the new government: the extent of policy and structural changes, the impact of such changes upon the stability and effectiveness of the political system, and the degree to which the conditions of disagreement and stalemate which led to the Grand Coalition persist.

Under such conditions, the present political system would probably continue as the bureaucratized arena of minimal decision-making, increasingly alienated from oppositional tendencies in the public. Given the potential explosiveness of the foreign policy issues still confronting West Germany, such a situation, particularly under conditions of economic stress, would probably be unstable and the political system could become the prey of extremist groups claiming to overcome the alienation between government and public, between "politics" and pressing national problems.

III. THE GRAND COALITION IN ACTION

By late 1967, little could be said with certainty about the actual stand taken by the Grand Coalition. Nor does this essay intend to review policy discussions under the Grand Coalition. The Grand Coalition had existed for too brief a period to enable it to confront directly some of the central problems upon which it promised action. It planned to remain in office at least until the election of September 1969. Thus, this essay will simply present some central themes based on its first year of existence to guide observation of it.

The New Style

Obviously, the new government introduced a new style to West German politics, but the extent of actual changes in policy was less clear. The new government enjoyed the usual "honeymoon period" of new governments. In the spring of 1967, polls showed a high degree of public acceptance of both Kiesinger and the government. The early months of the Grand Coalition were characterized by a good deal of successful public-relations work on behalf of the government (a product of the joint expertise of CDU/CSU and SPD) and some new departures in policy. By mid-summer 1967, however, the "honeymoon period" clearly was over. Press criticism increased and public favor fell. Significantly, this rising criticism coincided with difficulties within the government concerning economic policy for the following four years and with a public struggle between Kiesinger and Defense Minister Schroeder over the military budget.

The style of the Grand Coalition was based upon the rhetoric of unity and decisiveness in the pursuit of sound policies, upon Kiesinger's effectiveness as a symbol of leadership, and upon the consistent defense of the Grand Coalition by the chief SPD participants: Wehner, Brandt, Schmidt, and Karl Schiller, Minister of Economics. The Grand Coalition derived considerable legitimacy from the fact that it arose out of crisis and its spokesmen continued to emphasize the many problems with which it had to deal. The time required to master these problems was emphasized increasingly and, to a certain extent, the goals of the Grand Coalition were re-defined subtly. As time passed, structural reforms, such as a new electoral law and a revision of the federal-state relationship particularly with respect to tax distribution, received less emphasis and policy matters, such as budget balancing and stimulation of the economy, received more.

The tradition of "Chancellor Democracy" insured that considerable attention would be focused upon Kiesinger, despite the fact that he came to office as something of an outsider. The Chancellor rapidly established himself in the public eye as the spokesman of the new government. In May 1967, after brief discussion in the party, he also assumed the party chairmanship of the CDU/CSU. In state elections in Rhineland-Palatinate and Schleswig-Holstein in April, and in Lower Saxony in June, Kiesinger campaigned effectively for the CDU, which registered gains in all three states. At least superficially, the CDU/CSU refurbished its image to a considerable extent with Kiesinger as its leader. Yet Kiesinger's position within the Cabinet was by no means as authoritative as that of Adenauer, or even Erhard in his early months in office, and to the extent that his popularity increased, it stimulated his compatriots, notably Brandt, Wehner, and

Schroeder, to self-assertion. Moreover, his popular strength appeared relatively fragile, dependent upon the future successes of the Grand Coalition.

The Chancellor was a particularly articulate foreign policy spokesman. He functioned as the interpreter and defender of initiatives toward Eastern Europe long advocated by Wehner and Brandt. Toward France, he made demonstrative verbal overtures. Toward the United States, he alternated frank criticism with reassurances of cooperation. During the winter of 1966–67, the proposed non-proliferation treaty for nuclear weapons was criticized violently in the West German press. Strauss and Adenauer were among its most vociferous critics, charging that the United States failed to consult with Bonn and that West German scientific research might be impaired. Kiesinger joined in this criticism with frankness, but in much milder tone. His main objective was to emphasize that West Germany will gain more respect from Washington by expressing independent opinions than by playing the role of junior partner.

The Grand Coalition sought to emphasize West Germany's increasing role in world affairs generally. Brandt, Wehner, and the SPD placed most emphasis upon initiatives in *Ostpolitik*, Kiesinger and the CDU/CSU most emphasis upon independent judgment in policies toward the United States, Western Europe, and NATO. Together with the emphasis upon unified action to provide for a sound budget and a growing economy, this created the early style of the Grand Coalition. Kiesinger's abilities as a speaker earned him the title of a purveyor of "cascades of words," and greatly influenced this style.

Words and Substance

The potential for a gap between words and actions is great under a Grand Coalition. This gap had become more evident by late 1967. It was rooted in the barriers to policy successes created by the persistence of tensions within and between the parties, and by the objective difficulty of policy choices. Both parties, but especially the SPD, had an enormous stake in the Grand Coalition. Therefore, the difficulties of effective action created pressure to continue the coalition until it achieves successes at the same time that they led to doubts about the wisdom of continuing it. Within the parties, this contradiction found expression in growing indications of differences between party leaders in the Cabinet and party leaders outside the Cabinet. Both parties constantly sought to attract attention by verbal declarations, since each party feared losing its independent public image.

The Grand Coalition achieved several demonstrable early successes in economic and foreign policy. In January, the Cabinet agreed upon budgetary cuts to reduce the 1967 deficit and reached agreement with the states on distribution of tax revenues for the year. Pressure on Washington over the non-proliferation treaty and offset payments question led to a temporary compromise solution permitting West Germany to purchase American securities instead of making all offset purchases in arms. An economic stabilization measure, strengthening the power of the federal government to stimulate the economy, was rapidly approved. Diplomatic relations with Rumania were established, more rapidly than would have been possible under the Erhard government. The Grand Coalition declared that it regarded the Munich agreement of 1938 as no longer valid, and several months later concluded an agreement for exchange of trade missions with Czechoslovakia.

Ostpolitik formed one of the main interests of the Grand Coalition. In reality, however, the government acted cautiously. Much of its policy consisted merely of general statements of interest in normalizing relationships. The government declared its belief in detente and distanced itself from the concept of the "Cold War." It followed the "bridge-building" approach suggested in Johnson's speech of October 7, 1966, which created anxiety in West Germany at the time because of the feeling that Bonn's foreign policy was increasingly isolated. The Grand Coalition indicated its intention to develop new forms for relationships with Eastern Europe, but it did not develop a specific content for these new forms. This was especially true with regard to relationships with East Germany. Bonn emphasized the improvement of contacts with East Germany, but continued to insist strongly that it will not recognize the legitimacy of the East German State. It did not abandon its claim to be the only legal representative of all Germany. Moreover, relations with Poland made little progress and Bonn did not accept the Oder-Neisse line. The underlying principle of the "Hallstein Doctrine," although greatly weakened, was still official policy.

Finally, the Grand Coalition's relations with the Soviet Union continued frigid. Moscow reacted unfavorably to Bonn's attempts to strengthen ties with Eastern Europe. Yet, astute observers believed that relations with the Soviet Union ultimately would have the most to do with the success of Bonn's Eastern policy and particularly with the reunification problem.[22] The question of West Germany's relations with the Soviet Union was connected with West Germany's relations with the United States and its membership in the Western security system. There was no agreement about the extent to which one commitment hampers the achievement of new policy toward the other side.

Brandt increasingly emphasized the long-range nature of the project of improving relationships with Eastern Europe. Yet this emphasis was not completely in accord with the rhetoric of the Grand Coalition or with the expectations which accompanied its founding. Moreover, the SPD felt under increasing pressure to demonstrate new successes in foreign policy rapidly. Also, difficulty in doing so was caused by the continued influence in the CDU/CSU of conservative forces, suspicious of new initiatives in *Ostpolitik*. Thus, the SPD concentrated on verbal pronouncements which it found difficult to give substance.

The dilemma indicated by the two imperatives—need for rapid successes in order to strengthen the prestige of the government and the difficulty in achieving them—was a fundamental weakness of the Grand Coalition. Here, the continuing difficulties of West Germany's international position—cultivating relationships with the East while remaining tied to the West, seeking reunification while being unwilling to accept all the changes in established foreign policy positions which were probably prerequisites to any progress whatsoever—showed themselves highly significant for the operation of the political system. In brief: the foreign policy choices had no easy answers, but the Grand Coalition encouraged the belief that it would bring them about.

Of first importance among proposed structural changes was an electoral reform to discourage minor parties and solidify the trend toward a two-party system. The electoral reform was seen as a weapon against the FDP and as a guarantee against the influence of extremist groups. Whether such a law actually would offer the latter guarantee is open to some question. Two-party systems may not prevent a rise of anti-democratic groups under all conditions. Quite aside from this consideration, however, the Grand Coalition was unable to agree on a new electoral law and a noticeable tendency to postpone the question developed, despite the work of both party and government commissions. It became clear that the electoral law would not change before the 1969 election, implying that the Grand Coalition would continue till at least 1973, unless one partner withdraws. Evidently, a number of electoral plans were under consideration and serious disagreements within and between the parties concerned the plan to be put into effect. The Grand Coalition did secure agreement on a comparatively minor party law, but electoral change is a far more sensitive issue.

Other structural changes and social legislation were, for the most part, still undecided by late 1967. Plans for reform of federal-state relationships with regard to taxing powers required constitutional revision, and were not yet agreed upon by the Cabinet. The so-called "emergency law" had been discussed for years, was a particularly sensitive subject for the SPD, and was hotly disputed outside the government. The emergency legislation was to displace the still-existing rights of the former occupation powers to assume governmental powers in West Germany in case of an internal or external attack or serious threat of such an attack upon the state.

By far the most serious problem confronting the Grand Coalition in late 1967 was that of financial planning and economic growth. The Erhard government had been characteristically unable to adhere consistently to financial plans. Under pressure from interest groups and their spokesmen in the CDU/CSU, Erhard had temporized and given way. Moreover, the government had failed to develop adequate measures to cope with economic recession. The Grand Coalition promised economic sobriety and a consistent policy for economic growth. However, agreement on economic policy has become increasingly difficult to achieve. The summer of 1967 was marked by severe disagreements about intermediate-term financial planning for 1968–71. This controversy, revealing once again the splits within the CDU/CSU, as well as tensions between the coalition partners, had wide implications for the functioning of the Grand Coalition. Moreover, because economic policy is closely related to levels of military expenditures, the disagreements touch upon issues of foreign policy as well.

The issues involved in West German controversy about economic policy were, of course, not peculiar to that country. It is not surprising that there was competition for economic benefits and controversy about distribution of resources. However, the Grand Coalition had based much of the rationale for its existence upon its presumed ability to deal more effectively than previous governments with economic policy, and since the West German economy is notoriously sensitive to psychological forces, governmental ineffectiveness would itself hamper economic recovery.

In early July, Kiesinger postponed a scheduled trip to Washington and proclaimed a "week of truth" for the discussion of economic policy. Finance Minister Strauss emphasized that the effectiveness of the Grand Coalition was at stake. The Cabinet held an exhausting three-day meeting which resulted in few definite decisions and led to the open controversy between Kiesinger and Schroeder. The latter was the major victim of proposed restrictions on spending during the next several years. He replied by a public announcement that, should the budgetary restrictions remain, West Germany would be forced to reduce its armed forces by some 60,000 men. Schroeder's tactics led to a sharp reaction from Washington and to a public controversy with Kiesinger and Strauss on one side and Schroeder on the other. The Chancellor responded by demanding that Schroeder produce an alternative defense policy which would permit cutbacks in troop levels or possibly other defense sectors while maintaining West Germany's military capabilities. This suggestion led to disputes about the composition of the armed forces and the usefulness of its nuclear delivery systems. Moreover, Schroeder consciously stimulated unfavorable reactions from other NATO powers in order to strengthen his hand in the Cabinet. Thus, issues of West Germany's relations with its Western allies were never far in the background. The earlier failure of the Defense Ministry to examine the existing defense establishment thoroughly in the light of changing requirements was clearly related to uncertainties about the future of NATO's strategy.

This controversy indicated difficulties in decision-making within the Grand Coalition. It was not the only indication. While the SPD supported restriction of the military budget and had for some time been advocating re-examination of West Germany's military planning, it had its own internal difficulties because its Cabinet representatives supported tax increases which were opposed outside the Cabinet. The press increasingly compared the Grand Coalition with Erhard's government in its inability to maintain discipline within the Cabinet, in its gingerly attempts to curtail the subvention system, and in its difficulty to reach or adhere to concrete decisions on the coordination of budgetary policy (including tax measures) and government spending to stimulate the economy. In a meeting of the CDU central committee in mid-July, Kiesinger was criticized for indecisiveness in financial planning and for his "unconvincing performance" in the field. At the same time a cascade of robust boos greeted mention of his name at the national meeting of the powerful farmer's organization. A German Trade Union publication charged that "the nightmares of the past are becoming alive again. . . . The Grand Coalition is losing itself in compromises based on no real concepts." Meanwhile, CDU/CSU conservatives attacked the influence of Labor Minister Katzer, of the left-wing of the party, for his largely successful fight against curtailment of welfare expenses, and the SPD for its verbal pronouncements on contacts with East Germany.

Despite these signs of the breakdown of confidence in the Grand Coalition, the government had substantial strength, rooted above all in the lack of alternatives available to the two parties, and in the motives each had to remain in power. The coalition was unlikely to collapse by withdrawal of one of the partners. A coalition of either with the FDP was unlikely because that party was rent by conflict between a conservative business wing and a group of younger reformers who wished the party to follow a more progressive line and who had offered the most daring suggestions on relations with East Germany (including a proposal for eventual recognition) of any faction of any party. Moreover, the FDP's electoral strength was falling, as the most recent state elections had demonstrated. Barring participation by the FDP in a new government, only a minority government or dissolution of the Bundestag, with new elections, was possible if one of the coalition powers were to withdraw. Dissolution is so difficult that the latter possibility was, in any case, extremely doubtful, quite aside from the fact that the major parties were hesitant about an election following a major dispute between them and preceding electoral reform.

Thus, the Grand Coalition derived strength from the unlikelihood that an alternative government could be formed. Moreover, the NPD was beset by quarreling between its two chief leaders, with the former chairman having withdrawn to form his own splinter group. The party secured 6.9 per cent of the vote (4 seats of 100) and 5.8 per cent (4 seats of 73) respectively in elections in Rhineland-Palatinate and Schleswig-Holstein in April, and 7 per cent (10 seats of 149) in Lower Saxony in June. In view of the fragmentation within the group, these results were not unimpressive, but they were considerably below what might have been expected on the basis of the earlier successes in Hesse and Bavaria and the substantial reservoirs of potential right-wing voters in these three states. On the Left, there was considerable unrest, stimulated by opposition to emergency legislation and by the uproar in West Berlin in June 1967, following the killing of a student by West Berlin police. However, the Left was disorganized, and hardly in a position to create a substantial new party.

Thus, speculation about the durability of the Grand Coalition has less point than does discussion of the barriers to its effectiveness and the implications of its mode of operation for Bonn's political system. Whether the Grand Coalition will transform West German political patterns or will be largely a façade behind which the old disagreements and dilemmas are reflected depends largely upon its ability to overcome these barriers.

The Government and the Parties

The first task confronting the government is to secure agreement within the Cabinet; the second to secure agreement of party leaders outside the Cabinet. The first task is achieved more easily than the second, but even here the appearance of agreement may be deceptive. The Cabinet members are under dual pressure: from their particular interest constituencies outside the Cabinet and from their party. During the entire existence of the Bonn Republic, considerations of *Proporz,* or the representation of religious and interest constellations, have played a major role in CDU/CSU

Cabinet composition. This element contributed to the filling of Cabinet posts under the Grand Coalition as well. Kiesinger is a Catholic from the South, Schroeder a Protestant from the North. Katzer represents the labor wing of the party, Minister of the Treasury Kurt Schmücker business groups. Hassell remained in the Cabinet as Minister of Refugee Affairs mainly because he is a Northern Protestant. *Proporz* is not such an important factor in the SPD, but the ministers of that party are scrutinized by trade unions and the Bundestag delegation. The pressures in part inhibit the choice of the most effective leaders for ministerial posts. In addition, they render the ministers indecisive in adhering to Cabinet decisions and encourage them to violate Cabinet discipline.

Moreover, the parties are tempted to reap propaganda rewards at the expense of one another, for while they are partners in the Grand Coalition, they are also potential electoral opponents and both fear a loss of their independent image. The pressure for opposition arises primarily—particularly in the SPD—from the party outside the Cabinet. The experience of the long-standing "black-red" coalition in Austria showed that the partners inside the Cabinet were able to negotiate arrangements among themselves. This tendency, despite the various interests within the Cabinet, was also at work in West Germany. The situation was less harmonious between the Cabinet and party figures outside. For example, Helmut Schmidt, who became leader of the SPD parliamentary party when the Grand Coalition was formed, harbored political ambitions of considerable scope, and he showed increasing interest in establishing a position independent of the Cabinet. In June, a public dispute arose between Wehner and Schmidt. Within the CDU/CSU, Schmücker sought to mobilize support as that party's shadow "Minister of Economics," in opposition to Schiller.

Considerable speculation focused upon the fate of the Bundestag under the Grand Coalition.[23] That body had shifting majorities, the two major parties did not support Cabinet proposals unanimously, and the number of requests by deputies for policy information increased somewhat. Yet it can by no means be demonstrated that Parliament's role in decision-making increased or that its critical function became more meaningful. Initiative lay firmly in the hands of the Cabinet, and insofar as there was even the semblance of a "front" against the Cabinet, it came, not from Parliament as such, but from party politicians outside the Cabinet who happened to have their arena of activity in the Bundestag. Others, however, were active primarily in state governments. Due to the federal system and the strength of the state parties, state political leaders, particularly in the CDU/CSU, have greater influence on actual policy-making in the Cabinet than do Bundestag parliamentarians.

Of necessity, Kiesinger functioned in this Cabinet primarily as a negotiator and moderator. Yet, the greater the extent to which the Grand Coalition confronted large issues, the more he had to assume a leadership role in order to obtain agreement on policy. The more he attempted to do so, the more his position was endangered. Kiesinger's controversy with Schroeder illustrated the difficulty of decision-making in the Cabinet, revealed the continuing splits within the Cabinet, and showed that "Chancellor Democracy," which for many years appeared to be institutionally anchored, is, in fact, greatly dependent upon the party constellation.

Through his election as party chairman and his designation of Bruno Heck, a fellow Württemberger, to the newly created post of general secretary of the CDU, Kiesinger sought to strengthen his independence and win additional weight for leadership in the Cabinet. These moves, together with his alliance with Strauss and the CSU, which was decisive for his selection, gave a decided Southern and Catholic tone to the leadership (Heck and Strauss are also Catholics). Along with Schroeder's continuing ambitions for the Chancellorship and known preference for a coalition between Christian Democrats and Free Democrats in 1966, this was an important ingredient in the controversy on the military budget. An incipient conflict between northern Protestant CDU and southern Catholic CDU and CSU loomed in this controversy. Neither side could afford a complete break, for each depended upon the other, but their disagreement was sufficient to lead to possible stalemates. This possibility was decisive for the functioning of the Grand Coalition. For, as has been seen throughout this discussion, the Grand Coalition was not simply "another government," but an unusual government upon whose success or failure much depended.

At least one other CDU/CSU Cabinet minister was known to

harbor ambitions for the Chancellorship: Franz-Josef Strauss. One could not discount an eventual all-out struggle between Strauss and Schroeder, if Kiesinger became unable to hold the party together on policy questions and became dispensable. Whether such a struggle would be for the leadership of an immediate campaign against the SPD, or for replacement of Kiesinger as leader of the Grand Coalition, depended upon a number of circumstances which could not be predicted reliably. Strauss systematically attempted to win support from SPD leaders, and he would certainly seek to establish his own independence of action in some manner if the difficulties of the Grand Coalition under Kiesinger mounted.

The SPD faced considerable difficulties in seeking electoral advantage from existing or potential disagreements in the CDU/CSU. Though the CDU had failed to overcome its neglect of thorough party organization at local levels, state elections in 1967 brought it gratifying victories. It increased its pluralities in Rhineland-Palatinate and Schleswig-Holstein, and cut the SPD's lead in Lower Saxony. Probably, these results were influenced even more by local or temporary factors than are state elections generally (Adenauer's death, streamlined campaign techniques by the CDU in Rhineland-Palatinate) and they took place before emerging controversies about the budget, yet they increased criticism within the SPD about participation in the Grand Coalition. Fear that the CDU/CSU might benefit from this alliance was reinvigorated. Party leaders were forced to advance the date of the next national convention, and to plan a special meeting of leaders. The tension between Wehner and Schmidt was an expression of the SPD's dilemma. The party hoped to benefit from tensions within the CDU/CSU, but the wish was not equivalent to the fact. Attempts to create or accentuate a split between Kiesinger and other Christian Democratic politicians carried with them the danger of stalemate in the work of the Coalition, with its likely damage to the reputation of the SPD. In terms of electoral calculations, the party confronted the paradox of simultaneously hoping for the success of Kiesinger's Cabinet and hoping for the failure of its leader and its Christian Democratic members.

In this situation, the natural inclination of the SPD leadership, as well as of many other spokesmen of the Grand Coalition, was to emphasize the slow but steady progress of the government, to point to the objective difficulty of policy choices as a ground for slowness, and to perpetuate the alliance, with everyone endeavoring to have major influence in various areas of governmental activity. Yet, this tendency ill comported with the legitimation of the Grand Coalition at its birth—the ability of such a government to make rapid and fundamental decisions which would place the political system on a sounder basis. Moreover, because of the tensions which have been sketched earlier, the stability of the government was always problematical, and the stability of the political system as a whole open to some doubt.[24]

Finally this tendency substituted, for the public confrontation of personalities and issues, struggles and disagreements behind the scenes and confusing and ambiguous personality confrontations in the public arena. In this way, it encouraged the impoverishment of public life, the development of patterns of bureaucratic decision-making, and suspicions about the relevance of "politics" to real life. For it is not the fate of political ambitions or political parties which is of ultimate importance in contemporary political life, but the fate of popular sovereignty, of the modern experiment to combine popular participation with wise and stable government. The fate of this experiment will certainly not be decided in West Germany alone, but it has been the peculiar habit of Germany in modern times to foreshadow, or express in exaggerated form, conditions at work in other lands. The events of 1966 and 1967 in West Germany are, in many ways, instructive indices of central characteristics of contemporary politics.

NOTES

1. The proper translation of the German term *Grosse Koalition* is "Large" or "Big" Coalition, which is without the value overtones of the English expression "Grand Coalition." However, the latter term has become customary and is used in this essay.

2. Cf. Karl Dietrich Bracher, "Wird Bonn doch Weimar?" *Der Spiegel*, XXI, No. 12, March 13, 1967, pp. 60–67.

3. A statement made by Erhard in his declaration of policy following the election of 1965 and the formation of his new Cabinet.

4. The latter has been a major theme of critics in West Germany for years. Cf. also Anatole Shub, "Can Germany Ever Go Left?" *Encounter,* vol. 28, No. 2, Feb. 1967, pp. 27–32.

5. Cf. Eugen Gerstenmaier, *Neuer Nationalismus?* Stuttgart, Deutsche Verlags-Anstalt, 1965.

6. Comment of a Bavarian official during Erhard's speech before the CSU convention in Munich, quoted in Thilo von Uslar, "Strauss—Attack mit Platzpatronen," *Die Zeit,* Oct. 18, 1966.

7. Cf. Werner Kaltefleiter, "Die Grosse Koalition: Verfassungspolitische Aufgaben und Probleme," *Aus Politik und Zeitgeschichte,* (Beilage zur Wochenzeitung "Das Parlament"), XVII, Nos. 18–19, May 10, 1967.

8. E. H. Kunze, "Wer von Subventionen lebt . . ." *Die Zeit,* March 15, 1966.

9. Cf. Kaltefleiter in *Aus Politik und Zeitgeschichte* and Karl Dietrich Bracher, "Germany's Second Democracy—Structures and Problems," in Henry W. Ehrmann, ed., *Democracy in a Changing Society,* New York: Praeger, 1964, pp. 134ff.

10. For a recent review of Bonn's foreign policy, see the October 1966 issue of *Survey,* which is devoted to Germany (No. 61).

11. Bracher in Ehrmann, ed., *Democracy in a Changing World,* p. 137.

12. Richard Loewenthal, "The Germans Feel Like Germans Again," *The New York Times Magazine,* March 3, 1966.

13. Cf. George K. Romoser and Charles R. Foster, "Saftey First—The West German Election," *Bulletin of the Atomic Scientists,* XXI, No. 10, December 1965, pp. 37–39.

14. Rudolf Augstein, "Obstruktion bis zur Erschöpfung," *Der Spiegel,* XX, No. 42, October 10, 1966, p. 25.

15. Cf. Strauss' book *The Grand Design* New York: Praeger, 1965, as well as his article, "An Alliance of Continents," *International Affairs,* XLI, No. 2, April 1965, pp. 191–203.

16. On this subject, see the essay by Pierre Hassner and John Newhouse, "Alliance Politics and Arms Control: Sides of a Coin" in their pamphlet *Diplomacy in the West: Out From Paradox,* New York: 20th Century Fund "Tocqueville Series," May 1966, pp. 1–43. This essay points out that France is the most active West European exporter of aerospace products, and indicates the great importance large powers give to export of arms in their relations with other states.

17. *The New York Times,* February 12, 1967.

18. Bracher in Ehrmann, ed., *Democracy in a Changing World,* p. 134. Cf. also his paper "Chancellor Democracy and the Party State," read at the annual meeting of the American Political Science Association, Washington, September 1965.

19. Kaltefleiter in *Aus Politik und Zeitgeschichte,* pp. 18–19.

20. Werner Kaltefleiter and Vera Gemmecke, "Die NPD und die Ursachen ihrer Erfolge," in Ferdinand A. Hermens, ed. *Verfassung und Verfassungswirklichkeit;* Jahrbuch 1967, Teil I, Cologne: Westdeutscher Verlag, 1967, pp. 23–45. Cf. also: Hans Bachem, Gerhard Elschner and Bernhard Gebauer, *Material zum Problem des politischen Extremismus in der Demokratie,* Bonn: Politische Akademie Eichholz der Konrad-Adenauer Stiftung für politische Bildung und Studien-

förderung, 1967, and Walter Laquer, "Bonn is not Weimar," *Commentary,* vol. 43, No. 3, Mar. 1967, pp. 33–42.

21. Cf. Otto Kirchheimer, "The Waning of Opposition in Parliamentary Regimes," *Social Research,* XXIV, No. 2 (Summer 1957).

22. Cf. Kurt Birrenbach, "Wiedervereinigung—reicht unser Atem?" *Die Zeit,* May 2, 1967.

23. On the Bundestag see the thorough new study by Gerhard Loewenberg, *Parliament in the German Political System,* Ithaca, New York: Cornell University Press, 1966.

24. Cf. the forthcoming book by Erwin K. Scheuch, *Politische Strukturen der Bundesrepublik.*

Change in Soviet Policies after Khrushchev's Fall

by John A. Armstrong

I

MOST CONTEMPORARY STUDIES IN POLITICAL SCIENCE BEGIN WITH *process*—the way in which the political system operates and the social forces which are involved in it. Frequently, only after an investigation of these basic features does one proceed to examine *policy*. In studying the political system of the Soviet Union there are two major advantages in reversing this approach. The first arises from the difficulty of direct examination of process in the Soviet system. With rare exceptions the U.S.S.R. is closed to outsiders employing such refined research techniques as participant-observation, survey research, and depth interviews. At the same time, the Soviet elite consistently endeavors to conceal basic features of the political decision-making process. What information Soviet sources do provide on this process relates either to the purely formal aspects or to extraordinary conflict within the elite. Even in the latter case information is often presented years after the conflict has been decided, and represents only the "truth of the victors." In contrast to the preceding decade, the years 1966–68 have witnessed few revelations even of this limited nature. Policy pronouncements or actions from which policy may be inferred have, on the other hand, been numerous.

A second reason for beginning a study of Soviet politics by examining policy is the exceptionally inclusive nature of Soviet politics as compared to other sub-systems of Soviet society. In the major Western European and North American states which we commonly call "pluralist," centralized decision-making (by governmental and para-governmental bodies) does impinge on most aspects of the social system. Nevertheless, in practice as well as in theory, thousands of decisions which have an enormous cumulative impact on the entire society are made by autonomous bodies. Probably even more important, these autonomous bodies very frequently do not make decisions in accordance with an overall concept of the nature and direction of the social process. Each pluralist society contains, as a rule, several value systems. Moreover, most of the value systems present in a pluralist society explicitly reject comprehensive decision-making by a single center.

As an "ideal type" the Soviet political system is almost the opposite of the pluralist system, even though (as we shall see later) the difference is not so great in practice. Only one ideology, Marxism-Leninism, is officially recognized. This ideology purports to: (1) provide an understanding of the nature and direction of the entire social process; (2) prescribe the ultimate goals of policy-making within this social process; (3) prescribe certain basic strategies for attaining these goals; (4) designate a single institution for making authoritative decisions for all aspects of the social system. All specific policy decisions are referred to (2) and (3), i.e., are ostensibly designed to achieve the prescribed goals in accordance with the sanctioned means. Since, however, ideology only prescribes a limited framework of basic means, actual policy decisions reflect (in accordance with the formula of "the unity of theory and practice") the interaction of these prescriptions with the external social environment.

Marxism-Leninism defines the single decision-making body as the Communist Party, and denounces all efforts to formulate competing positions within the Party as "factionalism." Consequently, all "within-puts" by segments of the bureaucratic elite participating in the decision-making process must be formulated in terms of universal societal interest (as defined by the ideology) rather than particular group interest. If, however, we make the assumption that all political systems contain groups with differing interests, we can expect that at least some of the policies advanced as furthering the universal interest will in fact advance particular interests. Inferences concerning these particular interests may be obtained by examining the social characteristics of elite groups, but first one must identify the policy changes which the groups have affected.

Obviously, this approach depends heavily on inference rather than demonstration. Nearly always, alternative inferences may be made from the same set of circumstances associated with a given policy. When, however, numerous related policies can be examined the method becomes somewhat surer: if all can be inferred to point in the same direction in terms of group interests, the probability of correct inference is heightened. Because of the special nature of the choices confronting the Soviet elite since 1964, a wide range of seemingly related policy changes has been made. In the following pages we shall examine the most important of these to see whether one can infer (1) a common direction in the changes; and (2) an elite group interest behind them. While we can hardly hope to attain certain results, the exercise may help us obtain a coherent view of the Soviet system.[1]

II

In November 1961, the Twenty-Second Congress of the Communist Party of the Soviet Union adopted its first new program in forty-two years. In many respects the 1961 Program was simply a reiteration of the teachings of the "classics" of Communism—Marx, Engels, and Lenin. The basic goal—the attainment of world-wide Communism—was reaffirmed, though Lenin's teaching on the inevitability of war was sharply modified. The fundamental aspects of the full Communist society envisaged by the Program did not differ from the prescriptions of the classics: A classless society in which antagonistic group interests would be eliminated; the development of a new human personality experiencing co-operative work as a natural imperative; an economy of abundance in which "from each according to his ability, to each according to his needs" would be attainable. Also, the Program reiterated basic means by which such a society will be attained. The fundamental means for eliminating class antagonism (after revolutionary seizure of power by the proletariat) is still the "socialization" of all means of production. In order to carry out this process, a powerful state—the "dictatorship of the proletariat"—is needed for a time. As in the U.S.S.R. by 1961, this state will become the "state of the entire toiling population" after an initial period of repressing hostile elements and socializing basic production. The state will also have a highly significant educational function in preparing the "new man" of Communist society. Further (though this question lies outside the scope of our study), the state will have an even longer-range task of defending the socialist society against remaining imperialist states and helping the world-wide spread of Communism. But eventually the state as a coercive organization will disappear. In contrast to Marxist-Leninist classics, however, the Program and associated writings implied that the Communist Party is eternal.

The fundamental difference between the Program and the Marxist-Leninist classics was that the former set a timetable for achieving the goal of Communism. The final, emphatic words of the Program were *"The Party solemnly proclaims: the present generation of Soviet people will live under Communism!"* The term "generation" is not precise, but it certainly implies that complete Communism will be attained not later than the year 2000. The operational aspects of the Program were placed in 20-year perspective, i.e., the period through 1980. In that time span the "material and technical base of Communism" will be created and a "Communist society will be built in the main in the U.S.S.R.," though completion of the construction of this society will take place subsequently.

This solemn proclamation of a timetable for achieving Communism undoubtedly reflected a basic policy decision. As will appear in subsequent sections, the proclamation not only committed the prestige of the Soviet regime, but implied a whole series of related policies. We do not know how the basic policy decision was made, but it was proclaimed at a time when Khrushchev seemed to be at the height of his power; the Program seemed to be in line with numerous previous policies which he had personally introduced; and he committed his personal prestige to the Program by constantly emphasizing it in his public speeches. Throughout the remaining period of Khrushchev's ascendancy (November 1961–October 1964) the 1961 Party Program received enormous publicity as the charter for "building Communism." It served as a principal text for study groups in the Party and its auxiliary organizations like the Communist Youth Organization (Komsomol). Very soon after Khrushchev's ouster in

October 1964, the 1961 Program ceased to receive major attention in the Soviet press. In April 1966 the Twenty-Third Party Congress (the first after 1961) met. In their enormously lengthy speeches the delegates mentioned the 1961 Program *only 15 times*.[2] Instead, there was a tendency to refer to the decisions of the 1966 Congress as the "program for building Communism," though these decisions were not formally labeled a "Party program." The decisive difference is that the 1966 decisions, in contrast to the 1961 Program, did not set a timetable for achieving Communism.

Subsequent commentaries indicated that "the period of the evolution of socialism into communism will no doubt take a rather long time," and referred to a required growth of production "in the course of the next few decades." [3] In 1967, the Party General Secretary, L. I. Brezhnev, stated that the "years of our country's second half century will also be marked by new accomplishments." Evidently he was quite unwilling to forecast the ultimate attainment of a Communist society even by the year 2017. But Brezhnev insisted that the 1961 Program would eventually be achieved.

By 1968 it was becoming increasingly apparent that Khrushchev's optimistic timetable had been based on gross miscalculations. Part of these miscalculations concerned the domestic economy. The 1961 Program boasted unequivocally that "in the current decade (1961–1970), the Soviet Union, in creating the material and technical basis of Communism, will surpass the strongest and richest capitalist country, the U.S.A., in production per head of population, the people's standard of living and their cultural and technical standards will improve substantially, everyone will live in easy circumstances . . ." Even before Khrushchev's ouster these boasts sounded hollow; by 1968, with most the decade gone, they were patently absurd. Soviet industrial production continued to increase substantially, but the rate of increase slowed, while the American rate of industrial growth rose rapidly beginning in the early 1960's. Soviet agricultural production in the period 1962–65 suffered a real setback, causing (especially in 1963) significant scarcities in many foodstuffs. As a result (the matter is treated in section IV below) the regime's basic attitude toward stimulation of economic growth urgently required revision. Even more serious threats to confidence in rapidly achieving Communism were Soviet setbacks in the international field. At the Twenty-Second Congress Khrushchev held up "the shining image of a party which is marching forward victoriously throughout the entire world." A good part of this glow had derived from the spread of red over the world map as Communist regimes were established in Asia and Eastern Europe. The split with Chinese Communism, already looming in 1961, became increasingly bitter in the succeeding years. As a result, the existence of Communist regimes no longer seemed to be a guarantee of cooperative progress toward a Communist world. Equally important, probably, was the Soviet regime's recognition that major capitalist countries (particularly the United States) would remain as obstacles to the spread of Communism for a very long period. Instead of Khrushchev's optimistic image, by 1967 Soviet writers were envisaging generations during which the "petty bourgeois" West would adversely influence the psychology of Soviet people.

III

A New Man

A basic element of the 1961 Party Program was the transition from conformity based on state coercion to conformity arising from social pressure. The ultimate "Communist society will be a highly organized community of working men [in which] universally recognized rules of Communist conduct will be established whose observance will become an organic need and habit with everyone." In the transitional decades, "comradely censure of anti-social behavior will gradually become the principal means of doing away with manifestations of bourgeois views, customs and habits. The power of example in public affairs and in private life, in the performance of one's public duty, acquires tremendous educational significance." In other words, the "new man," who has always been an ultimate goal of Marxism-Leninism, will be developed. At no time, however, did the Soviet leaders envisage a purely spontaneous approach to securing conformity. Even under complete Communism, the Party would remain as a guiding organization, and in the meantime it directed a whole complex of social pressures.

The most obvious of these pressures were designed to prevent the infiltration of bourgeois views from outside the U.S.S.R. and to suppress organized ideological opposition inside the country. Significantly, in these areas the role of coercion did not slacken after the 1961 Program was proclaimed, nor has abandoning the Program led to demonstrable relaxation.

Religion

The only organized ideological opposition which the regime tolerates even nominally is religion. Like all preceding Marxist-Leninist statements, the 1961 Program stressed the importance of "overcoming religious prejudices" by persuasion: "It is necessary to explain patiently the untenability of religious beliefs . . . this can be done by making use of the achievements of modern science . . . leaving no room for religious inventions about supernatural forces." In practice, Soviet policy toward religious groups has varied from praise of "patriotic" stands by churchmen to violent persecution of religious bodies which explicitly opposed the regime's measures. In the late 1950's pressure on all religious organizations sharply increased, apparently because the Khrushchev regime believed that religion offered a potentially dangerous ideological alternative to Communism, but that for the time being convinced supporters of religion were too few to offer serious resistance. All religious bodies were harassed by severe limitations on printing of religious items, impediments to recruitment and training of clergy, and closure—on various pretexts—of houses of worship. Evidently the regime was particularly concerned with those churches which made strenuous efforts to provide religious training for the young. These included various sects, such as offshoots of the main Baptist Church, Jehovah's Witnesses, and Pentecostalists. Shortly before the Twenty-Second Congress a Pentecostalist elder was sentenced to five years' imprisonment for "forcible conversion" of his own ten-year-old daughter and other children. Two years later a Soviet publication wrote approvingly that a young man who had abandoned the Baptist Church planned to remove his younger brothers and sisters from his religious parents' home. In 1962 S. P. Pavlov, the head of the Communist Youth League, told its national congress:

It must be an object of our special concern to protect children from the influence of believing parents and relatives. The freedom of conscience that is set down in the Constitution applies to adult citizens who can answer for their actions. But we must not allow anyone to cripple a child spiritually, to do violence to his immature mind.[4]

It is not clear whether any real moderation of Soviet antireligious policies has occurred. A year after Khrushchev's fall an *Izvestia* article, referring to religious instruction for children, asserted that "no one has the right to impose on others and disseminate personally-held erroneous views hostile to the public consciousness." Severe sentences were given to those spreading religious literature. On the other hand, the chairman of the Supreme Court's Criminal Collegium cautioned against convicting persons merely for belonging to religious sects and disseminating their views, and noted that in 1964 there had been only one-third as many convictions for illegal acts "under the guise of performing religious rites" as in 1962. Even more significantly, he appeared to contradict the "activist" principle of removing children from religious influence by writing that relatives were entitled to raise them in a religious spirit. As will appear later, however, what is legally "correct" may not always reflect practice. In 1967, in an unprecedented group protest, priests of the numerically predominant Orthodox Church alleged that the hierarchy remained subservient while the regime quietly closed hundreds of churches.

Nationalism

In contrast to religion, nationalist organizations have never been accorded even minimal legal toleration. Indeed, suspicion of "bourgeois nationalism" is one reason for Soviet attack on minority religious bodies. There has been no change in the absolute prohibition of the Ukrainian Catholic Church, which was intimately related to nationalism in the West Ukraine. An important ground for the especially harsh restrictions on Judaism has been its alleged connection with Zionism and the state of Israel. In the post-Khrushchev years there has been no let-up on the rigorous press attacks on Zionism. For a time, however, the new Soviet leadership seemed to recognize that earlier statements directed against the Jewish religion and Zionism had verged upon racist anti-Semitism. In September 1965 a *Pravda* editorial quoted Lenin's demand for an "unceasing struggle against anti-Semitism," though the context stressed his opposition to all nationalism. There is some slight evidence that (at least until the Soviet stand against Israel's policy in the summer of 1967) younger Jews in large cities have dared to express their feeling of solidarity during religious holiday periods.

Undoubtedly, the Soviet regime regards nationalism as its most dangerous domestic ideological enemy: "of all the vestiges of the past the nationalist ones are the most tenacious." However, emphasis on the nationalist danger probably is due to the peculiar composition of the Soviet Union rather than to theoretical opposition of Marxist-Leninist ideology to nationalism. In an age when the nation-state, regardless of its dominant ideology, is the typical political unit, the U.S.S.R. is an anomaly. Apart from scores of tiny ethnic groups, it includes some twenty large and well-defined nationalities. From the purely formal standpoint these nationalities constitute a federal union, but Marxism-Leninism demands complete centralization of decision-making. In practice, therefore, the distinct ethnic groups have less independence than municipalities in most pluralist systems.

Two alternative Soviet policies on the nationality question appear possible. One is to stress the ideological basis of the Soviet Union as the "fortress of world revolution," the base and model of the universal Communist system of the future. In line with Khrushchev's optimistic forecast of world Communist victory, the 1961 Program emphasized this alternative: "For the first time there emerged in the international arena a state which put forward the great slogan of peace and began carrying through new principles in relations between peoples and countries. . . . the union and consolidation of equal peoples on a voluntary basis in a single multi-national state." If all Soviet ethnic elements (and particularly the more mobile, ambitious strata) could be persuaded that they were privileged to participate in the proximate attainment of the millennial goals of Communism, national differences could be relegated to an insignificant level. Nevertheless, the 1961 Program did not entirely renounce the second alternative: creation of a unified nation-state. The Program did abandon the extreme suggestion (advanced in Stalin's later years) that the Russian language and culture were so superior that they would ultimately prevail in a Communist world. Nevertheless, the preeminent position of the Russians within the evolving Communist society of the U.S.S.R. was asserted. All Soviet citizens were urged to master the Russian language and all efforts of other ethnic groups to hold aloof from Russian cultural influence were denounced. The preeminence accorded Russian continued unchanged in the following years, for reasons which are clearly revealed in an article published in the Ukraine in late 1965:

The functions of a common language of inter-national contact under conditions of Soviet reality could not be successfully fulfilled by any other language except Russian. This role of the Russian language is caused by many social-historical factors, among which we wish to note the following: Russian is the native language of more than one-half of the population of the USSR; Ukrainians and Belorussians, who constitute nearly one-quarter of the population of the USSR, as a rule know the Russian language, which is closely associated with Ukrainian and Belorussian; a considerable part of the non-Russian population of our country knew Russian even before the October Revolution. Now it has become the second language of the intelligentsia of all non-Russians . . . Thus, more than three-fourths of the population of the USSR practically know Russian one way or another. The prominent and leading role of the Russian people in the overthrow of tsarism and liquidation of oppression by tsarist and local "native" oppressors, the fraternal help of the Russian people in the political, economic and cultural development of the national republics, also to a considerable extent contributed to the Russian language fulfilling the function of inter-national contacts among the nations of the USSR. Finally, historical tradition was of considerable importance in determining the Russian language as the language of inter-national contact, the role played by Russian culture and science in the history of the development of the cultures of nations of the USSR.[5]

Although there has been no change in the primacy accorded Russians, implementation of the policy has encountered serious difficulties. One of Khrushchev's most significant policy innovations was enhancement of the position of the Ukrainians and Belorussians, which (together with the Russians) comprise the closely related East Slav ethnic group. Though he was careful to stress his own Russian nationality, Khrushchev had been associated with Ukrainian affairs for many years. He placed many members of the Ukrainian apparatus in high all-Union posts; while not all of these were ethnic Ukrainians, their promotion provided some symbolic satisfaction for Ukrainians. Throughout Khrushchev's period of ascendancy Party membership of Ukrainians and Belorussians rose steeply, both absolutely and relatively. Recent data on Party nationality composition is meager, but the policy of symbolic concessions to Ukrainian and Belorussian national pride has definitely continued since Khrushchev's ouster. While N. V. Podgorny, former head of the Ukrainian Party apparatus, apparently failed to secure a commanding position in the elite, he was made Chairman of the Supreme Soviet Presidium. Thus, he was the first ethnic Ukrainian to become titular head of the Soviet state. However, while Leonid Brezhnev (a Russian) had a long association with the Ukrainian apparatus, the number of ethnic Ukrainians in key posts like the directorship of the police and the head of the cadres section has declined since 1964. More significant are the numerous indications of Ukrainian dissatisfaction (Belorussian concern is not evident) with the role of "younger brother" in the East Slav family. Even during Khrushchev's final years of power, Ukrainian writers publicly objected to the intrusion of Russian locutions in their language, and complained of the low proportion of Ukrainian-language publications. A few Ukrainian literary figures established contacts with anti-Soviet émigré circles; more, secretly circulated writings critical of Soviet nationality policy. In the late summer of 1965 the post-Khrushchev leadership arrested over a hundred Ukrainians—mostly intellectuals. While the arrests were concentrated in the Western Ukrainian territories acquired during 1939–45, and much more nationalist than the East Ukraine, a number were seized in the capital, Kiev. Many, including several prominent writers, were freed after long interrogation, a considerable number (reports suggest about 20) were sentenced to long terms of banishment and imprisonment for "spreading anti-Soviet propaganda." [6]

Even if educated Ukrainians are not convinced anti-Communists, they may wonder why they should be incorporated in a strictly centralized Soviet system unless this system is necessary for proximate achievement of the millennial goals of Communism. In abandoning the timetable for achieving Communism, and in de-emphasizing its spread throughout the world, the post-Khrushchev leadership has weakened its claim to the *ideological* allegiance of Ukrainians. Even if the regime could secure their allegiance on purely nationalist grounds, as members of the Russified East Slav group, it would encounter equal difficulties in a different direction. Russians comprise nearly 55 per cent of the Soviet population, Ukrainians 18 per cent, and Belorussians 4 per cent. Together, therefore, the East Slavs have an overwhelming majority. Ethnic groups of utterly different background occupy highly strategic areas of the Soviet Union, however. This is especially true of the large minorities of Moslem background (mostly speaking Turkic languages) predominant in huge frontier areas of the Caucasus and Central Asia. With some 26 million members (and a disproportionately high birthrate) these nationalities are numerically important and culturally cohesive. In religious, linguistic, and cultural characteristics they closely resemble the peoples of the neighboring independent states of Turkey, Iran, and Afghanistan. Yet the territories of the Soviet nations of Moslem background have been heavily infiltrated by Slavic colonists, who hold a large proportion of the key political and economic positions. In many respects, therefore, these Soviet territories resemble European colonies—which in other parts of Asia have disappeared before the tide of nationalism. So far the position of the Soviet regime has been to boast of the economic progress attained in these Moslem territories; the lack of ethnic discrimination; and the model these areas provide for future Communist societies in developing countries. Once again, the Soviet claim is necessarily based on asserting that the USSR is the base for establishing world Communism. Undoubtedly this consideration—and pragmatic concern over the spread of liberalization from Czechoslovakia to the USSR—led the Soviet regime to flout world opinion by invading Czechoslovakia in August 1968.

The situation is further complicated by Soviet determination to take advantage of the differentiated functional utilities of the various nationalities. Thus, while the regime encourages urbanization and industrialization in all parts of the USSR, a recent Soviet analysis points out that equal urbanization of all union republics is undesirable. Some (Central Asia is mentioned specifically) must continue to specialize in agriculture. Though the analyst denies that rural conditions necessarily imply lesser opportunities for advancement, all experience in the USSR (and elsewhere) demonstrates that a predominantly rural ethnic group does not get its share of elite positions, that the relative life-chances of its members are lower than among urban ethnic groups. In the East European Communist bloc, concern with being relegated to a "colonial" supplier of agricultural products and raw materials has been a major force behind the unwillingness of even the Rumanian Communist leadership to follow Soviet directives. If the Soviet regime continues to impose "specialization" of this nature upon the non-Russian elements of the USSR population, a similar reaction from the growingly self-conscious minorities may be anticipated. In the last three years, therefore, one can conclude that fundamental continuity in an ambivalent nationality policy has merely increased Soviet difficulties.

Intellectuals

As in other parts of the world, intellectuals are the carriers of national disaffection in the USSR. But the Soviet regime's problem with intellectuals is not confined to minorities. Russian intellectuals also exhibit numerous signs of dissatisfaction. The problem is intensified by the fact that the Soviet system has never been content with negative devices for preventing expression of disaffection, but has regarded positive loyalty by intellectuals as a cornerstone of the indoctrination process. As the 1961 Program put it, the writer's duty is "faithful and highly artistic depiction of the richness and versatility of socialist reality, inspired and vivid portrayal of all that is new and genuinely Communist, and exposure of all that hinders the progress of society." Khrushchev evidently hoped to secure intellectual conformity by relaxing the rigid, arbitrary controls imposed by Stalin while maintaining more subtle sanctions. For example, Boris Pasternak was denounced for sending *Dr. Zhivago* (a novel questioning the basic worth of the Revolution) abroad for publication. But he was not imprisoned or even forbidden to go to Sweden to receive the Nobel Prize in literature, though he was warned (effectively) that, if he did, his manifest lack of patriotism would prevent his returning to the USSR. After his death, however, the woman who was his close collaborator was quietly sentenced for currency violations. In this way, the regime maintained a pose of aloof contempt for its intellectual opponents, while hinting at harsher sanctions. In more than a dozen cases, a more sinister tactic was employed: writers like Valery Tarsis who circulated strong (and apocalyptic) denunciations of the

Soviet system were adjudged insane. Quite possibly the regime was experimenting with the possibility of declaring that, as the new Communist personality developed, all overt deviation would be classed as mental incompetence.

In some instances (notably that of Iosif Brodsky) dissident intellectuals were punished through application of the "anti-parasite" legislation enacted in 1958 and later. Generally, however, this legislation was designed not to secure intellectual conformity as much as to enforce standards of orderliness and industriousness needed for the transition to Communism. Eventually, the 1961 Program asserted, "labor for the good of society will become the prime and vital requirement of everyone, a necessity recognized by one and all . . . high standards of organization, precision, and discipline . . . are insured not by compulsion, but thanks to an understanding of public duty, and are determined by the whole tenor of life in Communist society." But this goal (which has remained unchanged since Marx's time) could, the Program continued, be achieved only by instilling in the people "conscious discipline and a Communist attitude toward labor" in the transitional period. The practical necessity of disciplinary measures had been equally apparent to Stalin, who used harsh compulsion. Khrushchev hoped to replace these sharply resented legal and police procedures by social pressures guided by the Communist Party. The general policy was stated in the 1961 Program: "As socialist democracy develops, the organs of state power will gradually be transformed into organs of public self-government. . . . Comradely censure of anti-social behavior will gradually become the principal means of doing away with manifestations of bourgeois views, customs, and habits." Some measures, which the Program described as implementations of this policy, were already in effect. One was the establishment of Komsomol patrols authorized to discipline youths behaving in a rowdy or offensive manner in public. This elastic disciplinary authority resulted in such abuses as stripping a "loud" sport shirt from a vacationer. "Comrades courts" had equally vague authority; they were set up in places of work to insure discipline, as well as in apartment houses to guard against slovenliness and rowdy behavior. In the spring of 1964, a letter to *Izvestia* asked that comrades courts even punish persons who told anti-Soviet jokes. As extra-judicial tribunals nominally constituted by neighbors or fellow-workers of the delinquents, the comrades courts epitomized the policy of utilizing social pressure in place of legal coercion. Their powers were restricted, however, to imposition of reprimands and small fines. Much more serious, potentially, were the "working peoples collectives" at places of employment; in 1961 they were empowered to deport "parasites" to Siberia or other designated areas for up to five years. Neither the comrades courts nor the working peoples collectives were bound by legal procedure; members served as accusers and judges, though they had no special legal training. Behind both types of tribunal stood, of course, the local Party organization, which could use them for exposure and summary punishment of those it felt impeded the movement toward Communism.

It now appears clear that even in Khrushchev's time the comrades courts were not very effective. They tended to be regarded as neighborhood scolds rather than as serious curbs on delinquents. The working peoples collectives rarely met to deport "parasites." The parasite sanctions were rigorously and frequently invoked, however, by the alternative method envisaged by the 1961 decree: summary trial in the lowest echelon of the regular court system. In these trials the formalities of Soviet criminal proceedings (already lax by Western standards) were minimized. "Public accusers" (presumably sent by the Party) entirely unacquainted with the defendant, denounced his behavior on the basis of hearsay. Sometimes proceedings resulting in years of banishment lasted only a few minutes. Once the accused was convicted of parasitism he was turned over to the police (who had often instigated the proceedings in the first place) for transportation to the designated area. On his arrival there, the local police kept the deportee under a kind of parole supervision to see that he worked diligently at his assigned job. If he did not, he was confined in a regular "corrective labor camp." Obviously the role of state agencies in social and labor discipline enforcement was dominant. But the official emphasis on instruments of social conformity provided superficial evidence of the diminution of state coercion as Soviet society moved toward Communism.

While the evidence is not entirely satisfactory, it seems safe to hypothesize that the social conformity measures proved inadequate on three counts. The lack of formal safeguards for the defendant ran counter to the emphasis on "socialist legality." From 1953–57 (i.e., prior to Khrushchev's defeat of his rivals) legal reforms had played a major part in reversing Stalin's arbitrary police regime. When, in 1958, deportation by workers collectives was first introduced (in Central Asia), prominent jurists publicly complained that the lack of formal safeguards for the accused violated socialist legality. Partly, no doubt, as a result of these protests, the deportation procedure was not introduced into the larger Russian Republic for three years. A second, possibly more important, reason for continuing to utilize the courts and the police was the weight of bureaucratic inertia, which found the old arrangements (somewhat modified to permit speedier and more arbitrary judgments) more comfortable. A third reason why social conformity measures were inadequate was the strong tendency of Soviet citizens to sympathize with the "parasites" and literary dissenters or at least not to join the regime in prosecuting them.

Having abandoned the timetable for achieving Communism, and lacking a personal stake in asserting the diminution of state action, Khrushchev's successors were in a position to take positive steps to recognize the dominant role of state coercion. In the last years of Khrushchev's ascendancy and for some months after his fall, considerable attention was devoted to drafting a new Soviet constitution; but in the last two years this project has received very little attention. Instead, the importance of the "state of the entire people" has been emphasized. The Soviets (legislative bodies) are hailed as "the most inclusive of all public organizations," but the 1961 Program's dichotomy between "organs of public self-government" and the state is negated by noting that the Soviets are "simultaneously agents of state power." Moreover, the coercive power of the state is set forth in detail:

Coercion by the state comes into force only when manifestations of bourgeois ideology, remnants of private-property mentality and morality or prejudices become the basis of anti-social actions and lead individuals into conflict with the norms and laws of socialist society. . . .

The socialist state plays a great role in strengthening Communist discipline and inculcating a highly conscious attitude toward labor for the good of society. . . . The safeguarding of public order is an important type of activity by the Soviet state promoting the education of the people in the spirit of Communist discipline and organization. . . .

The construction of Communism is the creation of its material and technical base and at the same time the development of social relations, the growth of social relations into Communist relations. This presupposes the upbringing of people in accordance with the special features and principles of a Communist society, the molding of a new man possessing a high level of consciousness and comprehensive spiritual culture. Only when this process has been completed will the need for regulation by state and law and, consequently, the state itself wither away. But there is only one path to this—the all-round use of the socialist state for construction of the economy and culture, for comprehensive development and Communist upbringing of every toiler in the socialist society.[7]

A generally more pessimistic note has appeared in Soviet discussions of human behavior. As noted earlier, fears are expressed that "bourgeois" influences from the capitalist countries will affect Soviet citizens for generations to come. Another article quotes Lenin on the persistence of "excesses by *individuals*" even after crime "as a social phenomenon" has disappeared in the Communist society.

Theoretical recognition of the state's coercive functions has been matched by practical implementations. In September 1965, the 1961 anti-parasite decree was substantially modified. The scope of deportations was somewhat restricted geographically, but the main change was elimination of all reference to "working peoples collectives." Instead, the local Soviets (along with the lower courts) were given exclusive power of deportation. Thus two types of state agencies replaced the earlier "organs of public self-government." The restoration of overt state coercion in dealing with intellectual dissent is even more significant. The new Soviet legal codes adopted in 1960, like their predecessors, make "agitation or propaganda carried on for the purpose of subverting or weakening Soviet authority," including circulating literature, a felony. Occasional hints that this provision might be invoked appeared in the Soviet press during Khrushchev's ascendancy. For example, in 1961, *Izvestia* denounced a United States Information Agency handbook on how to answer Soviet citizens' questions as "criminal activity." The following year the magazine *Nedelya* noted that the police had formal grounds for bringing a young man who had written "subversive poems" to trial. In practice, however, the Russian Republic criminal code Article 70 on anti-Soviet propaganda seems to have been invoked rarely if ever in Khrushchev's time. In August 1965, however, a British school-teacher was convicted under this Article alone for distributing émigré publications. The following spring the far more sensational case of the prominent Soviet writers, Andrei Sinyavsky and Yuli Daniel, hinged entirely on Article 70. Like Pasternak they had sent their writings (which could be interpreted as fundamentally critical of the Soviet system) abroad for publication. In contrast to the extra-legal pressure used in Pasternak's case, the Soviet regime brought Sinyavsky and Daniel to formal, public trial, and sentenced them to several years' imprisonment. Dozens of students and writers were imprisoned for protests related to this trial. During 1967–68 several lesser literary figures were tried on similar charges, but the ominous accusation of links to anti-Soviet emigre organizations was added. Writers who protested against these in-fringements on literary freedom were fiercely attacked in the Soviet press, which refused to publish their works.

The use of legal provisions to stifle dissent is as ancient as the history of authoritarian systems. Except in ambiguous statements designed for foreign consumption, the Soviet regime has never pretended to respect unqualified freedom of expression. To a num-ber of Western legal observers, Soviet resort to formal legal pro-cedure in the Sinyavsky-Daniel case seemed at least a minimal recognition of the concept *nulla poena sine lege*—no penalty without a prior legal provision. Even the obviously biased atmos-phere of the Soviet court seemed preferable to the unstructured and potentially arbitrary proceedings of a working peoples col-lective. But the regime also continues to apply harsh censorship and to hold closed meetings where dissenters are slandered as well as denounced.

To Soviet intellectuals, the open use of extreme penalties for verbal dissent was horrifying. An impressive instance of this effect was Svetlana Alliluyeva Stalina's reference to the trial as a major element in her decision to leave the USSR. Shortly after her self-imposed exile became known, the fourth Congress of the Union of Soviet Writers convened. Outwardly it was harmonious, but only because many outstanding writers were not admitted or voluntarily absented themselves. Soon after the Congress adjourned, a letter which the leading writer, Aleksandr Solzhenitsyn, had addressed to it, was published abroad:

Our writers are not supposed to have the right, they are not endowed with the right, to express their anticipatory judgments about the moral life of man and society, or to explain in their own way the social problems or the historical experience that has been so deeply felt in our country. . . . Even the simple act of giving a manuscript away for "reading and copying" has now become a criminal act, and the ancient Russian scribes were permitted to do that.[8]

Solzhenitsyn's appeal was especially poignant because his 1962 novel, *One Day in the Life of Ivan Denisovich,* had drawn on his personal experience to portray graphically the brutal repression of Stalin's era. Intellectuals had hoped that accounts like Solzhenitsyn's would serve as object lessons preventing a return to Stalin's tactics. After Khrushchev's fall, however, the official press again mentioned Stalin favorably, though with reserve. According to a survey by a perceptive literary critic, "despondency [is] displayed by members of the post-war generation who, having dreamed in 1962 of a breakthrough toward freedom of expression, now find themselves confronted once again with reactionary barriers." [9]

There seems little doubt that the intellectuals misgauged the nature of Khrushchev's toleration of anti-Stalinism. Since his principal rivals in the "anti-Party" group were more implicated in Stalin's crimes than he was, Khrushchev derived an initial political advantage from denouncing Stalinist repression. Later, he probably calculated that vivid literary descriptions of the Stalin period would make his own quasi-dictatorship look better by contrast. Indeed, one can speculate that the drastic alteration in methods for attaining Communism provided by the 1961 Program was deliberately designed as a contrast to Stalin's emphasis on state coercion.

One further intellectual trend in the post-1964 period should be noted: the revived emphasis on the continuity of the Russian cultural heritage. Such a trend was also apparent in Stalin's later years, when it apparently resulted from his fear of violent change. Today Soviet writers emphasize Russian culture as a reaction to Chinese writers' denigration of all pre-Communist culture. Here,

as in other recent Soviet developments, a conservative trend is reinforced by aversion to Chinese radicalism.

IV

While Soviet leaders have devoted enormous attention to educational and coercive measures for adapting human personality
to the requirements of Communism, they have never abandoned the
basic Marxist-Leninist tenet that this adaptation depends on the
relationships of production. The "new man" cannot be created
until an economy of abundance eliminates the attachment to rewards, with voluntary restraint in material demands developing
simultaneously with the confidence that all real requirements will
be freely satisfied.

Under Communism all people will have equal status in society, will
stand in the same relation to the means of production, will enjoy equal
conditions of work and distribution, and will actively participate in the
management of public affairs. . . . [In 1971–1980] the material and
technical basis of Communism will be created and there will be an
abundance of material and cultural benefits for the whole population,
Soviet society will come close to a stage where it can introduce the
principle of distribution according to needs . . .

The 1961 Program balanced this optimistic prediction with the
caution that

Communist construction must be based upon the principle of material
incentive. In the coming twenty years payment according to one's work
will remain the principal source for satisfying the material needs of
the working people.

Nevertheless, the Program called for starting immediately toward
the goal of social and economic equality. "The disparity between
high and comparatively low incomes must gradually shrink" it
said, and in fact economic analyses show that between 1961 and
1964 modest reductions were made in the high pay differentials
in Soviet industry. Perhaps more significant were the steps proposed for gradually eliminating incentives themselves. "As the
country advances toward Communism, personal needs will be
increasingly met out of public consumption funds, whose rate of
growth will exceed the rate of growth of payments for labor."

By 1980, the Program continued, the following benefits would be freely available to all: municipal transportation, water, gas, heat, housing, vacations, midday meals, children's boarding schools, disability care, medical services and medicine.

By 1966, a different emphasis appeared in the Soviet press. While it asserted that gradual steps were being taken to reduce income differentials, it harshly criticized the "principle of leveling, since it reflects petty-bourgeois attitudes and operates against the interests of the working people." Probably more important was the revised attitude toward public consumption funds. Noting, surprisingly, that 70 per cent of all payments and benefits from these funds are already related to earnings, an economist pointed out that suggestions for increasing this proportion, thus enhancing the incentive impact of public funds, should be considered. Apparently the implication is that "public consumption" items like social security benefits should be geared to a worker's achievement rather than his needs. Equally surprising is the simultaneous emphasis placed on pay-as-you-go medical care, for one of the sharpest Soviet criticisms against capitalism has been its money basis for care of the sick. A physician wrote in *Literaturnaya Gazeta* that

We need not fear the word "fees." There are polyclinics that charge fees; out of embarrassment we call them economic-accountability clinics. These polyclinics are extremely popular, partly because here a person can choose his doctor . . .[10]

The writer went on to propose fee-charging nursing homes for the dependent elderly. Obviously, paid medical treatment had existed in Khrushchev's time; but its public recognition reflects a new attitude toward incentives.

The change has been even more sweeping in the housing field. The 1961 Program promised eventual elimination of rent; for decades, in fact, publicly constructed apartments had rented far below cost. Unfortunately for the Soviet citizen such apartments were hard to find, cramped, and often squalid. In spite of large-scale building in the 1950's and early 1960's, very little quantitative improvement had taken place, as the following calculation indicates:[11]

Year	Urban Housing (million sq. meters)	Urban Population (millions)	Housing Space per capita (sq. meters)
1913	180	28.1	6.5
1926	216	26.3	9
1939	421	56.1	7.5
1958	832	99.8	8.5
1961	1,014	107	9.5
1967	1,350	131	10.3

Under these circumstances it is not surprising that many thousands of city dwellers were willing to put their savings and much personal labor into constructing their own housing. Most of the latter consisted of *dachas* (cottages) on the outskirts of the cities, though there was some cooperative construction of multi-family dwellings. In the early sixties, all private construction came under suspicion. The 1961 "anti-parasite" decree was directed specifically against those who built houses with "unearned income," but reports indicate that houses were confiscated even from those who had painfully saved the construction costs from their wages.

After Khrushchev's fall, official pronouncements adopted a radically different view of personal housing. Pointing out that a third of all urban housing was personal property, writers stressed "enlistment of the population's savings for building personal homes" as an indispensable aid in overcoming the housing shortage. Even provision of state credits as an encouragement to private construction was urged. Soviet editors sharply criticized correspondents who—a year or two behind the official line—continued to urge limitation on personal property like houses and automobiles. One letter writer, for example, was attacked for contending that personal property must be restricted at most to clothing, books, glasses, fountain pens, shoes, underwear, beds, and dishes; "indeed, the list should be reduced; this will bring Communism closer." Official commentators drew a sharp distinction between legitimate "personal property"—the result of personal labor and destined for personal consumption—and illegitimate "private property" used to produce income. In effect, property was praiseworthy if it served as a reward for work performed in accordance with the regime's requirements, criminal if it was the result of personal initiative.

Even this distinction, tenable on the whole in urban environments, broke down in agriculture. Since the early 1930's the predominant institutional unit has been the collective farm (*kolkhoz*). Under complete Communism this cooperative must give way to completely socialized ownership, but the matter is probably regarded as less significant than the persistence of outright private cultivation in the peasants' garden plots. In Khrushchev's period, agricultural economists recognized that the plots were indispensable sources of food. But as early as 1948 Khrushchev had advanced a plan for drastically restricting the plots; during the late 1950's he gingerly returned to the scheme. Like all earlier doctrinal statements, the 1961 Program pointed out that "supplementary individual farming" was incompatible with complete socialism (much less Communism) and optimistically predicted that the plots would be given up voluntarily when they were no longer necessary economically. From the Marxist-Leninist point of view, the main objection to the plots was not the time spent on them (though this was of great practical concern to Soviet agricultural directors) but their use to earn income through private initiative. During 1961–63 the collective farm markets where peasants sold their produce were harassed by the police; anyone dealing in large quantities of food was likely to be arrested as a "speculator." Official agencies were urged to buy up the peasants' produce directly, "to create an economic situation in which there is no room for parasites."

After Khrushchev's dismissal, Soviet publications continued to state that in the final analysis the plot is "not compatible with the ideals of Communism." As early as November 1964, however, articles praised the peasants' efforts on these "private plots" and criticized collective farms which had reduced the area allotted to private farming. Such efforts hurt the more industrious farmers, leaving them worse off than the improvident who had resorted to trickery to "expand their own farming operations." Since then, the incentive role as well as the practical necessity of the plots and the collective farm markets have been emphasized. In early 1966, one article pointed out that 16 per cent of all food consumed in the USSR was sold through these markets. The police were condemned for stopping trucks (under the guise of fighting speculation) carrying fruit and vegetables to the markets, and collective farms were instructed to provide transportation for the peasants' produce. The operation of the law of supply and demand in the farm market was admitted, although state stores were urged to offset drastic price fluctuations.

Heightened incentives in agriculture could hardly be avoided if the near-catastrophic food situation of 1963–65 was to be overcome. Just before Khrushchev's ouster there was some reduction in the use of the large brigade employed to work the collective-farm fields. Under this system, peasants could hardly count on a return proportional to their individual efforts, nor could they team up with relatives or close friends to accomplish distinguishable tasks entitled to specific rewards. In the succeeding years the small work team (*zveno*) has made rewards proportioned to accomplishments more feasible. Other measures, such as minimum wage guarantees and earlier distribution of farm profits, have heightened incentives. State agencies (like the Ministry of Agriculture) have partially regained the administrative authority they had lost to the Party between 1953 and 1962, but the collective farm as a unit enjoys more autonomy. Most of the measures for increasing incentive, and more strictly economic policies such as the increase of the fertilizer supply, are too technical to be covered here. The net effect in agriculture has been a moderate but definite shift toward rewards proportional to abilities, even though the result is social differentiation which in the long run is counter to the transition to Communism.

Admission that social differentiation is increasing rather than diminishing is apparent in other areas of Soviet life. Beginning in 1958, school regulations required nearly all students to work for a time before proceeding from high school to college. A large proportion of high-school students was assigned to vocational schools, and artisan training was introduced into the primary schools. One reason for this shift in educational policy was the general manpower shortage, but Khrushchev's distrust of white-collar tendencies to hold aloof from the "proletariat" was a cogent factor. Recruitment of workers into the Party itself was highly stressed. Together with the reduction of income differentials, these measures reflected the egalitarian aspects of Khrushchev's policy. They have not been wholly discarded since 1964. Nevertheless, there has been a leveling off of the proportion of workers admitted to the Party: in 1956–61 workers were 40.6 per cent of new members; in 1961–65 they were 47.6 per cent; in 1966 the proportion admitted dropped slightly to 46.8 per cent. As early as March 1965 the Minister of Higher and Secondary Specialized Education reported that "procedures . . . for reserving for production workers up to 80 per cent of the places in the general admission plan [for higher education] did not justify themselves." The trivial and wasteful aspects of work-training in the schools, which had been the cause of complaints even in Khrushchev's time, received more attention, and requirements were modified. All of these changes are likely to operate in favor of the intellectually capable student, encouraged and aided by educated, white-collar parents. The trend, therefore, appears to perpetuate social stratification.

Very recently Soviet analyses have moved cautiously to admit that such stratifications are significant even where class differentiation is eliminated: "The new phase of intra-class relations intrinsic to the socialist society leads to rearrangement of the structure of the working class." In essence, the "intra-class" distinctions are recognized as arising from differing skill levels, which in turn result from differences in education—a trend which is, in fact, the principal basis for social differentiation in all modernized societies. Yet the 1961 Program had called for the elimination of distinctions between mental and manual work, and the ability of the individual to alter his occupation freely. Soviet analyses still contend that in "Communist society . . . social homogeneity of occupations and free exchange of occupation will exist"; but they caution that "we shall have to deal for many a year to come with differences among workers according to complexity of work." Like the elimination of incentive, complete social equality must await the indefinitely postponed millennium of abundance, for only "petty bourgeois theorists" favor the establishment of "a society of the poor but equal."

Renewed admission of inequality and the indefinite necessity of material incentives were accompanied by sweeping changes in managing the Soviet economy. These reforms, which are frequently associated with the name of the economist Yevsei Liberman, are among the most important policy changes of recent years, but their substance is too technical to permit full exploration here. To put the matter in a brief, necessarily over-simplified fashion, the "command economy" was to be partially replaced by the "cost accounting" principle. Instead of being judged by their success in producing a specified assortment of goods, factory managers were to be evaluated on their ability to make a profit by keeping costs below income from sales of their product. Superficially, the extension of the cost accounting principle seems like another aspect of the emphasis on incentives. A word of caution must be entered, however. The "profit" achieved by a manager was indeed to be a criterion of his success; but the profit accrued to the state's budget, not to the manager's personal account. Bonuses and other rewards for the manager are related to his degree of success, but that had been the case under the command economy principle as well; only the criterion of success was altered. Furthermore, the cost accounting principle had long been established in theory. In most areas of production, it had, however, been secondary to material output criteria.

The Liberman reforms were, in fact, a search for more effective "socialist" management rather than a surrender to capitalist principles. Since Leninist theory never established fixed criteria for evaluating management success, it is quite possible that the "simulated" capitalist criterion of financial profitability would be an acceptable working principle even under complete Communism. To date, however, implementation of the profitability criterion has been very limited. The range of the manager's discretion is severely restricted for he must still produce an assortment of goods stipulated in terms of quality as well as quantity by central authorities; must deliver these goods to specified consignees according to a fixed schedule; and must obtain his supplies in a similarly prescribed manner. The main difficulty appears to be the price system, which has borne little relation to real production costs. Since the regime is quite unwilling to surrender direct control over goods allocation, letting the laws of supply and demand determine prices, it confronts the extremely difficult task of setting prices by fiat. In the summer of 1967 the whole price system was overhauled, but it remains to be seen whether the change will be effective in compelling managers to minimize costs.

Although there is no necessary connection between profitability as a managerial criterion and social inequality, there may be some psychological tendency to equate the search for enterprise profits with the renewed emphasis on material rewards for accomplishment. In addition, the economic reform has brought a renewed stress on leadership as a talent setting some men above others. In Stalin's time the managers were informally described as "princes"; today an article refers to "the commanders of production—from enterprise director to foreman."

V

Consideration of the changes in enterprise direction is inseparable from consideration of the general reorganization of economic direction since 1964; the latter, in turn, is a major component of the political realignment which took place following Khrushchev's ouster. Thus far we have been able to identify a number of policies with Khrushchev's personal interest and initiative, and to trace their reversal by his successors. It is now apparent that Khrushchev was never an absolute dictator. Very probably his power to set policy varied considerably even during the years (1958–64) when he was head of both state and Party. Nevertheless, his influence on policy was always considerable, and his personal style affected the whole tone of Soviet political life. In contrast to his detailed (if exaggerated) denunciation of his rivals, Khrushchev's successors have never provided an account of their disputes with him before his ouster, or even of the sequence of events immediately preceding his forced resignation. Whereas the Twentieth Party Congress (1956) witnessed Khrushchev's violent denunciation of Stalin, the Twenty-First Congress (1959) saw his henchman castigate the "anti-Party" group, and the Twenty-Second Congress was the forum for attacks on both Stalin and Khrushchev's anti-Party rivals, the Twenty-Third Congress speeches did not refer to Khrushchev by name. As will appear shortly, the difference in style is significant. Nevertheless, policy criticisms there and at preceding Central Committee plenary sessions clearly pointed to Khrushchev.

As was described above, Khrushchev's optimistic emphasis on rapid transition to Communism has been criticized as "adventurism" and the basic policies taken in accord with this emphasis have been wholly or partially reversed. Criticism on this score has, however, been indirect and muted. By far the most severe attacks have been directed against Khrushchev's organizational measures. Though the new leadership is necessarily concerned with policy, the locus of its interest seems to be revealed by this concern with the workings of the bureaucracy.

Khrushchev and his supporters had won their 1957 victory over the "anti-Party" group to a large extent on the basis of organizational change: the decision to move from central industrial ministries (associated with Kaganovich and Malenkov) to more than one hundred councils of popular economy (sovnarkhozes) at the provincial level enhanced the authority of the provincial Party apparatus, which was Khrushchev's strongest ally. In the following years, however, Khrushchev found the sovnarkhoz defective on two counts. From the purely administrative standpoint the sovnarkhozes were too numerous. As a result, they were difficult to coordinate; they absorbed a large overhead of administrative personnel; they tended to favor "autarchical" provincial interests over the general economic interest. Sovnarkhoz operation also tended to hinder technical innovation badly needed in the maturing Soviet economy. Research and development in each major industrial field was carried out by state committees in Moscow; but these bodies had no authority to require sovnarkhozes to introduce changes which might be highly productive in the long run but caused short-run disruption of schedules. The conservative bias of the sovnarkhoz operation was probably increased by the fact that the provincial Party first secretaries were more influential than the state officials directing the sovnarkhozes. Yet the Party officers had neither the time nor the skills to direct industrial affairs. A large majority had limited educations (acquired, for the most part, in agricultural vocational schools and Party in-service training) whereas the problems of Soviet industry increasingly required scientific and engineering expertise.

Confronted with these difficulties, in late 1962 Khrushchev undertook a major reorganization of the Party as well as the industrial direction.[12] The number of sovnarkhozes was drastically reduced so that there were typically three provinces in each sovnarkhoz district. The Party organization was bifurcated, with distinct branches (up to the Union republic level, except in frontier regions and certain small provinces) for agriculture and industry. A majority of the "old" provincial first secretaries was assigned to head the agricultural organizations; they retained their titles but their jurisdiction was drastically reduced. A few "old" first secretaries, nearly all with advanced technical educations, were assigned to head the industrial Party organizations in the new consolidated sovnarkhoz centers. A large number of "new" secretaries (apparently mostly with technical educations also) were assigned to head other provincial Party industrial organizations.

The reorganization clearly reduced the power of many important officials. Quite possibly it heralded an even more severe future reduction in their status, for it seemed logical to extend the reorganization by reducing the number of *provinces* to correspond to the number of sovnarkhoz districts (Leninist ideology has always asserted that—apart from nationality considerations—the basis for territorial subdivision should be economic administrative convenience). This reduction would have meant that a majority of the "old" first secretaries would have lost their posts or been subordinated to their erstwhile peers.

So far, the conclusion that the provincial first secretaries constituted an elite interest group opposed to the bifurcation has been entirely based on inference. Khrushchev's ouster afforded more direct evidence. While the authority of the majority of provincial first secretaries was reduced in early 1963, they remained members of the Party Central Committee, which is not normally altered until a regular Congress. Yet the Central Committee elects the chief Party Secretary, and in 1957 Khrushchev had set the precedent of appealing to the body when his rivals sought to oust him. In October 1964, however, exactly the reverse occurred; Khrushchev's critics in the Party Presidium called a special meeting of the Central Committee. The latter, dominated by provincial Party secretaries, apparently voted his removal without hesitation. Within two months after Khrushchev's ouster, bifurcation was completely undone. At the provincial level, the "old" secretaries, with few exceptions, regained their unified authority, while the "new" secretaries resumed subordinate posts. At the *rayon* (district) level, the return to the territorial *status quo ante* was not quite so complete, since part of the consolidation of small districts remained in effect. Displacement of rayon first secretaries has always been frequent, however; it appears that the 1962–65 turnover of top Party personnel at this level, as at the province level, was no greater than the normal attrition rate.

Beginning with the October 1964 plenum, Khrushchev's Party bifurcation was bitterly criticized as confusing, unviable, and a violation of Lenin's principles on unified Party direction in a given territory. At a very early stage this line of criticism was turned against the sovnarkhoz system as well. Obviously, the large sovnarkhoz region was difficult for Party secretaries to cope with, since typically it embraced three Party provincial organizations even after the reversal of bifurcation. Yet the small sovnarkhoz had demonstrated its inefficiency; it is also likely that Party secretaries had come to recognize, between 1957 and 1962, that the task of directing industry, however gratifying the prestige might be, was practically beyond their ability. The solution reached (in December 1965) was complete abolition of the sovnarkhoz. Later (at the Twenty-Third Congress) the Party leader, Brezhnev, declared that the territorial system of administration of manufacturing led to depression of the direction of the branches of manufacturing in many economic regions. The unity of technical policy was broken; scientific-research organization was detached from production. This hindered working out and introduction of new techniques.[13]

In place of the sovnarkhoz the central ministry resumed overall direction of each branch of industrial production, including the state committee's research and development function. Not only were the central ministries restored as organizations but the ministers themselves were, for the most part, men who had long held posts in high central industrial direction. At least one-third (of the initial appointees) had been chairmen or deputy chairmen of the corresponding state committees between 1957 and 1965; at least eight (including some of the former chairmen) had been ministers or deputy ministers before 1957. Among the new ministers appointed in 1965 there was a scattering of former sovnarkhoz chairmen, but very few ex-Party officials. At the Twenty-Third Congress, central industrial directors also regained a measure of the importance they had enjoyed in elite bodies. About one-fourth of the newly elected Central Committee (full and candidate members) consisted of central governmental officials, mostly industrial ministers. The same category in 1961 had included less than one-sixth of the Central Committee, and sovnarkhoz chairmen had constituted an insignificant minority. Proportionately, however, the territorial Party secretaries did not drop much below the 40 per cent of the Central Committee which they comprised in 1961; the main relative losses were to local governmental offices and the like.

The central industrial ministries did not, however, regain the power they had had in Stalin's time, for the Liberman reform (incomplete as it was) devolved much more authority to the enterprise manager than had been the case earlier. As a result, the provincial Party secretaries could view the restoration of their 1957 rivals to ministerial posts without fearing a serious reversal of the Party primacy established at that time.

Analysis of post-Khrushchev organizational restoration has suggested that a major motive of the elite was preservation of its own position. Relatively minor organizational changes at the Twenty-Third Congress, such as the dismantling of the Russian Republic Party Bureau and its Secretariat apparatus, seem to point in the same direction by reducing the diffusion of power which had helped Khrushchev play one elite group against another. Changes in the Party rules bear directly on this point. In 1961 the Party Statutes (not to be confused with the Program) were amended to impose limits on the number of times Party officials could be reelected as secretaries or as members of Party committees. In 1966 these provisions were rescinded, as "not justified in practice." At the same time, the emphasis on rejuvenation of the apparatus, which these formal provisions had exemplified, was greatly diminished. At the Twenty-Second Congress the number of delegates had been vastly inflated; possibly the availability of larger facilities in the new Kremlin Palace of Congresses was a factor permitting this expansion, but it also provided an opportunity to introduce as delegates a high proportion of young persons who had recently entered the Party, *without* correspondingly diminishing the number of older officials. Even in 1961, the turnover in the far more significant Central Committee membership was low; the proportion of middle-aged members with long Party service was overwhelming. As yet age data on the 1966 Central Committee members is incomplete, but the following comparison of Party entrance dates suggests that the middle-aged element (now approaching 60 years old) has probably retained its dominance as has the pre-World War II group of Party entrants:

Composition of Central Committee (Full Members)

Year of Party Entrance	1961 (%)	1966 (%)
Up to 1917	3	4
1917–20	6	4
1921–30	32	26
1931–40	36	44
1941–45	16	17
1946–55	5	4
1956–	1	1

There was a suggestion at the Twenty-Third Congress that the pragmatic evidence against continued rejuvenation of the elite reflected a deliberate policy decision. Brezhnev remarked that "measures of the past years" had led to introduction of some incapable cadres. "We need young and old cadres," he said, "including those who have gone through the school of practical activity in the localities."

The evidence of an aging, relatively uneducated elite maneuvering to maintain its dominant position may appear as a purely selfish trend. But the observer must recognize that this perpetuation of oligarchical power has combined with extraordinary stability (in Soviet terms) and avoidance to overt factional strife. As noted earlier, the Twenty-Third Congress was remarkable for its muffling of past intra-Party conflict; rivalry in the present ruling group was even harder to detect. The number of full members of the Politburo (11) remained identical with the number immediately after Khrushchev's ouster; two candidate members were added to make a total of eight. Only two full members, A. I. Mikoyan and N. M. Shvernik, were dropped; in both cases advanced age could serve as plausible grounds. The dropped candidate, L. N. Yefremov, was more clearly demoted. This substantial continuity made Brezhnev's explanation of the redesignation of the Presidium as the Politburo more meaningful, "as better expressing the character and activity of the high political organ of our Party." Two other high Party officials were even more explicit in hailing the return to the Leninist name of the "organ which directs the work of the Central Committee in the period between plenary sessions." [14] Since the formal basis for Khrushchev's defiance of the Presidium in 1957 was that it was not entitled to direct *him* between Central Committee plenary sessions, the unchallenged implication was that the Politburo had been elevated to be the standing committee of the oligarchy, above any individual official.

One must point out that the restoration of the title "General Secretary" for the Party chief implied a balancing increase in Brezhnev's prestige; but the change did not receive as much attention or applause as the Twenty-Third Congress delegates accorded the Politburo restoration. In contrast to the later periods of Khrushchev's and Stalin's ascendancy, the positions of Chairman of the Council of Ministers (held by A. N. Kosygin since Khrushchev's ouster) and Party leader have been kept separate. The General Secretary therefore lacks the prestige abroad associated with the head of the Soviet government. Control of the Party Secretariat remains a position of immense potential influence, however; there seems little doubt that Brezhnev is the most powerful figure in that body. In 1965 N. V. Podgorny, a strong potential rival, was "kicked upstairs" to be formal head of state. Another powerful secretary, A. N. Shelepin, was relieved of his government powers; more recently he has apparently lost his influence over the police through the removal of his protégé V. Y. Semichastny. Shelepin and other personages like M. S. Suslov, whose prominence antedates Brezhnev's, remain significant balancing forces in the Secretariat, however. Since the Congress, Brezhnev has adopted a slightly more impressive public style, but compared to Khrushchev he (and all other Soviet spokesmen) are colorless. This bland style may be deliberately fostered by the oligarchy to prevent individual leaders from acquiring undue prominence. During the 1968 Czechoslovak crisis, the Soviet press stressed that all decisions were made by the Politburo. The drabness of the Twenty-Third Congress itself may well have arisen in part from a general feeling that spectacular pronouncements would inevitably enhance the prestige of the officials who made them.

Given the tumultuous course of factional strife in the Soviet Communist Party, it would be rash to predict lasting harmony. Each year that goes by strengthens the precedent for settling disputes (surely *some* occur) behind closed doors, possibly by demoting, but certainly not by disgracing the losers. The stronger these precedents become, the more likely that political succession can be accomplished without upheaval. The removal of Khrushchev was frictionless compared with the four-year struggle following Stalin's death; and even that struggle was mild compared to the protracted, bloody aftermath of Lenin's passing. If the Soviet system has matured to a stage in which conflict no longer results in the losers' political destruction, in which leadership change is accomplished by a quasi-legal mechanism like a Central Committee vote, its gain in stability is incalculable.

It must be stressed that the gain so far has resulted from the perpetuation of an aging oligarchy. Within less than a decade a large majority of these men will die or become ineffectual through old age. Despite the precedents they establish, a new generation may revert to older patterns of Soviet political history. In all the crises of Soviet rule, however, conflict has at least formally remained within the Party, which acts as the supreme legitimizing institution. While, at times Stalin practically reduced the Party to a secondary position, he and his lieutenants never formally deviated from acknowledging its primacy, as Khrushchev put it in 1940:

The Party is responsible for everything. Whether it is Army work, Chekist work, economic work, Soviet work—all is subordinate to the Party leadership, and if anyone thinks otherwise, that means he is no Bolshevik.[15]

This principle was repeated in virtually unaltered form by a *Pravda* writer in February 1967:

The Communist Party is the highest form of organization of the working class and all the working people, and it alone is capable of guiding and must guide all state and public organizations, including the army and state security bodies; only under this condition can they successfully carry out their functions and act in a coordinated way.[16]

VI

It is, perhaps, judicious to close our survey of substantive changes in the Soviet system during 1965–68 with the emphatic expression of continuity in basic aspects just quoted. The oligarchical tendencies which now seem dominant were strong under Khrushchev, who never possessed the personal dictatorial powers Stalin held. Even the latter necessarily relied on a bureaucratic elite. In many respects, therefore, it is preferable to regard the past four years as a period of continuity rather than drastic change. Nevertheless, there does appear to be an intimate connection between the triumph of bureaucratic oligarchs and the numerous policy changes described earlier. Unquestionably, by 1966, abandonment of the timetable for achieving Communism was unavoidable unless the regime was willing to engage in desperate belligerence abroad or carry out a social upheaval at home. But certainly an aged, oligarchical leadership is less likely to resort to such "adventurism" than an individual leader. Experience suggests that committees are cautious, and elderly committees are super-cautious. No doubt the 1961 Program secured the support of the bulk of the elite because world and domestic developments appeared to favor the Soviet cause, and because the Soviet people required a morale stimulus. The Program seems to represent, however, the logical culmination and consolidation of Khrushchev's earlier innovations, and to express his optimistic temperament. When his optimism proved unfounded he had to go, and it was to be expected that his successors would consolidate their position rather than pursue ultimate Communist goals at all costs.

Many trends since 1964 have been contradictory and much is obscure. It seems possible, however, as discussed in the preceding sections, to detect mutually consistent trends in specific policies as well as in the tempo of the overall drive toward millennial goals. Economic direction represents a compromise between return to the central mechanisms, which the oligarchs became familiar with in their more vigorous years, and innovation (begun, indeed, under Khrushchev) in use of simulated profit criteria. Apart from the caution evident in the later step, the reliance upon elite managers probably makes this kind of innovation more acceptable to the leadership, which unqestionably recognizes the need for improved economic performance. Retreat from social equality is more closely in line with oligarchical perpetuation at the top and is closely related to the practical man's reemphasis on the incentives which, under the slogan "to each according to his work," characterized Soviet socialism for decades prior to 1961. Reliance on state coercive mechanisms, the traditional resort of authoritarians, would also seem to reflect the mood of aging oligarchs. Outright censorship of alarming literary productions and indignant condemnation of fundamental criticism probably appear simpler, more effective, and more righteous than social pressures. At the same time, some, at least, of the present oligarchy may have been appalled by the prospects of absolute conformity (as opposed to outward compliance) implicit in some of the social control measures envisaged in the 1961 Program. In spite of this, avowed enemies of Communist ideology, religion and nationalism, are treated as sternly as ever, for the present leadership is no more inclined than Khrushchev to recant its basic faith in Marxism-Leninism.

It remains to be seen whether reiteration of this doctrine, in the absence of expectations of proximate realization of its millennial promise, will sustain the regime. There is a kind of "revolution of rising expectations" in the USSR as elsewhere. Substantial increases in consumer goods have been made in the last three years (notably through the phenomenal harvest of 1967, which may owe something to more abundant fertilizer as well as to good luck), but they may not be adequate to secure more than grudging acquiescence for the regime, especially among the skeptical peasants. Intellectual dissent, enlisting a large portion of the educated youth, has almost surely grown stronger and more courageous in the past three years. Events like the demonstration outside the court where Sinyavsky and Daniel were tried are almost unprecedented. If the regime can present neither a humane nor a dynamic image, it will lose the most sensitive portion of the population.

Most dangerous of all, perhaps, is the nationality problem. It is intimately involved with most of the other foci of disaffection—minority religions, non-Russian intellectual expression, and dominantly peasant cultures. It is tied to the Soviet Union's difficulties in maintaining control of the Communist bloc on the one hand,

and to the seemingly irresistible rise of nationalism in the developing world on the other. For decades, the Soviet leadership legitimized its control over national minorities by its assertion of a unique millennial mission. If this messianism is tacitly shelved, force alone may not hold the USSR together.

Alongside all these problems is the problem of the new generation of the elite, which the old oligarchs have so far kept from the seats of power. From the actuarial standpoint alone the new generation's hour must come within a very few years. When it does attain power, it will be faced with an awesome complex of problems, but it will also enjoy the self-confidence based on persistence of the Soviet system through more than a half-century of desperate crises. Perhaps the greatest question in its (and our) future is whether the new Soviet generation will consider Communist ideology an expendable encumbrance or a heritage which demands implementation.

NOTES

1. The average reader of this essay is probably more interested in general sources for studying current Soviet political developments than in the specific sources I have used. Consequently, I have provided note references only for longer quotations and a few highly significant data. In addition to Soviet newspapers and periodicals (not many Soviet books are useful for changes as recent as 1965–68), I have relied very heavily on the *Current Digest of the Soviet Press.* This weekly not only provides convenient translations, but selects from a range of Soviet publications which the individual scholar can hardly find time to examine. A very useful supplement (particularly on nationality matters) is the monthly *Digest of the Soviet Ukrainian Press.* The *New York Times,* in addition to its reports, prints many original documents (such as the official Soviet translation of the draft Party Program, August 1, 1961, which is the source of my Program quotations). The student of Soviet affairs can keep up with current developments fairly well by spending a few hours a week on the sources just listed, even if he does not know Russian. Unfortunately, there is no interpretative survey in English comparable to the splendid *Osteuropa* series (*Osteuropa,* a monthly, for general topics; *Osteuropa-Recht; Osteuropa-Wirtschaft; Osteuropa-Naturwissenschaft*) in German. *The Bulletin of the Institute for the Study of the USSR* (Munich) and *Est et Ouest* (Paris) provide considerably less systematic monthly or biweekly surveys, while *Soviet Studies* (Glasgow) and *Problems of Communism* (United States Information Agency, Washington) provide more selective quarterly or bi-monthly reviews. Im-

portant articles on Soviet affairs appear frequently in less specialized periodicals. The excellent series of books on Soviet affairs which provide our background for interpreting current developments are usually unavoidably several years behind current developments. I believe, however, that the discussion in the second edition of my introductory textbook, *Ideology, Politics and Government in the Soviet Union* (F. A. Praeger) is factually accurate up to mid-1967. In the following discussion, I have assumed that the reader has at least an outline knowledge of the background of Soviet politics.

2. Guenther Wagenlehner, "Ideologie: Der Parteitag der stillen Revision," *Osteuropa,* XVI, 1966, 462.

3. "Fifty Years of Great Victories of Socialism," *Pravda,* November 4, 1967, trans. *Current Digest,* XIX, No. 44, p. 11.

4. *Pravda,* April 17, 1962, trans. *Current Digest,* XIV, No. 16, p. 5.

5. Y. Desherieyev, M. Kammari, and M. Meiliyan, "Development and Mutual Enrichment of the Languages of the Nations of the USSR," *Ukraïns'ka Mova i Literatura v Shkoli,* No. 12, December 1965, trans. *Digest of the Soviet Ukrainian Press,* No. 2, p. 24 (with minor stylistic adaptations).

6. *They are Still in Prison: A Report on the Arrests and Trials of Ukrainian Intellectuals, 1965–66,* New York: Prolog Research and Publishing Association, Inc., 1967.

7. D. Chesnokov, "The Educative Role of the Soviet State," *Pravda,* February 27, 1967, trans. *Current Digest,* XIX, No. 9, pp. 6–7.

8. *New York Times,* June 5, 1967 (originally published in *Le Monde,* Paris).

9. Marc Slonim, "Writers in Moscow," *New York Times Book Review,* May 21, 1967, p. 20.

10. A. Luk and V. Tardov, "The Patient and His Relatives," *Literaturnaya Gazeta,* December 8, 1966, trans. *Current Digest,* XVIII, No. 50, p. 9.

11. Based (except for 1967) on statistics in A. G. Kharchev, *Brak i Semya v SSSR* (Marriage and the Family in the USSR), Moscow, 1964, p. 161.

12. I have analyzed these changes and subsequent organizational changes through 1965 in "Party Bifurcation and Elite Interests," *Soviet Studies,* XVII, April 1966, pp. 417–29.

13. *Pravda,* March 30, 1966, p. 3.

14. V. S. Tolstikov and P. E. Shelest in *Pravda,* March 31, 1966, p. 3.

15. Quoted in my book, *The Soviet Bureaucratic Elite,* New York: F. A. Praeger, 1959, p. 145.

16. I. Pomelov, "The Communist Party in a Socialist Society," *Pravda,* February 20, 1967, trans. *Current Digest,* XIX, No. 8, p. 9.